Sells Like Teen Spirit

Sells Like Teen Spirit

Music, Youth Culture, and Social Crisis

Ryan Moore

NEW YORK UNIVERSITY PRESS
New York and London

NEW YORK UNIVERSITY PRESS
New York and London
www.nyupress.org

Library of Congress Cataloging-in-Publication Data ·

Moore, Ryan, 1970–
Sells like teen spirit : music, youth culture, and social crisis / Ryan Moore.
p. cm.
Includes bibliographical references and index.
ISBN-13: 978-0-8147-5747-5 (cl : alk. paper)
ISBN-10: 0-8147-5747-2 (cl : alk. paper)
ISBN-13: 978-0-8147-5748-2 (pb : alk. paper)
ISBN-10: 0-8147-5748-0 (pb : alk. paper)
1. Punk rock music—Social aspects—United States. 2. Alternative
rock music—Social aspects—United States. 3. Punk rock music—
History and criticism. 4. Alternative rock music—History and
criticism. I. Title.
ML3918.R63M65   2009
306.4'8426—dc22   2009026855

New York University Press books are printed on acid-free paper,
and their binding materials are chosen for strength and durability.
We strive to use environmentally responsible suppliers and materials
to the greatest extent possible in publishing our books.

Manufactured in the United States of America
c   10 9 8 7 6 5 4 3 2 1
p   10 9 8 7 6 5 4 3 2

Contents

Acknowledgments

This book has been a long, long time in the making, sort of like my own version of *Chinese Democracy* (I can only hope it gets better reviews!). When I began doing ethnographic research in the San Diego scene way back in 1995, I had the good fortune to be shown the ropes by a number of musicians and all-around hipsters, particularly Rob Crow, Julie D., Brock Gallard, Dale Harris, Gary Hustwit, Hugh Kim, Aaron Mancini, Patrick Padilla, Armistead Burwell Smith IV, Jenny Stewart, Stimy, Mark Waters, and Mitch Wilson. Bob Beyerle, Larry Harmon, and John Lee not only granted me extensive, candid interviews but also lent me zines and photographs that were indispensable for my research. Tim Mays and everyone else at the Casbah furnished a second home during my grad school years, and their cooperation was essential. Paul O'Beirne and Pete Reichert not only caused me to rock out on countless occasions while they were playing with Rocket From the Crypt but also poured a good pint and talked a lot of shit as bartenders at the Live Wire. Last but certainly not least, from the beginning Matt Reese served as my guide through this scene and its history, granting colorful, humorous, and thoughtful interviews and also allowing me to rummage through a lifelong collection of old punk zines, photographs, and flyers.

In graduate school at UC San Diego, I was incredibly fortunate to find a community with whom I could debate ideas, grade papers, and party (though not necessarily all at the same time!). We also walked picket lines together, and some of them served with me on the UC Strike Committee while we waged an eventually victorious struggle to unionize academic student employees at the University of California. So, in the outdated parlance of the 1990s, I would like to "raise the roof" for my posse of Kelly Becker, Eric Boime, Krista Camenzind, Kathleen Casey, Mark Collier, Abbie Cory, Rod Ferguson, Susan Fitzpatrick-Behrens, Rene Hayden, Rafiki Jenkins, Beth Jennings, Christina Jimenez, Dan Johnston, Melisa Klimaszewski, Tom Lide, Adam Linsen, Alberto Loza, Kelly Mayhew,

Anthony Navarette, Molly Rhodes, Sarah Schrank, Matt Stahl (aka Bourbon LaMonde), Angie and Charlie Thorpe, Mark Warshaw, Glen Whitehead, and Mark Wild. Among the faculty, George Lipsitz simply led by example as a scholar, teacher, and activist. Finally, not enough could be written here about the importance of Rebecca Klatch, without whom I could not have survived graduate school. Her faith and encouragement enabled me to endure some tough times, her critical eye and diligent readings improved my scholarship immeasurably, and her open-mindedness exemplifies the best of the sociological profession.

I would also like to acknowledge the literally thousands of students I've taught at UC San Diego, the University of Kansas, Colgate University, and Florida Atlantic University in my post-PhD years as a semi-employable vagrant sociologist. Obviously I can't thank you by name even though so many of you deserve it, but remember what I probably told you in class: you're utterly powerless as individuals, but there's no limit to what you can accomplish if you get organized as a collective, and as a whole you've certainly had an immeasurable impact on my life. Big doses of gratitude also go to those colleagues who befriended me along this journey: Bob Antonio, Dan Carey, Eve Clark, Brian and Natalie Donovan, Ophra Leyser, Hilary Lowe, Bill Staples, Robert Vodicka, and Norm Yetman for keeping me entertained in Kansas; Lesleigh Cushing, Chris Henke, Carolyn Hsu, Jason Kawall, Spencer Kelly, Meika Loe, and Ben Stahlberg for keeping me warm at Colgate; and Farshad Araghi, Liz Atzberger, Dan Bass, Ann Branaman, Amy Broderick, Stephen Charbonneau, Peter Fine, Eric Freedman, Mark Frezzo, Mark Harvey, Phil Hough, Marina Karides, Anna Lawrence, Chris Robé, Derek Taylor, and Patricia Widener for keeping me cool in Florida.

A big thank-you goes to Ilene Kalish and Aiden Amos at NYU Press for believing in my project and putting up with this neurotic, long-winded, and technologically inept writer. I also want to thank the anonymous reviewers whose reports on various drafts have undoubtedly improved the quality of this book. I would have been hard-pressed to find the time to finish this project without the support of a Scholarly and Creative Activities Fellowship from Florida Atlantic University's College of Arts and Letters.

The most significant people in my life haven't been named yet. The whole damn world doesn't need to know how we met or why you rule, but I bet you still want to see your name in print and I know better than to forget about you, so here goes: Brad Augusta, Brian Augusta, Gary

Baker, Kim Clouse, Stephanie Cornwell, Alicia Cox, Mike Diefenderfer, punk rock Erin, Aaron Gilbreath, Kirsten Grobien, the Helton family, the Hopeless Variety, Amy Marshall, Julie Miller, Jen Mongoven, Renee Morgan, Shawn Nanna, Jen Nevergole, Lance Parton, Mike Roberts, Sarah Schrank, Lori Seay, Lisa Smith, Tara Stephenson, Jay Tow, Lisa Vetere, the West Boca Jaywalkers, Bob Westergaard, Steve Westergaard, and Pete Williams. We haven't spent much time together, but I need to thank Mike Watt for teaching the meaning of punk rock to another dude from Pedro. They can't read these words, but I still want to thank Rosie O'Doggell and Abbie Paw-man for getting me out of bed every day for our morning walk and keeping me company while I write. Superhumongous doses of love go to Katy Livingston for all the support. Special thanks go to the world's greatest mother, Lucy Moore; my father, George Moore (the real DIY writer in the family); and Carol Moore, all of whom have extended so much unconditional love and periodically saved me from starvation. There is also big love for my little brother, Kevin Moore, despite the fact that he got all the musical talent in our family, and for his wife, Lauren Stephenson-Moore, for maintaining a second home for my all-too-infrequent trips back to the Bay Area. And I want my sister, Karen Moore, and her little army of munchkins, named Benjamin, Isabella, Antonio, and Mateo, to know that they continue to inspire me to fight for a better future.

In making this list I've realized how lucky I am to have so many fabulous people in my life. So I've decided to dedicate my book to all of you.

1

Anarchy in the USA

Whenever governments have imposed sweeping free-market programs, the all-at-once shock treatment, or "shock therapy," has been the weapon of choice.

—Naomi Klein[1]

Gimme gimme shock treatment.

—The Ramones, "Gimme Gimme Shock Treatment"

New York City, 1975: The events that would later be heralded as the origins of punk were taking shape. During the previous year, the band Television had begun performing regularly at a music club buried in the depths of the Bowery, CBGB's. Television's gigs were soon paired with the Patti Smith Group, and both bands found an audience among New York's art rock crowd. Meanwhile, four self-styled hooligans from Queens had also formed a band and named themselves the Ramones; by 1975 their performances at CBGB's—renowned for their ferociousness and brevity—had garnered considerable attention and a recording contract with Sire Records. With their leather jackets, mop haircuts, and streetwise personas, the Ramones' depiction of juvenile delinquency was balanced by a cartoonish sense of humor, enabling them to personify an emerging punk sensibility of minimalism and postmodern irony.

Before the end of 1975, two local writers had christened the burgeoning New York scene with the publication of a fanzine called *Punk*. For Legs McNeil, one of the magazine's cofounders, the term "punk" was used because it "seemed to sum up the thread that connected everything we liked—drunk, obnoxious, smart but not pretentious, absurd, funny, ironic, and things that appealed to the darker side."[2] In 1975, the New York scene comprised an extraordinarily eclectic cohort of musicians—including the

The Ramones in front of CBGB's in 1975. From *No Thanks!* Chrysalis Music, 1978.

preppy Talking Heads, the trashy Heartbreakers, and the sultry Blondie—and thus "punk" was less descriptive of a specific style of music than a general sensibility, particularly one of opposition to mainstream rock music and the hippie culture. A London-based countercultural entrepreneur named Malcolm McLaren visited the New York punk scene twice in the mid-1970s, and according to legend he was captivated by the style of chopped hair and torn clothing donned by Richard Hell, along with the nihilism supposedly expressed in his song "Blank Generation."[3] McLaren exported this look and sensibility back to London, where it created a new style of fashion for SEX, the boutique he owned with Vivienne Westwood. McLaren also drew from Richard Hell and the New York punks in shaping the attitude and music of the band he had begun managing, the Sex Pistols. The rest is punk rock history.[4]

In 1975, the city of New York was also in the middle of a major fiscal crisis that brought it to the brink of bankruptcy. The emergency began when financial institutions refused to continue lending money to the city as its municipal debt grew, and it famously reached its peak in October 1975 when president Gerald Ford rebuffed the city's requests for a federal bailout, prompting the *New York Daily News* to run the headline "FORD TO CITY: DROP DEAD." Deindustrialization had driven the city's unemployment rate up to 10 percent, and the decline from 7.9 million inhabitants in 1970 to 7.1 million in 1980 represented the largest population loss in New York City's history. While tax revenues flattened, New York City was also committed to providing an array of public services and municipal jobs that had been secured by a mobilized working class over the course of the twentieth century. As New York plunged into crisis, a cabal of financiers and ideologues seized the opportunity to loosen the city's responsibility for these public services and employment, thereby remaking New York City into a model of neoliberal capitalism divorced from social democracy and the welfare state. Officials from New York City and New York State did eventually negotiate a loan to avoid bankruptcy, but only after agreeing to severe austerity measures, including cuts in public services.[5]

New York City's fiscal crisis became one of the earliest instances of what Naomi Klein has called the "shock doctrine," in which social or natural disasters provide opportunities for local and global business elites, working with free market ideologues, to dismantle social programs and policies once secured by an organized working class.[6] Business elites and right-wing economists used the city's crisis to seize a larger slice of wealth and undo working-class power in the process. William E. Simon, secretary of the treasury in the Ford administration and a major proponent of laissez-faire capitalism, testified that any federal aid to New York should be on conditions "so punitive, the overall experience made so painful, that no city, no political subdivision would ever be tempted to go down the same road."[7] The restructuring of New York was not simply a grab for wealth and power but also an ideological surge against the perception of the city as a safe haven for lazy welfare cheats, liberal intellectual elites, unproductive union workers, and morally depraved miscreants. The changes instituted during the fiscal crisis included layoffs and wage freezes for thousands of municipal employees, the charging of tuition fees for the first time at the City University of New York, fare hikes throughout the public transit system, and budget cuts imposed on schools, hospitals, and public services. With mass unemployment and a deterioration of services, New York in the mid-1970s is often remembered as a time "when daily life became grueling and the civic atmosphere turned mean."[8]

The most desperate conditions were to be found in the South Bronx, where the official unemployment rate among young people reached 60 percent, with even higher estimated rates in some neighborhoods. During the 1950s, "urban renewal" had involved the construction of the Cross Bronx Expressway, conceived by the city's notoriously autocratic urban planner Robert Moses. The Cross Bronx accelerated the process of suburbanization and "white flight" while at the same time plunging its surrounding neighborhoods into a downward spiral of economic and infrastructural deterioration. In the 1970s, the economic recession and fiscal crisis suddenly accelerated the processes of deindustrialization and urban decay. The South Bronx was thrust into the media spotlight in 1977, first in July when a power outage led to a night of looting and vandalism, and then in October when sportscaster Howard Cosell announced that "the Bronx is burning" as a fire broke out near Yankee Stadium during game 2 of the World Series. But in reality the immolation of the South Bronx had been ongoing for years, as some 30,000 arson fires were set between 1973 and 1977, typically at the behest of landlords seeking to collect insurance money. The South Bronx thus emerged as a tragic symbol of the shift in American urban policy from a "war on poverty" to "benign neglect."[9]

As the punk scene was developing in lower Manhattan, the elements of what we now know as hip hop music and culture were coming together around the same time in the Bronx. In 1973 DJ Kool Herc began hosting parties with his sister, Cindy, in the recreation room of her apartment building at 1520 Sedgwick Avenue—now officially designated by the New York State Office of Parks Recreation and Historic Preservation as the "birthplace of hip hop"—and it was here that Herc developed his style of isolating and repeating the instrumental breaks on funk records to provide dancers with prolonged periods of rhythmic intensity. As these dance parties became increasingly popular, Herc moved his sound system into the streets and plugged into lampposts to generate power. Meanwhile, since at least the late 1960s some disempowered young people had been spray painting their signature "tags" on New York City subway trains in what could be seen as pleas for visibility and efforts in spatial mobility. Such graffiti art was a crucial source of inspiration for early hip hop culture in celebrating the command of urban space, the stylish "making a name" for oneself, and the defiance of police and state repression. During the second half of the 1970s, the practices of break dancing, deejaying, graffitiing, and rapping became the focal points in a transformation of social relations among African American, African Caribbean, and Puerto

NYC mayor Abraham Beame holding the infamous issue of the *New York Daily News*. Mayor Beame ripped up the paper after the photograph was taken. From *Working Class New York: Life and Labor Since World War II*. Joshua B. Freeman. New York: The New Press, 2000.

Rican youth concentrated in the Bronx. These social relations took the form of "crews" that competed with one another in displaying their graffiti or break-dancing skills, with DJs fashioning an accompanying musical mix of beats, raps, and turntable scratching. DJs battled for followers and jurisdiction over neighborhoods in the way that street gangs had done, most prominently in the case of the Zulu Nation, founded by Afrika Bambaataa to redirect youth in the Bronx from gang violence to rap music with an Afrocentric message.[10]

Subcultures and Music in the Age of Neoliberalism and Post-Fordism

In this book my aim is to illuminate the points of intersection between music and youth subcultures on the one hand and the transformation of political economy and social structure on the other. With regard to the latter, I refer to neoliberalism and post-Fordism as a series of economic and political changes that began in the mid-1970s. Neoliberalism is an economic theory that champions privatization and condemns state interventions in the free market, and as official policy it has been imposed by the institutions of global finance and trade (the World Bank, IMF, and WTO) with a fundamentalist zeal since the 1970s, when neoliberals began gaining the upper hand in their offensive against Keynesianism.[11] Following the work of David Harvey, I contrast the age of neoliberalism with the "embedded liberalism" that was instituted after World War II, which was distinguished by greater state intervention in capitalist economies and a sort of class compromise among capital, the state, and organized labor. Embedded liberalism produced high rates of economic growth throughout the 1950s and most of the 1960s, but it began to show signs of malfunctioning in the late 1960s before plummeting into "stagflation" (an unanticipated combination of inflation and high unemployment) in the 1970s. The failures of embedded liberalism gave momentum to the neoliberal theory espoused by Milton Friedman and other economists at the University of Chicago, whose ideas were applied in renewed attacks against labor and the welfare state, beginning in Chile after the overthrow of the Allende government in 1973. The fiscal crisis of New York City in 1975 can also be seen as a pivotal moment in this transition, as Harvey has argued:

> The management of the New York fiscal crisis pioneered the way for neoliberal practices both domestically under Reagan and internationally through the IMF in the 1980s. It established the principle that in the event of a conflict between the integrity of financial institutions and bondholders' returns, on the one hand, and the well-being of citizens on the other, the former was to be privileged. It emphasized that the role of government was to create a good business climate rather than look to the needs and well-being of the population at large.[12]

The change from Fordism to post-Fordism is related to the rise of neoliberalism, but more pertinent to the social processes of production and consumption than to the relation between states and markets. Fordism took its name from Henry Ford's strategy to pay his autoworkers five dollars per day in 1914 in the hope that high wages would allow workers to become consumers of the very products they were being churning out on the assembly line while also ensuring submission to the discipline necessary for mass production. Fordism subsequently took shape as a system of mass production and mass consumption, and in later decades it dovetailed with Keynesian strategies to stimulate consumption through government spending. After World War II, government subsidies for housing, education, and highway construction, coupled with steadily increasing wages, increased consumer demand by swelling the ranks of the middle class. With the crisis of the 1970s, however, mass production began to be forsaken in favor of more "flexible" strategies of accumulation with the crucial advantage of enhancing capital's spatial mobility in the search for cheap labor. The breakdown of Fordism has been followed by an increasing reliance on outsourcing and subcontracting, as the post-Fordist political economy depends on greater numbers of temporary and part-time workers who are easily disposable and usually not entitled to good wages or benefits. At the same time, in the realm of consumption, the mass markets and mass culture of the mid-twentieth century have splintered into an array of niche markets and lifestyle cultures. Thus, the changes in production and consumption, or work and leisure, have been mutually reinforcing in creating a form of social life that is more fragmented, decentralized, impermanent, and individualized.[13]

As revealed by David Harvey's analysis, neoliberalism and post-Fordism are complementary terms that describe different aspects of the restructuring of capitalism that has taken place since the 1970s. In total, this process of restructuring has allowed transnational corporations to extend their global reach, granted capital greater autonomy from regulation by the nation-state, privatized resources and formerly public industries, eviscerated the welfare state and social democracy, disenfranchised organized labor, accelerated the commodification of everyday life, exacerbated inequalities of wealth, and supported a culture of antisocial individualism and materialism. Such changes cannot merely be described as "economic," for they have given rise to a whole way of life where time and space are compressed, social relations are more fluid and ephemeral, and the commodity form infiltrates every aspect of everyday life.

As New York City became a test case for neoliberal and post-Fordist restructuring after the fiscal crisis of 1975, the punk scene of the 1970s has also come to be seen as both a beginning and an endpoint in the history of rock music and subcultures. The musicians in the New York scene sought to create sounds that were distinct from the forms of rock music that by the mid-1970s had achieved a dominant position within the music industry and FM radio. Although the New York scene accommodated a range of musical styles—from the sinewy guitar epics of Television and the dreamy retro pop of Blondie to the brutish racket of the Ramones—there was a general consensus about the exhaustion of mainstream rock music and the desire to create something different. Likewise, there was a collective feeling that the styles and sensibilities of hippie culture had become stagnant or even reactionary within the social context of the 1970s—that the "counterculture" had been absorbed by the commercial culture. Punk therefore comprised darker and more threatening forms of imagery than did the colorful and mellow hippie culture. For these reasons, the emergence of punk has been seen as a response to the demise of rock and the failure of Sixties utopianism.

My argument is that rock music and the hippie counterculture were shaped by a rebellion against the qualitative consequences of Fordism and embedded liberalism, and that punk was the signal that these movements were exhausted and co-opted in the new social context of the 1970s. By "qualitative consequences" I mean the ways that young people rebelled against the forms of meaning and identity set out for them by the new middle-class and mass society after World War II—the soulless consumer materialism, the rationalization of education, the conformity of the "organization man," and so forth. Although the counterculture represented a revolt against the "technocracy," to use Theodor Roszak's terms, it was also a product of that postwar system, for its optimism and self-importance depended on the apparently limitless abundance of the American economy, which privileged young people and allowed them to experiment and "drop out."[14] The Sixties counterculture mocked the stability and predictability of Fordism and embedded liberalism while taking their productivity for granted, thus creating visions of a postmaterialist future where the values of leisure, spontaneity, and self-expression would triumph over work, discipline, and instrumental rationality. By the mid-1970s, the counterculture's utopian vision had been exhausted, and a collective sense of dread had developed with the onset of economic recession, political crises, and cultural malaise. The Fordist economy and mass society against which young rebels had defined themselves was disintegrating into a new system of individualized labor and niche markets that could more easily incorporate the symbols, rhetoric, and music of the counterculture into the consumer culture and the creative economy. During the 1970s, the counterculture dissolved into a hodgepodge of spiritual, ecological, and artistic movements, and rock music was solidified as a commercial genre at the center of the lucrative music industry and gradually became distanced from the Sixties' call to social change. Punk arrived in this context with the message that rock was corrupted and possibly even "dead," hippies were the new "mainstream," and society was regressing to a meaner and more chaotic state that made the counterculture's utopianism irrelevant.

After Malcolm McLaren brought it across the Atlantic, punk took root amid a social crisis in the United Kingdom that had similar origins but was much more dramatic and devastating than the one affecting the northeastern United States at the time. An incipient scene may have been thriving in New York by 1975, but punk did not fully enter the spotlight of popular culture until late 1976 and the tumultuous year of 1977, specifically with the emergence of the Sex Pistols and all the assorted scandals surrounding them. This was a time when unemployment levels reached their highest levels in the United Kingdom since World War II, with a disproportionate impact on working-class youth. On the verge of bankruptcy while watching the value of the pound collapse, in late 1976 Britain's Labour government turned to the International Monetary Fund for a loan, which came with a mandate to slash public expenditures and set the stage for a neoliberal turn in the British political economy. Beyond economics, this was a social crisis that both signaled the demolition of the "liberal consensus" that had been in place since World War II and brought the authoritarian Margaret Thatcher into the leadership of the Conservative Party.

British youth found themselves in a society embroiled in racial and class conflicts, from the violent battles between police and Caribbean youth at the Notting Hill Carnival of 1976 to the racist attacks on Asian immigrants ("Paki-bashing") to the growth of the neofascist political party known as the National Front. A range of styles developed in this context as punk variously mixed with older working-class subcultures like the mods and skinheads, reggae and ska music from the Caribbean, and the postmodern sensibilities circulating in the glam rock scene and British art schools. On the whole, punk's main thrust was in resistance to the new social (dis)order; this opposition could be organized in political campaigns like Rock Against Racism, but was also more diffusely evident in punk's practices of symbolic provocation, juxtaposition, and annihilation.

At approximately the same time that punks were taking the world by storm and the elemental forms of hip hop were emerging in the South Bronx, a subgenre of heavy metal had also developed from the most extreme facets of rock music. Heavy metal picked up the loudest and gloomiest sounds to emerge from blues-inflected rock at the end of the 1960s, and as style it merged the hippie counterculture with the hypermasculine, proletarian image of the motorcycle gang. Heavy metal's musical conventions were largely established by musicians from industrial cities (e.g., Birmingham, England; Detroit; London's East End) in the 1970s, and its fans were most likely to be young, working-class, white males with symbolic investments in rebellious masculinity. If punk was sometimes romanticized as "dole queue rock" or the authentic voice of exploited youth, heavy metal was almost unanimously ridiculed by rock critics and other arbiters of taste, for the music was thoroughly commercialized and the fans could be caricatured using the enduring stereotype of the duped mass audience.

Rather than directly confronting the powers that be, heavy metal created fantasy worlds where power, domination, and resistance were represented by way of mythology and the supernatural. By the time it entered the age of MTV, heavy metal had established a secure niche within popular music, and new subcultures began developing as young people formed local scenes where heavy metal was mixed with punk or other styles of music and performance. In the United States, heavy metal split into two opposing camps during the 1980s: at one end was a "thrash" scene, which accelerated heavy metal music to the pace of hardcore punk and utilized the imagery of power, violence, and alienation; at the other was a "glam" scene, which celebrated spectacular styles of performance and the hedonistic rock 'n' roll lifestyle as means of escape from disempowerment and dullness.

Meanwhile, after punk's moment had passed and the less confrontational elements of "new wave" were digested in the early years of MTV, localized scenes that were variously labeled "postpunk" or "alternative" sprouted on the margins of popular culture and managed to survive through the 1980s. These scenes developed in bohemian urban enclaves and college towns and were defined less by a particular sound or sartorial style and more by the social relationships forged among musicians, audiences, and cultural producers like fanzine writers. Live performances served as the primary medium for organizing these social relations, while independent record labels, fanzines, and college radio provided an infrastructure of media for connecting scenes to one another across space. After mostly ignoring them for more than a decade, the music industry took an interest in localized music scenes during the early 1990s with the success of Nirvana and Seattle's "grunge" scene, as "alternative" became a new advertising buzzword in marketing to young people.

Inside these scenes, the creation of independent media was supposed to provide a buffer from the corporate world and ensure at least relative autonomy from the demands of commerce, and thus a notion of authenticity was invested in the idea of localized alternative scenes as sincere and small-scale. It was precisely this image of the authentic as something other than a commodity, however, that became the basis for a new marketing strategy when advertisers turned their attention in the early 1990s to an allegedly cynical, media-savvy demographic known as Generation X. In chapter 4 I will discuss how alternative music became absorbed into post-Fordist forms of capitalism in which culture has a crucial economic role in promoting commercialized forms of individuality, creativity, and diversity. The ideological opposition between art and commerce that alternative culture inherited from bohemia, romanticism, and modernism collapsed in this new age of capitalism where markets absorb new trends faster than ever before and the consumer culture thrives on expressions of difference, novelty, and authenticity.

The corporate use of "alternative" as a commercial genre only lasted a few years, and in fact many young people rejected and ridiculed both the appeals to "Generation X" and the music industry's incorporation of grunge and alternative rock. As I argue, these marketing strategies grew out of a crisis of legitimacy within consumer capitalism; far from resolving this crisis, however, the episode exposed capital's continuing inability to simulate authenticity in the commodity form. The music industry's search for talent inside local alternative scenes had more significant consequences, but the production of music in what came to be known as "indie" rock largely continued after the industry had liquidated "alternative" of its cultural cachet. Once the vogue for alternative passed, the styles and sounds of indie rock increasingly looked to the past to cultivate a "retro" aesthetic that pinched from genres like country, the blues, swing, rockabilly, and soul to create new musical hybrids such as alt.country, the mid-1990s swing revival, and the latest incarnations of garage rock. There are several ways to interpret this retro turn: as a symptom of creative exhaustion within rock and youth culture, a sense that "it's all been done"; as a variation of postmodern techniques of pastiche that recycle and recombine images of the past in ironic or incoherent ways; as a historical dialogue with styles and genres that recall the past to critique the present; or as an expression of anxieties about the social identities of gender, race, and class, and a symbolic attempt to resolve those anxieties by revisiting a past that appears more solid. I consider each of these possibilities in an analysis of retro culture and music in chapter 5.

In the chapters that follow, I discuss the development of these forms of music and subculture—punk, hardcore, straightedge, heavy metal, thrash, glam, grunge, alternative rock, indie rock, and various retro hybrids—in relation to the transformation of social structure that has occurred since the 1970s. In the final chapter, I consider the possible futures for music and youth culture in an industry where, on the one hand, power is more concentrated in a handful of transnational conglomerates, but new digital technologies are also democratizing the means of musical production and distribution. Nevertheless, this is not meant to be an exhaustive history and it would not be possible to cover all the forms of youth culture and music that have arisen since the 1970s. Many significant forms of subculture and music are neglected here: to name just a few, new wave and industrial music, goth subculture, dance music and club cultures, emo, and fans of jam bands who inherited the Deadhead culture.[15] There are certainly many important bands and entire scenes that I do not discuss at all—even within genres of punk and heavy metal—despite the fact that they may be able to shed brilliant light onto sociological questions, a task I hope other researchers will undertake. Above all, however, the most significant musical genre and subculture omitted here is hip hop. I hope that my comments about the origins of hip hop in the opening pages covey some sense of how important I believe hip hop has been in responding to the social crises of our times, but it is beyond the scope of this book to offer anything more than passing comments at different points in the narrative. Fortunately, the flourishing field of hip hop studies also makes my analysis unnecessary, for the interested reader can easily consult the outstanding work of many scholars who situate hip hop within the larger economic, political, and cultural context of post-1970s American society.[16]

Marxist Theory and Postmodern Culture

I will draw these links between music, subculture, and society using Western Marxist theories of culture. Because of recent historical developments, I believe the analytical tools of Marxism are more relevant than ever. In short, neoliberal, post-Fordist capitalism has assumed a predominant place in contemporary social life, and Marxism provides the best means of understanding the relationships among culture, the marketplace, and the commodity form. The point of departure for Western Marxism is the separation between the "base" of the economic mode of production and the "superstructure" of culture and ideology. The designation of "Western Marxism" refers to intellectuals living in the advanced capitalist societies of Western Europe and North America who challenged the orthodox Marxist view that changes in the base automatically determine corresponding changes in the superstructure.[17] Raymond Williams was one of the most trenchant critics of this form of orthodox Marxism, arguing: "We have to revalue 'determination' towards the setting of limits and the exertion of pressure, and away from a predicted, prefigured and controlled content. We have to revalue 'superstructure' towards a related range of cultural practices, and away from a reflected, reproduced or specifically dependent content."[18] Western Marxism thus upholds the idea that economic forces play a primary role in shaping social relationships, but it also allows for the relative autonomy of culture and social institutions in rejecting the notion that the superstructure is simply a passive reflection of the mode of production.

A key factor mediating between economics and culture that I will invoke at various moments in the chapters that follow is postmodern culture or the postmodern condition. By referring to the postmodern as a culture or a condition, I am following a number of scholars who have looked beyond postmodernism as a style in the arts, literature, theory, and so forth in developing the broader notion of a postmodern society or "postmodernity." In particular, David Harvey and Fredric Jameson elaborated complementary analyses of the condition of postmodernity as the consequence of post-Fordism (Harvey) and postmodernism as the "cultural logic of capitalism" (Jameson).[19] I do have some trepidations about using the term "postmodern," however, as it was evoked so frequently and often recklessly by intellectuals during the 1980s and 1990s that it became virtually meaningless and an occasion for the parody of the obtuse vacuity of academic discourse. Nevertheless, one useful attribute of all the various strands of postmodernism is the notion of a crisis of representation. A postmodern crisis of representation is apparent in myriad changes in social life, where it has become increasingly difficult to know where the sign/image/identity/simulation ends and the meaning/reality/self/object begins: art and architecture become a pastiche of recycled styles; identity and language become not simply the means but the ends of political struggle; philosophers and scientists reflect on the constructed nature of their claims to truth; literary theorists deconstruct intertextual discourses rather than uncover the meaning of the text; popular culture becomes ironically self-referential; and youth cultures create style from retro objects and fashion. The political economy of late capitalism is such that representations are more important and valuable than the objects they purport to represent, for today it is the swoosh or the golden arches, not the shoes or the burgers, that generate the commodity's value.

The evolution of the postmodern from an artistic sensibility to a widespread social condition occurred approximately between the 1960s and the

1980s. Jameson identified an early postmodern approach in Andy Warhol and the pop art movement of the 1960s, which recycled and reproduced the simulacra of celebrities and commodities; conversely, rock music emerged as a form of popular culture while absorbing the aesthetic conventions of individual brilliance and authenticity that developed within high culture and the avant-garde. Jameson also singled out the 1960s as a moment of origins due to the "generational rupture" that "swept so much of tradition away at the level of *mentalités*," allowing women, people of color, and a multitude of subjugated identities to occupy the cultural field and challenge the standards of high culture.[20] It was not until the 1980s, however, that Jameson designated postmodernism as a "cultural dominant." His prime examples were taken from architecture, where form is most closely bound to capital and its command of urban space, and cinema, where Jameson noted a trend toward retro stylizations and an even deeper sense of temporal confusion, which he oxymoronically called "nostalgia for the present." During the 1980s, the emergence of postmodern popular culture was also signaled by MTV, where there was no boundary separating programming from advertising, as well as television shows like *Miami Vice*, a drama that more closely resembled an extended music video.[21] But probably nothing ushered in the arrival of postmodern society more than Ronald Reagan, the former actor who referred to the presidency as "the role of a lifetime" and championed trickle-down economics and neo-imperialist foreign policy with references to *Dirty Harry*, *Rambo*, *Star Wars*, *War Games*, and even espionage films starring Reagan himself.[22]

In New York City, postmodernism developed in the cross-fertilization among art, music, fashion, and the intelligentsia, with the punk and hip hop scenes playing a reciprocal role in both being shaped by and giving form to postmodernism. Punk and hip hop evolved within an environment of creative destruction in which the industrial economy, working-class neighborhoods, and the industrial working class were being destroyed at the same time that an emerging class of creative workers and consumers was accumulating both economic and symbolic forms of capital in a new urban economy of aesthetics, real estate, and culture. In 1970s New York, the real estate economy was merging with the art market in the transformation of SoHo. The expansion of the cultural economy led to greater employment opportunities for people in the arts, fashion, and decor.[23] As the culture of hip hop was developing within the incendiary atmosphere of the South Bronx, aspects of it (e.g., graffiti and break

dancing) were subsequently absorbed into New York's cultural economy of art and aesthetics. The links between punk and art in New York
spanned from the New York Dolls' performances at the Mercer Arts Center in 1972–73 to the integration of poetry and art in the music of Patti
Smith, Television, and the Talking Heads to the interchanges between art
and punk/"no wave" music at the Mudd Club from 1978 to 1983.[24] New
York's punks played with the continually eroding pop/art distinction, and
in doing so they gave punk music and style a decidedly postmodern look
and feel; the results, however, were variations on postmodern culture that
dramatically differed from the pop/art crossovers of the 1960s in expressing the bleakness of the 1970s.

For my purposes, one of the most significant consequences of postmodern culture is found in the realm of social psychology, in what Jameson called "the waning of affect": "As for expression and feelings or emotions, the liberation, in contemporary society, from the older *anomie* of
the centered subject may also mean not merely a liberation from anxiety
but a liberation from every other kind of feeling as well, since there is
no longer a self present to do the feeling."[25] I interpret "affect" as having
a double meaning here, referring to an emotional state or dramatization
of the self (to cultivate an affectation) and a capacity to influence or understand the process of causation (to affect change). The postmodern
subject experiences a waning of affect in both senses of the word: he or
she becomes emotionally numb, or at least strikes a pose of indifference,
and senses an inability to cause change or comprehend cause and effect.
In fact, these are related: the individual becomes emotionally indifferent
because one cannot make sense of the world or imagine making a difference. This waning of affect yields a predisposition for self-reflexive irony.
Assailed by overhyped spectacles, absurd advertising claims, and pointless
celebrity gossip, the postmodern subject grows increasingly jaded but still
embraces the trash of popular culture from a knowing distance. Ironists
are experts in deconstructing how images are fabricated, and they know
that everyone is always trying to sell them something. The ironic sensibility spills over into real life, as images and identities can be adopted and
discarded without any emotional commitment—it is a life lived in quota-
tion marks. In postmodern society, signs can be played with from a safe
distance once they have been separated from their referents. Even con-
formists can go along with the system with tongue firmly lodged in cheek;
as Todd Gitlin once quipped, "Choose one: the resulting ironic spiral either mocks the game by playing it or plays it by mocking it."[26]

Along with Lawrence Grossberg, I argue that the waning of affect is particularly evident within contemporary rock music and youth culture. Grossberg has revised Jameson's thesis in noting that affect has not disappeared but rather has been dislodged from ideology and the possibilities for change: "It is not so much that nothing matters—for something has to matter—but that there is no way of choosing, or of finding something to warrant the investment."[27] Like Grossberg, I historically locate a significant rupture in the affective possibilities of rock music and youth culture with the failure of Sixties utopianism and the emergence of punk as a form of cultural opposition divested of any sources of hope. The emotional detachment of postmodern life is reinforced by the constant commercial solicitation of young people, who have become increasingly "media savvy" when it comes to detecting and decoding a sales pitch. In recent years this has created a serious problem for the marketing machine that is constantly searching for new methods to target this coveted demographic of consumers. Some advertisers have begun to utilize some self-consciously ironic sentiments in marketing to young people. In other cases, advertisers have tried to latch on to subcultures and musical forms that symbolize authenticity for young people. But this too has deepened the cynicism of youths who are sensitive to the ways that their rebellion has been appropriated by corporations and sold back to them.[28]

The Decline of the "Middle Class"

The triumph of neoliberalism and post-Fordist capitalism has involved the steady erosion of what is commonly but imprecisely called the "middle class" in American society. This too is an important mediating factor in the relationships between global political economy, postmodern culture, youth, subculture, and music. In the decades after World War II, the compromises among capital, labor, and the state had guaranteed rising wages and a better standard of living for working people. Inequalities centered on race and gender would come to the fore in the social movements of the 1960s, but class conflicts were temporarily suspended as the gap between the haves and the have-nots shrank. The reversal of the trend toward equality began in the 1970s, as manufacturing jobs that had brought union wages and job security were steadily eliminated or outsourced.[29] Manual laborers and people of color were initially those hardest hit by deindustrialization in the 1970s, but in the 1980s and 1990s "downsizing" began affecting white, well-educated, and well-paid employees in white-collar professions. Meanwhile, although millions of new jobs have been created in the service sector during the last few decades, most of them do not measure up to their predecessors in terms of wages or benefits. The political economy of post-Fordism depends on a surplus of part-time or temporary employees, the bulk of whom perform service work, are not entitled good wages or benefits, and are easily disposable during hard times.

The transition from Fordism to post-Fordism and embedded liberalism to neoliberalism has been characterized by two radically different trends in the distribution of income and wealth. From 1949 to 1979, the incomes of all American families, from the poorest to the richest, increased by roughly 3 percent every year and therefore doubled in that 30-year span. Since that time, however, low-income and middle-income Americans have not increased their earnings—and actually experienced a decline in their net household worth—while the rich, and especially the richest of the rich, have enjoyed extraordinary increases in income and wealth.[30] This abundance of wealth has become quite visible in part because of popular culture and celebrity lifestyles, thus creating a sense of what sociologists call relative deprivation. For example, Juliet Schor found that the amount of income Americans say they would need to "fulfill all their dreams" doubled from $50,000 in 1987 to $102,000 in 1994, a mere seven years later.[31] Likewise, Robert Frank has argued that rising inequality harms the middle class because the wealthy have launched an "expenditure cascade" that has increased the costs of the benchmarks of middle-class life, especially housing.[32] Thus, the price of the American Dream has ballooned while incomes have remained stagnant, with the predictable consequence being a growing crisis of personal debt that has imperiled the financial security of the typical American household.

Young people have been greatly affected by downward mobility. In media and popular culture young people continue to be symbols of wealth, either as celebrities or instant millionaires profiting from economic boom times, but for the vast majority of American youth the reality is much different. As young people are told that they can have it all and watch a few of their peers achieve overnight success and fame, they are confronted with the realities of increasing competition in college and postgraduate admissions, a contracting market for good jobs, and higher costs of housing, health care, and child care. In short, the gap between the expectations created by an individualistic culture and the reality of a declining middle class is especially acute for the younger generations. The consequences are readily apparent in the increasing rates of anxiety, depression, and loneliness stemming from an atomized culture in which rootlessness is a precondition of occupational mobility. In the words of psychologist Jean Twenge, young people today are "more confident, assertive, and entitled" and also "more miserable than ever before."[33]

At the same, the increase in inequality and the visibility of extraordinary wealth in popular culture have intensified the spirit of cutthroat competition, selfish individualism, and social Darwinism. The rewards of success or good fortune have never been greater, but there is little in the way of a safety net for those who fail. This "all-or-nothing" scenario has led to greater incidents of cheating in schools, sports, and business as individuals pursue narrow self-interest without regard to the consequences for other people.[34] While downward mobility has destabilized the American Dream, corporate scandals and the casino economy (in which wealth appears to magically multiply) have further undermined the popular notion that success is a result of hard work. Cynicism can only grow deeper as Americans see athletes get an edge by taking steroids, students get into elite colleges by cheating on their exams, and businesses inflate the value of their stocks with bogus accounting practices. As this cynicism hardens, otherwise law-abiding people begin to assume that they too must cheat and act selfishly just to keep up with their competitors.

The title of this chapter refers to the Sex Pistols' anthemic song "Anarchy in the U.K.," and it is meant to suggest a connection with youth culture in general and punk rock in particular, but in actuality the true source of anarchy in contemporary society is unrestrained capitalism. Deregulation and privatization have exposed everyone to volatile markets that change instantaneously, obey no code of ethics, and appear impossible to control. The words of Marx and Engels in *Manifesto of the Communist Party* now seem prophetic: capitalism has debased the relationships between people to little more than "naked self-interest" and "callous 'cash payment'"; values and cultural practices that were once considered sacred have been "drowned . . . in the icy water of egotistical calculation"; commodification has reduced "personal worth into exchange value" and the concept of freedom to "that single, unconscionable freedom—Free Trade"; formerly honorable occupations have been converted into mere "paid wage-laborers"; in short, capital has created a world of "naked, shameless, direct, brutal exploitation."[35]

Rhythm, Noise, and Music as a "Structure of Feeling"

Having conceptualized postmodern culture and the decline of the middle class as crises of affect, I will now outline a method for analyzing music as an emotional register of social change. Raymond Williams formulated the notion of a "structure of feeling" to describe cultural practices that capture the spirit of their times by mediating between social structure and everyday life. Williams sought to identify not only the ideological but also the emotional dimensions of culture, the "specifically affective elements of consciousness, not feeling against thought, but thought as felt and feeling as thought."[36] Although Williams used it in developing a theory of literature, "structure of feeling" can also be effectively applied to music, because music's meaning is so often communicated through moods and emotions rather than ideas or beliefs.[37] The notion of music as "thought as felt and feeling as thought" is supplemented by the insight that a singer's voice conveys meaning and emotion in the way he or she sings, perhaps more so than through the lyrics that are actually sung; the French semiotician Roland Barthes called it "the grain of the voice."[38] In the chapters that follow I consider the meaning and impact of a number of vocal styles: the bellowing rage of the hardcore punk; the screeching wails of the heavy metal singer; the lethargic or sarcastic mumbling of Kurt Cobain or any number of other alternative rockers during the 1990s; the shrieks of riot grrrls, overflowing with both anger and pleasure; and the tongue-in-cheek smirks of retro garage bands who appropriate the past with a sense of irony. Each of these can shed fresh light on various dimensions of the social conditions that have reshaped not only the fields of cultural meaning but also the channels of emotional expression.

Along with the grain of the voice, music's affective significance can be measured in terms of its rhythm and its noise. I refer to rhythm and noise not only in their literal sense as elements of music, but also as allegories for the different roles of music in society and social change. Noise, as Jacques Attali observed, is that which disturbs and disrupts.[39] In evading or mocking the established conventions of music, noise expresses social disorder, and so it is no coincidence that authorities routinely work to repress and censor it. By pushing the envelope and testing the boundaries of what is sonically agreeable or acceptable, noise is a form of innovation that dissolves the illusion of harmony and recurrence, allowing musicians to explore new possibilities beyond the established order. This is what gives music its power of "prophecy," according to Attali: "Its styles and economic organization are ahead of the rest of society because it explores, much faster than material reality can, the entire range of possibilities in a given code. It makes audible the new world that will gradually become visible."[40] Thus, music retains the capacity to anticipate social change insofar as noise is ahead of its time: "What is noise to the old order is harmony to the new."[41]

Rhythm, on the other hand, suggests a cyclical, as opposed to disruptive, experience of time, and it works in social space through the body to cement social relationships. At the end of his storied life as a Marxist philosopher, Henri Lefebvre sought to develop a method he called "rhythmanalysis," which introduced much of what I mean here by rhythm as both musical element and mode of social experience. As Lefebvre defined it, rhythmanalysis "situates itself at the juxtaposition of the physical, the physiological and the social, at the heart of daily life."[42] Lefebvre believed that capitalism has sought to replace the rhythmic, cyclical experience of time embedded in nature and the body with a quantifiable sense of linear time more amenable to work schedules and commodity novelties. Rhythms continue to spontaneously break out in everyday life as something like a return of the repressed, however, because there are inherent limits to capitalism's ability to colonize the reproductive processes of nature and physiology. Lefebvre found rhythm alive in cities of modern capitalist societies, both in music itself but also in gatherings and rituals where ecstatic moments of communal joy could be recovered. "The festival," he wrote, "which in other respects has been recuperated and commercialized, is restored, together with features that had been done away with: rupture, transgression, ecstasy."[43]

Rhythm and noise are in some ways conflicting tendencies in the aesthetics and cultural politics of music. Noise can be understood as antisocial, composed by musicians who strive to be ahead of their time by standing apart from tradition and annihilating conventions. Meanwhile, rhythm might be seen as a communal practice in which there is no firm distinction between performer and audience and the act of dancing fuses individuals with the collective. But rhythm and noise can in fact complement each other, and the musical and sociopolitical impact of either is stunted in the absence of their counterpart. Without rhythm, noise can protest and destroy, but it lacks the power to affirm an alternate conception that reconstructs social relations and different uses of time and space. In the absence of noise, rhythm can more easily be integrated into the smooth functioning of the dominant society, particularly the times and spaces of consumerism.

Since the 1970s, a few performers have demonstrated the potential to transcend this opposition between rhythm and noise. In punk rock, the Clash, Gang of Four, and the Minutemen fused punk noise and funk rhythms, and all three bands expressed fervent dissent and imagined alternate forms of social relations. In hip hop, where rhythm typically prevails, Public Enemy achieved synthesis by integrating political critique and a devastating sound: as Hank Shocklee, leader of their production team (known as the Bomb Squad), once put it, "We took whatever was annoying, threw it into a pot, and that's how we came out with this group. . . . We believed that music is nothing but organized noise."[44] Nonetheless, these kinds of musical and political synthesis are rare. In the histories of punk, metal, and various forms of alternative rock we consider in the following chapters, noise is the predominant musical element and structure of feeling, while rhythm is sorely lacking. As both a consequence and a symptom of rhythm's absence, subcultures have been severed from a utopian vision of reconstruction that might effectively complement their noisy proclamations of defiance and disorder.

The reasons behind noise's predominance over rhythm are social and historical. There was greater equilibrium between rhythm and noise at the crest of the counterculture's growth in the late 1960s, as rock music maintained closer ties to rhythm and blues, and rock festivals gave young people a forum for communal celebration. By the early 1970s, the faith in revolution and liberation had evaporated, and a sense of defeat and exhaustion settled over young people. Punk and heavy metal emerged in the aftermath as expressions of youthful rebellion but also as barometers of the dystopian and cynical mood of the times. Building on the Sixties spirit of resistance but jettisoning the faith in change and progress, punk and heavy metal tipped the scales toward noise and away from rhythm. Punk famously spat in the face of the hegemonic society, but it was largely a form of white noise that divorced rock music from rhythm and blues while signaling the exhaustion of Sixties ideals of experimentation and transcendence. In heavy metal, volume and noise articulated the declining fortunes of the white working class while facilitating the transformation of rock festivals into more commercialized spectacles.

To examine structures of feeling we must therefore examine the affective elements encoded in music through the grain of the voice and the balance of rhythm and noise. This is a notoriously difficult task, which calls to mind Elvis Costello's statement that "writing about music is like dancing about architecture—it's a stupid thing to want to do."[45] Indeed, I must admit that I frequently find it impossible to translate the moods and emotional impact of music into words. Like many scholars in the inter-disciplinary field of cultural studies, I tend to write more around the so-cial context of music rather than directly about it, and the danger is that the presentation may seem more reductionist than I intend in connecting music to subcultures and society. When the music itself is considered, I fear I am also guilty of relying too much on lyrics despite what I have said about the importance of noise, rhythm, and the grain of the voice. Obvi-ously, as so many other scholars and critics have discovered, it is more convenient to quote lyrics even if one knows there is something far more significant being expressed in the music. Musicologists of popular music have gone to some lengths to correct this bias in recent years, but most rock music cannot be smoothly translated into traditional musicological categories and discourses, and in any case I have no training in musicol-ogy and don't even play a musical instrument.[46]

In searching for words to convey the affective power of music, I have sometimes incorporated writing styles derived from rock criticism and advanced by writers in various fanzines and musical periodicals. This is not usually or easily done, for it necessitates crossing the boundaries that separate sociology from aesthetics, and the role of sociological ana-lyst from that of the rock critic and fan. Particularly in the later chapters, there are moments in the text where I write about musical performers in a way that tries to convey some of the bang and the oomph of the music. Rather than hiding my enthusiasm as a fan, I have sought to utilize a little of it to communicate why a band matters and why, not just how, they rock. The criteria involved with which bands I have chosen to write about are inevitably subjective, selected from a standpoint that looks for both social and sonic significance, whether it is heard in protest music that directly confronts society or a form of music that more subtly expresses some collectively shared meaning or feeling that can be traced to wider social changes.

Youth, Subcultures, and Scenes

The eminent German sociologist Karl Mannheim once wrote that the consequences of social change are most noticeable in "the problem of generations." Whereas adults filter novelty through a framework of usable past experience, young people are less bound to tradition and more dra-matically influenced by new events, ideas, and values.[47] Youth and youth

culture occupy a privileged position relative to modernity's spirit of novelty and innovation—in a natural sense because age predisposes them to
look to the future and cast history aside, but also because "the newest" and
"the modern" are constantly advertised to them by the culture industry,
which covets the lucrative youth market. Youth, which has been defined
as the stage of life that entails a "psychosocial moratorium" from adult responsibilities and thus enables experimentation with identity, is a product
of the economic development and affluence of Western societies in the
twentieth century.[48] The extension of higher education, postponement of
work, and advancement of birth control technologies are among the social changes that have created youth as an "in-between" phase of the life
cycle. This life stage routinely catalyzes rebellion, especially those forms
of rebellion in which the young embrace leisure, creativity, and instant
gratification in opposition to thrift and instrumental reason. Commercial
interests have capitalized on these youthful qualities as the consumer culture expanded during and after the twentieth century, marketing to youth
by promoting themselves as both sponsors of pleasure and saviors from
adult authority.

I believe that youth culture, along with music, can once again illuminate the social changes that have developed since the 1970s. One of the
hallmarks of the new economic order and contemporary American society, however, is its splintering into an array of niche markets and cultural
differences. We have no one central generational style that can provide a
complete picture of social change, but rather an assortment of subcultures
that have mixed together to form new hybrids and styles over the course
of the past 30 years or so. Generation is in this sense an outmoded concept, a relic of the era of mass society, mass culture, and mass markets
that reached its breaking point in the late 1960s. The most recent attempts
to name generations as "13th Gen" or "Millennials," primarily motivated
by the demographic methods of marketing, have never really caught on
as labels to describe the culture of young people, in part because contemporary youth culture is now fragmented into a smorgasbord of musical
tastes, fashions and styles, and uses of technology.[49]

Various subcultures can provide more partial viewpoints on particular aspects of recent social changes. The concept of subculture originated
with the famed Chicago School of sociology in the first half of the twentieth century to describe the various cultures that emerged in a developing
urban context, largely among immigrants and their children, and were
thus characterized as "deviant" in comparison to the assumed core values

of the American middle class.[50] The concept was revived in the 1970s by British scholars at the Contemporary Centre for Cultural Studies, better known as the Birmingham School, to describe how youth cultures from teddy boys to punks performed symbolic acts of resistance against the hegemonic social order. The main idea has been that subcultures take on a spectacular form by appropriating commodities and using them in innovative and unintended ways that assign them new, subversive meanings in the process of creating style.[51]

The Birmingham School's earliest studies developed the notion that the symbolic gestures of subcultures provide imaginary or "magical" solutions to problems or contradictions rooted in socioeconomic conditions. Writing about subcultures that emerged during the 1950s and 1960s, Birmingham School scholars identified two main sources of structural change: the decline of working-class communities as a result of urban redevelopment, and the evolution of mass culture, which threatened to supplant traditional working-class culture. Different subcultures responded to these changes in seemingly opposite ways. Phil Cohen, for example, observed that skinheads costumed themselves as a "caricature of the model worker," a ghost of the hypermasculine, proletarian past. Mods, on the other hand, employed "dress and music [that] reflected the hedonistic image of the affluent consumer," thus personifying the pursuit of upward mobility embodied in the emerging consumer culture.[52] Some years later, in writing about Britain's first generation of punks, Dick Hebdige traced a "homology" of disorder and defiance evident across the various forms of punk music, styles of dress, and rituals of performance. Recalling the concept of noise that I introduced in the previous section, Hebdige concluded that "subcultures represent 'noise' (as opposed to sound)" in the sense that they function "not only as a metaphor for potential anarchy 'out there' but as an actual mechanism of semantic disorder: a kind of temporary blockage in the system of representation."[53]

In recent years a number of scholars have proposed that the Birmingham School's theory of subcultures is outdated and needs to be replaced. The main point of contention is that the Birmingham School exaggerated the extent of unity and coherence within subcultures and constructed a rigid analytic boundary separating subcultures from hegemonic society. The terms "neotribes" and "postsubcultures" are among those that have been nominated to succeed subcultures in describing youthful gatherings that are more fluid and ephemeral in fashioning hybridized forms of music and style.[54] According to these critics, this conceptual change is warranted by social changes that have fragmented the cultural landscape into a plethora of identities and styles from which individuals are free to choose and combine in any number of ways.[55] As a result, youth cultures are not only more splintered and transient, but the boundary distinguishing them from the mainstream has eroded as society has increasingly comprised multicultural niches of taste and identity.

These critics of the Birmingham School have raised a number of important points, but I do not believe they necessitate an abandonment of "subculture," and so I will continue to use the concept to refer to the meanings expressed through music, style, and performance within youthful communities that are relatively distinct from popular culture. It is certainly true that the number of subcultures has multiplied in recent decades, and so I will accordingly discuss not only punk and heavy metal but also various spin-offs and hybrid combinations like hardcore, straightedge, thrash, glam, grunge, and riot grrrl. In this sense I believe subculture can be effectively contrasted to the term "generation," which suggests a unity and homogeneity of youth culture that has not existed since the 1960s. Moreover, the "sub" in subculture signifies not only plurality but also subordination and subversion in relation to dominant culture, and I believe this aspect of the concept can be retained as long as we acknowledge that the niche marketing of post-Fordist capitalism allows the music and style of subcultures to be commercially absorbed into popular culture at an accelerated rate. In other words, participants in subcultures continue to construct identities based on authenticity and difference from an imagined "mainstream," and sometimes based on active resistance against society, but a post-Fordist form of capitalism that blurs the boundary between subculture and popular culture increasingly threatens these identities.

Along with subcultures, I will continue to refer to "scenes" as localized forms of community and social networking that comprise face-to-face interaction at live performances and other spaces such as record stores. The crucial distinction here is that I speak of scenes as local forms of social relations and cultural production, while subcultures are more translocal, and increasingly virtual, fields where scenes are connected to one another across space through media.[56] If subcultures are held together through commonalities of musical taste and style, scenes are constituted by the social relationships among individuals involved in the production, consumption, and intermediate valuation of music. Although there is still a disjuncture between the realms of production, cultural artifacts, and consumption, the relations between musicians and audiences are closer within localized scenes, where those integrated into the local scene as fans or musicians produce the media of recording, distribution, and performance.[57] For instance, even bands like Metallica and Nirvana who would eventually sell millions of records began as fans of different musical genres and were socialized through interactions with other participants in their respective local scenes.

The social relations within subcultures and local scenes are analogous to the social interaction and organization of art worlds as described by Howard Becker.[58] In music scenes as in art worlds, cultural meanings circulate not only between performers and audiences but also through the mediating discourse of music critics and respected insiders. Musicians and fans inherit a set of conventions about what is aesthetically good, and aesthetic judgments and debates among performers, critics, and audiences continually change or update those conventions. Like many artistic works, the production of a musical recording or performance typically requires more people than we tend to realize, and frequently involves a rather intricate division of labor. For these reasons, it is advantageous to examine music as a social product as much as or more so than the work of individual creators, though some individual musicians are certainly more innovative than others in mastering conventions, mixing forms, and creating new standards. Subcultures and local scenes mediate between music and society as collective processes in which creative work is performed, cultural symbols and emotions are circulated, and aesthetic conventions are upheld, revived, discarded, or dismantled. When it develops at the local level of the scene, musical performance is the product of social interaction and reciprocal symbolic exchanges with its audience. Thus the music created by musicians immersed in these scenes can be interpreted as a register of meanings that are at least partially shared and circulated within a larger subculture. In each of the following chapters, I discuss a number of musical performers as emblematic of recent historical moments in American society with the proposition that collective processes of symbolic production within scenes and subcultures mediate between music and society.

Music and subcultural styles tend to attract certain types of individuals. Music has famously become a refuge for the more creative and sensitive young people, who often experience intense alienation from social institutions. This sense of alienation can propel young people toward politically progressive forces, but in some cases it has fueled reactionary forms of anger, and probably the most common result is nihilism or resignation.

In turn, young people use music and style to communicate their disaffection, and their involvement in a subculture can serve as the basis for a rebellious self-identity. The rebellion of these creative, sensitive, and at-odds-with-the-world youths is fought through music and a process of distinction in which the musical tastes of the majority or mainstream are reviled and ridiculed as indicative of a larger pattern of conformity and complicity. As a discourse, this is an amalgam of older criticisms of mass culture mixed with contemporary concerns about commercialization in the music industry and culture at large.

In 1950 the revered American sociologist David Riesman observed the ways that rebellion from larger social norms were expressed through music, as he found "two polar attitudes toward popular music, a *majority* one, which accepts the adult picture of youth somewhat uncritically, and a *minority* one, in which certain socially rebellious themes are encapsulated."[59] His depiction of the minority taste group, which predates rock 'n' roll and was probably made with certain jazz fans in mind, is still remarkably prescient in describing many contemporary fans of different genres of independent rock that have developed with the spread of punk and college radio:

> The rebelliousness of this minority group might be indicated in some of the following attitudes toward popular music: an insistence on rigorous standards of judgment and taste in a relativist culture; a preference for the uncommercialized, unadvertised small bands rather than name bands; the development of a private language and then a flight from it when the private language (the same is true of other aspects of private style) is taken over by the majority group; a profound resentment of the commercialization of radio and musicians. Dissident attitudes toward competition and cooperation in our culture might be represented in feelings about improvisation and small "combos"; an appreciation for idiosyncrasy of performance goes together with a dislike of "star" performers and an insistence that the improvisation be a group-generated phenomenon.[60]

This discourse of distinction from the mainstream has political implications that are contradictory and complex. The aggressive disdain for stars, advertising, and commercialization that Riesman identified in 1950 translates today into contempt for the handful of global conglomerates that control most of the music business and a general distrust of corporations and "the media" as dominant social institutions. And yet there also is intrinsic elitism in this division of musical tastes. In the terms of Pierre Bourdieu, this is a process of distinction involving an accumulation of cultural capital, as musicians, critics, and devoted fans uphold an alternate hierarchy of prestige that is relatively autonomous and often hostile to the hierarchy based on market notions of sales and popularity.[61] This distinction equates autonomy from commercialism with authenticity and at the same time condemns mass culture as hopelessly corrupted and counterfeit.[62] In less academic terms, it is a narrative that has frequently been told about the commercialization of punk, grunge, and alternative subcultures: once upon a time, there was this little scene, where everyone knew each other and they weren't in it for the money, but then the media invaded and started hyping the scene, and the major labels instigated a feeding frenzy to sign the "next big thing." It is certainly true that the music industry, advertisers, and various commercial forces do scout for rebellious subcultures and styles that can be used to stimulate further consumerism, but I will challenge the assumption of critical scholars and jaded hipsters alike who conclude that commercialization automatically results in co-optation. The assumption is that corporations not only profit from the music and style but also gain control over its meanings and politics. In short, while the notion that capital appropriates youthful rebellion is beyond dispute, the widespread belief that this automatically depoliticizes subcultural resistance needs to be questioned.

When it is converted to an ideology or a political culture, these distinctions of taste and antimarket sensibilities give shape to the sort of progressivism most commonly found among the children of the professional middle classes. Again, Riesman described this conversion of musical taste into political ideology with stunning prescience:

> There are still other ways in which the minority may use popular music to polarize itself from the majority group, and thereby from American popular culture more generally: a sympathetic attitude or even preference for Negro musicians; an equalitarian attitude toward the roles, in love and work, of the two sexes; a more international outlook . . . ; an identification with disadvantaged groups . . . with or without a romantic cult of proletarianism; a dislike of romantic pseudo-sexuality in music, even without any articulate awareness of being exploited; similarly a reaction against the stylized body image and limitations of physical self-expression, which "sweet" music and its lyrics are felt as conveying; a feeling that music is

too important to serve as a backdrop for dancing, small talk, studying, and the like; a diffuse resentment of the image of the teenager provided by the mass media.[63]

Much of this worldview is still evident in young people who become intensely involved with music, including a greater appreciation of racial and cultural difference, a more global perspective, and identification with society's losers and misfits. Limitations and contradictions are also apparent, for example, when appreciation and identification slides into the romanticism and exoticism of racial and cultural difference that has characterized bohemia from its inception.[64] Riesman's distinction between majority and minority audiences also reveals an unconscious reproduction of sexist discourse, for even those who espouse an "equalitarian attitude" about sex roles continue to degrade majority audiences in the feminized stereotypes of passivity, sentimentality, and vanity. This finds a parallel in studies of subcultures that focus on public spaces that privilege boys, like the streets and nightclubs, rather than the private ones that girls have more access to, like homes and bedrooms.[65] In each case, the separation of minority and majority audiences replicates a gendered binary between active producers and passive consumers.[66]

Nonetheless, the participation of young women in subcultures and various music scenes has increased substantially since Riesman's time, especially with the advent of punk. For instance, in chapter 4 I discuss the riot grrrl subculture that formed as a means of incorporating feminist politics into the do-it-yourself punk media of self-published fanzines and independent record labels. Scenes and subcultures still tend to be male dominated, however, and some, like heavy metal, are more masculinist than others. With some exceptions, analyses of music and subculture have generally failed to theorize the symbols, music, and styles of subcultures in terms of masculinity and its social construction.[67] At various spots in the following chapters I do examine music, subcultures, and style in light of masculinity and its changing meanings in American society, such as the popularity of heavy metal's spectacular displays of power with young men or the way that retro styles and music revive images of mid-twentieth-century U.S. masculinity. Furthermore, I attempt to situate the changing meanings of masculinity in the context of socioeconomic processes like deindustrialization and the evolution of an image-based postmodern culture.

Methodology and Ethnography

One critique frequently leveled at subcultural studies is that its semiotic theories overestimate the depth of meaning in rituals and practices—that they "read too much into" style and music. This is partly a methodological problem, as the semiotic analysis of subcultural signs was rarely matched by ethnography or interviewing that would allow researchers to investigate how young rebels made sense of their style or how much of their resistance was intentional.[68] The primary method of my study has also been to develop cultural readings of music, style, and subcultural practices that connect and allow us to illuminate different historical moments as well as a long-term process of social transformation; nonetheless there is always a risk that readers will find that I read too much into music and signifying practices. As a supplement to these readings, however, I draw from three years of ethnographic research and interviews conducted primarily in the indie rock music scene in San Diego between 1995 and 1998. While this is not a study of thick description organized around qualitative data about musicians' sense of identity or experiences of community, I do draw from this research to enhance the framework for understanding the localized meanings of music and style and the relations among subcultures, media, and commercial forces.

I initially became immersed in this scene when I moved to San Diego in 1993 to enroll in graduate school and began to attend shows at a local venue. A few of the local bands had recently signed major-label contracts and there was some speculation that the San Diego scene was on its way to a breakthrough analogous to that experienced by Seattle-based grunge a couple of years before. I decided to study the San Diego scene in 1995 as a research project for a graduate seminar in field methods. I had yet to develop a specific focus for the study, but I was generally interested in the do-it-yourself ethic, the recent wave of major-label interest, and the resulting conflicts between the ideologies of independence and authenticity, on the one hand, and the threat of co-optation and "selling out." I began interviewing shortly after commencing fieldwork. I asked my interviewees open-ended questions about how they initially got involved in these activities, why it continued to be important to them, and what difficulties they encountered in attempting to make a living while trying to maintain creative autonomy. I also asked about family, school, and work to get a sense of how these activities of cultural production fit in with the rest of their lives, their identities, and their sense of community.[69]

The discussion of subcultures and music in the subsequent chapters is organized in a loosely chronological fashion. Chapter 2 examines punk, but I reach back to the end of the 1960s to show how punk was an outgrowth of the counterculture's demise and the crisis of Fordism. Chapter 3 begins at roughly the same time period in situating the origins of heavy metal. Both chapters 2 and 3 proceed to examine the different subcultures and musical subgenres that developed out of punk and metal during the 1980s. Chapter 4 covers the grunge and riot grrrl subcultures that emerged from the Pacific Northwest in the early 1990s along with the larger field of what came to be known as alternative rock. Chapter 5 considers the retro turn in music and subcultures during the 1990s, with an analysis of alternative reinventions of genres like country, rockabilly, and swing and the stylistic recycling of historical imagery and fashion. Chapter 6 brings us into the present and future of music and subculture with a deliberation on their roles in a hypercommercialized culture of digital technology.

All these chapters offer a distinctive angle on the political economy of post-Fordism and postmodern culture. Chapter 2 examines the different responses within punk to the postmodern waning of affect and the conservative turn in American and British politics. If punk is defined by a crisis of meaning, then heavy metal is defined by a crisis of power, and so chapter 3 considers deindustrialization and its consequences for working-class masculinity. Chapter 4 scrutinizes the commercialization of grunge and alternative as a microcosm of culture's role in post-Fordist economics and the uses of authenticity in marketing. Chapter 5 situates retro culture within debates about the fate of history and collective memory in postmodern culture. Finally, chapter 6 recalls the debate sparked between Theodor Adorno's vilification of the culture industry and Walter Benjamin's optimistic appraisal of mechanical reproduction to hypothesize the possibilities and limitations for music and subculture in an age of digital media and global conglomerates.

A number of music journalists and some interdisciplinary scholars have already extensively documented many of the subcultures I discuss, especially the punk scenes of the 1970s. The analysis in the ensuing chapters draws from many of these secondary sources in tracing the broader development of these subcultures, scenes, and musical genres.[70] There is a risk of repeating some facts and details that will be well-known to readers already familiar with such histories, but there is also a danger in writing as too much of an insider, and so I have done my best to maintain a balance between these two perspectives. My aim is to provide an original reinterpretation of these musical and subcultural events by viewing them in light of socioeconomic processes of restructuring. The perspective offered by political economy can reshape our understanding of these cultural practices, while in turn the analysis of music and style can shed new light on how social changes have been lived and felt.

The following chapters thus examine music, subcultures, and events that have occurred across and beyond the United States, but my ethnographic emphasis also gives considerable attention to the scenes in California, and Southern California in particular. The scenes in the various regions and cities of California can be thought of as both "local" and "global": local in the sense of being built on face-to-face social relationships and thereby possessing unique dynamics of style and music, but also global because the media spotlight shines so brightly on everything that happens there, especially in Los Angeles. My discussion of punk and hardcore thus provides more coverage of the scenes in Los Angeles, San Francisco, and San Diego than is typically offered in other histories, which put the focus on the original scenes in New York and London. Likewise, after tracing heavy metal's origins in postindustrial Britain, I examine the hybrid forms of thrash and glam that flourished in Northern and Southern California, respectively. The discussion of grunge and alternative rock necessarily begins in the Pacific Northwest, but my ethnographic fieldwork in the San Diego scene offers a unique perspective on a local scene that generated considerable hype but never broke into the mainstream. In terms of the sociological framework of post-Fordism, neoliberalism, and postmodernity I laid out earlier in this chapter, the focus on California scenes is also advantageous because this region is in many ways the geographic epicenter of those socioeconomic changes. The transformations in political economy since the 1970s have been global in their reach, but they also need to be understood in terms of a power shift from the industrial Northeast to the West Coast's distinctive style of laissez-faire capitalism, "not-in-my-backyard" conservatism, and cultural economics of image and entertainment. The various California music scenes were regionally distinctive responses to these conditions of post-Fordism, neoliberalism, and postmodernity, and so it is there that we begin the next chapter, with the presidential election of Ronald Reagan and the formation of the California punk scenes.

2

Reagan Youth

I wanna be anarchy.
—The Sex Pistols, "Anarchy in the U.K."

There is no such thing as society.
—Margaret Thatcher, interview published in
Women's Own, October 31, 1987

In 1980 the band that simply named itself X released their debut album, *Los Angeles*. The first cluster of punk bands that formed the Los Angeles punk scene in the late 1970s had been mostly imitative of their British predecessors, but X began to establish a unique regional style by recalling the images of Southern California that appeared in the hard-boiled pulp fiction and film noir of the 1930s and 1940s. Greil Marcus likened *Los Angeles* to "[Raymond] Chandler's L.A. without Phillip Marlowe" in the sense that "the songs are written and sung not from Marlowe's point of view but from the point of view of the losers and misfits he inevitably discovers at the fringes of big-money murders—or whose bodies he turns up."[1] In the context of the Great Depression, noir had depicted Los Angeles as a dystopian hellhole lurking beneath the surface of beauty and prosperity, where the little guy finds himself stuck in the middle of police corruption and gangster capitalism. In reaching back to the noir tradition, X bypassed the images of Los Angeles as a paradise of leisure and liberty, which reigned throughout the 1960s from banal surf movies to countercultural hallucinations. If Los Angeles had once represented the acme of Fordist modernity and the frontier's edge where material scarcity was a thing of the past, X was the first among a series of local punk bands who revisualized it as a depraved abyss buried

Ronald Reagan caricatured in a flyer for a show by some of the seminal bands of the Washington, D.C., scene. From *The Encyclopedia of Punk.* Brian Cogan. New York: Sterling, 2008.

under glossy ephemera. X's John Doe and Exene Cervenka would sing with, against, and over each other's voices, thus intensifying the feeling of conflict and desperation.

The year 1980 also saw the election of Ronald Reagan to the presidency of the United States. Reagan's victory was the culmination of a new conservative movement whose nucleus was the Orange County suburbs south of Los Angeles.[2] As governor of California during the late 1960s, Reagan had amassed political capital in large part through his condemnation of the counterculture and campus protests. In 1980, with American society reeling from economic stagnation and a perceived impotence in international affairs, and with a backlash against the movements for racial and sexual equality gathering steam, Reagan was able to win over a national electorate that had once perceived him as too belligerently right-wing. Reagan's election opened the doors to a zealous cohort of conservatives who commenced their quest to undo the social compact instituted in the decades since the New Deal and remake American society in the image of neoliberal capitalism. Reagan immediately became the most reviled and caricatured figure within the American punk subculture of the 1980s.

Some of the few voices of dissent against the Reagan agenda came from within the punk subculture. From San Francisco, the Dead Kennedys took their name from the violent extinction of Sixties idealism and cultivated their own satirically political style of punk music. In their first single, released in June 1979, the Dead Kennedys lampooned the hippie counterculture, which they perceived as becoming integrated with the political and economic establishment in the 1970s, with a song called "California Über Alles." It imagines that Jerry Brown, then the Democratic governor of California, has become president and instituted a uniquely California brand of fascism ruled by Eastern philosophy, health food, and laid-back lifestyles. As the music builds to a sinister beat, lead singer Jello Biafra sneers lyrics such as "Zen fascists will control you / One hundred percent natural / You will jog for the master race / And always wear the happy face." The Dead Kennedys changed their tune after Reagan's election, however, updating the lyrics in a new song called "We've Got a Bigger Problem Now." During the late 1970s, punks in the United States and the United Kingdom had attacked and ridiculed the hippies, but now it was clear that the political winds were shifting dramatically, and so the Dead Kennedys modified the verse quoted above: "Ku Klux Klan will control you / Still you think it's natural / Nigger knockin' for the master race / Still you wear the happy face."

The Dead Kennedys would continue to be a force of resistance against the Reagan Administration, big business, and the religious right. But by 1980 the punk subculture in the United States was undergoing a significant change as its initial wave of provocation fizzled and a new subculture was emerging that would be known as "hardcore." At virtually the same time that Ronald Reagan was moving into the White House, the new hardcore style and sensibility was taking root in Washington, D.C. The D.C. hardcore scene maintained punk's antiauthoritarian streak and expanded its do-it-yourself practices of independent cultural production, insisting that people should be active participants in forming their own bands, creating independent record labels, and writing for self-published fanzines. But hardcore was also more macho and thuggish than the original punk subculture, as hardcore shows routinely became spaces of violence; further, despite the rhetoric of rebellion and nonconformity, it typically enforced a rigid homogeneity of sound and style. This was especially evident in the suburbs of Los Angeles and Orange County, where the scene had shifted away from Hollywood and the artier bands like X toward a younger and more belligerent community. Even with its elements of resistance, I will argue that the dystopian structure of feeling within punk and hardcore overlapped with the larger political atmosphere of cynicism and hostility that fueled the widespread turn to the right.

Just Say No?

The story of punk's invasion of popular culture has reached the status of mythology. Greil Marcus described the Sex Pistols specifically and punk generally as acts of "negation" revealing that "if nothing was true, then everything was possible."[3] Jon Savage, punk's foremost historian, similarly concluded that "history is made by those who say 'No' and Punk's utopian heresies remain its gift to the world."[4] Extending the analysis beyond music to the realm of style, Dick Hebdige saw punk as the culmination of youth culture's subversion of bourgeois ideology: "Punk did more than just upset the wardrobe. It undermined every relevant discourse."[5]

Punk has thus been commemorated as a carnival of symbolic refusal whose ancestors date back to Dada and the Situationist International. A parallel, if less intellectualized, discourse circulates in popular culture in which 1970s punk is associated with rebellion against not only society but also the rock music establishment. Punk, as the story goes, exposed and ridiculed the commercialization of rock music and the hippie counterculture. It attacked the pretensions of progressive rock and restored the vitality and irreverence that had originally energized rock 'n' roll. Punk sought to elude and undermine the music industry with a do-it-yourself ethic and an underground network of independent record labels and fanzines. Alas, this story does not have a happy ending, as punk died a quick and violent death once it was absorbed by the media and fashion industry.

This chapter uses the advantage of hindsight to shed a different light on punk and its relationship to the historical circumstances that spawned it. My point of departure comes from the preeminent rock journalist Lester Bangs, who in writing about the punk scene at New York's CBGB's quipped, "Anytime you conclude that life stinks and the human race mostly amounts to a pile of shit, you've got the perfect breeding ground for fascism."[6] In brief, Marcus and others have brilliantly illuminated punk's negationist thrust, but in light of the stasis and cynicism of the last three decades, it is equally plausible to conclude that if nothing is true, then nothing is possible. Punk was a sign of the exhaustion of the faith in love, community, and possibility that had characterized the counterculture and the New Left during the Sixties. With the benefit of historical distance we can also see that punk emerged in a pivotal moment of transition in the global political economy, as the social democracy of Fordism gave way to a more unforgiving brand of unfettered capitalism. The story of punk's ignition therefore takes on further significance as a harbinger of the descent into a callous society devoid of alternatives.

Punk should be seen as the final stage in the collapse of Sixties utopianism and the broader conditions of economic affluence and cultural idealism that nurtured it. Therefore, in this chapter I will chart the emergence of punk by first going back to the counterculture and the social conditions surrounding it. From this perspective, punk is not an adversary of rock and the counterculture so much as it is the exclamation point on their decline into impotence, a decline that rock musicians had been self-consciously commenting on throughout the 1970s. Especially in Britain but also in the United States, punks were well aware that they were growing up amid a severe social crisis. But we can see now that this was not just a short-term convulsion but rather the beginning of a long wave of neoliberal capitalism, political conservatism, and social Darwinism that continues to this day. This restructuring slammed the brakes on the spirit of progress and experimentation that characterized the modernism of the Sixties. Punks ushered in the condition of postmodernity with cries of "no future" and "no values." After all, despite their opposing political trajectories, the parallel sensibilities of punks and neoconservatives were striking: both maintained that society was falling apart and that the Sixties' efforts to make the world better had failed.

What's So Funny About Peace, Love, and Understanding?

After World War II, American society engineered stability and growth through government programs to stimulate suburban migration and consumer spending by the middle class. An enormous generation of baby boomers was poised to inherit this society, assured that it would make history and direct the United States and the world to a better future. The baby boomers would be doted on in countless parenting manuals, courted as a multibillion-dollar teen market, and pack university campuses infused with military spending. Politicians, educators, and self-proclaimed child-rearing experts declared that this was a special group who would benefit from all the difficult sacrifices of the past and the infinite opportunities of the future. Advertising was also an important factor in the creation of generational consciousness, as marketers appealed to youth with the message that they were special, different from their parents, modern and with-it. The consumer culture constructed youth as a distinct and privileged identity long before "don't trust anyone over thirty" became a battle cry in the late 1960s.[7] "The result," as Theodor Roszak wrote, "was a uniquely pampered generation of children . . . who grew up to believe that every finger painting they brought home from kindergarten ought to be admired and every problem of high-school life ought to be a family obsession."[8]

As a result, even amid the mass rebellion of the 1960s the youth movements maintained this sense of self-importance and optimism. The New Left was propelled into action by the exclusion of African Americans from the bounty of postwar affluence, and its ranks swelled with popular opposition to the military-industrial complex's horrifying slaughter in Southeast Asia. But the movement was also motivated by an idealistic sense of the possibilities for personal as well as political growth. "The Port Huron Statement," the initial salvo of the Students for a Democratic Society, brimmed with faith in human nature, the potential for change, and the virtues of political commitment. In it, SDS asserted that "we regard men as infinitely precious and possessed of unfulfilled capacity for reason, freedom, and love."[9] The model for SDS and "The Port Huron Statement" was the vision of the "beloved community" put forth by the Student Non-violent Coordinating Committee in the wake of the lunch counter sit-ins of 1960. Along with the call to serve justice and equality, the young people of the New Left saw their activism as an antidote to the depersonalization and meaninglessness imposed on them as they were being trained to supervise the technocracy, famously describing themselves as a "generation, bred in at least modest comfort, housed now in universities, looking uncomfortably to the world we inherit."[10] Their optimism stemmed from the perhaps naïve faith that the United States could live up to its ideals and that youth would play a decisive role in shaping history, as so many adults had told them.

The hippie counterculture expressed similar levels of confidence in the ability to discover an authentic self and community through experimentation. The hippies venerated all things natural and advocated a return to the innocent playfulness of childhood. Like the New Left, however, they were also products of postwar affluence and technological innovation, yet their relationship to this heritage was more ambivalent than antagonistic. Sonic technologies allowed Bob Dylan to advance from the sincerity of folk to the surrealism of rock, gave the Beatles and the Beach Boys room to explore their recording studios, and powered the light shows, experimental jam sessions, and massive rock festivals. The sexual revolution depended on the accessibility of the birth control pill. As Kenneth Keniston remarked, expressions among hippies like "turn on," "tune out," or "blow your mind" suggested "a profound identification of the self with the electronic machine."[11] Perhaps nothing better symbolized the hippies' attempts to use modern science and technology to transcend modernity than LSD, the product of U.S. government and military funding that would be used in the Sixties to expand minds and raise consciousnesses—often "deconditioning" its users against the ideology of the very military-industrial complex that created LSD in the first place.[12]

Both the hippies and the New Left arose in opposition to the instrumental rationalization of the technocracy, the bureaucratization of higher education, and the conformity of mass culture. But they were also products of the organized system, and they drew their optimism and idealism from the apparently limitless abundance of the American economy. These were not merely movements of resistance but also experiments in renewal, growth, and possibility. Affluence was a buffer that allowed young people to drop out, but more generally it created the feeling of continuous development and infinite opportunity, which the Sixties generation took advantage of even in their acts of rebellion. Marshall Berman has thus written of the Sixties as the pinnacle of modernity's breathless pace of innovation: "It was easy, in those boom years, to live off the fat of the land. This made it easier to experiment, to take risks for the sake of our self-development, for we were secure in the knowledge that it was not only possible, but adventurous and exciting, to move on. Thus the growth and dynamism of the American economy provided for us—for an expanding and energetic new middle class—the same sort of support that Mephisto's money and mobility provide for Faust."[13]

These years saw the transformation of what had been known during the 1950s as rock 'n' roll into a much larger offshoot simply called rock, a musical medium that was expected to be more artistically significant, experimental, and authentic. Rock 'n' roll became rock when it added more noise to what had been a predominantly rhythmic form of music. There was a corresponding shift in aesthetic value whereby good rock music was expected to be socially relevant, artistically innovative, and sincerely intended. The musical events that precipitated this change are now enshrined as the lore of rock history. One moment involved the transformation of rock 'n' roll by its meeting with the aesthetic and political criteria of folk music in the mid-1960s, a cultural collision that was famously greeted with hostility by some of Bob Dylan's fans but in short time emerged as the hybrid of folk rock that would define a new California sound. At roughly the same time, the Beatles were setting new musical standards that advanced rock 'n' roll from a form of entertainment for teenagers to a more serious cultural statement to be studied by mature audiences.

Rock therefore originated with the erosion of two cultural boundaries, one separating rock 'n' roll from folk culture and the other separating it from high culture. Folk culture imported the notion that rock 'n' roll can and should address the sociopolitical issues of its time; a distrust of commercialism, the music industry, and mainstream audiences, with which rock 'n' roll had initially been tainted (the point of contention for Bob Dylan's folk fans); and finally, the idea that fans are not mere spectators or consumers but instead form a community where there should be minimal separation between performers and audiences, and where everyone should have access to the means of musical production. In the wake of the musical innovations by Bob Dylan, the Beatles, and the Beach Boys, rock music aspired to be reevaluated using the categories of high culture and the idea of the auteur musician, and by the end of the 1960s a set of aesthetic standards had developed within the rock music culture that claimed value for rock as a kind of art. These folk and art sensibilities created conflicts that continue to drive rock music and its ideology—between the ideals of the creative individual and the democratic community, for instance—but in other respects they overlap and reinforce one another, as in the mutual opposition to commerce and the assumption that music is too important to be just entertainment.

The evolution of rock occurred along with the rise of a new cohort of "cultural intermediaries" who conferred artistic or political legitimacy onto rock and also helped shape the aesthetic conventions and social commentary of the music itself.[14] While some of this theorizing about the significance of rock was done by musicians themselves, many of these intermediaries were critics and fans who were products of the student and youth cultures that developed among the baby boom generation. In the late 1960s a number of these intermediaries came to rock from the social movements that had formed on college campuses, and they judged rock on its ability or failure to serve as a kind of protest music, celebrated its power to unite young people in a festive environment, and lamented its complicity with commerce and corporate control. Another set of intermediaries gravitated to rock from other fields of culture to legitimate its value as music or poetry or opera. Before long, rock's cultural intermediaries had created their own press, facilitating an innovative style of journalism and indigenous criteria for rock criticism. The intermediaries between music, on the one hand, and politics and art, on the other, shaped the wider culture surrounding rock music, and they also influenced its economic intermediaries, those entrepreneurs within the counterculture who conceived of and promoted rock recordings or rock festivals not as mere commodities but as culturally significant statements or events.

In this brief but pivotal time, an ethos of experimentation took hold within rock music, and the primary feeling within the emerging counterculture was optimism about the possibilities for social and personal transcendence. The Beatles' innovations were famously responded to by Brian Wilson's experiments in the recording studio in the making of the Beach Boys' heralded album *Pet Sounds* (which then further spurred the Beatles in making *Sgt. Pepper's Lonely Hearts Club Band*). Jimi Hendrix took the lead in exploring new sounds and noises that could be created from the guitar, amplification, feedback, and distortion; in conjunction with a number of other guitarists, Hendrix also shaped a style of performance that made playing the guitar into a spectacle of power and male sexuality.[15] Whereas folk music had mainly focused on the past and expressed nostalgia for preindustrial traditions, folk rock evolved into psychedelic rock in California with the Byrds, the Jefferson Airplane, and the Grateful Dead. These and many other bands that started in the folk scene now had their sights set on a space-age utopian future, as their minds were expanded by hallucinogenic drugs and their music was opened up by the culture of experimentation and improvisation. To effectively complement the music, lyricists strove to have their words reach the standards of poetry, and lyrical themes of uplift and development rapidly became clichés, particularly when double meanings were encoded with reference to drug use and states of higher consciousness (e.g., "eight miles high," "get experienced," "break on through to the other side").

Bad Moon Rising

Intermediaries in social movements, the rock press, and the arts played a crucial role in theorizing the cultural significance of rock in the late 1960s, and in so doing indelibly put their stamp on the music. These individuals and emergent forms of cultural media can be situated within a larger social class composing creative and intellectual members of the middle class who "are fascinated by identity, presentation, appearance, lifestyle, and the endless quest for new experience."[16] All these sources of fascination can be channeled into the consumer culture's hierarchies of taste and distinction, but increasingly the new cultural intermediaries also find work specializing in symbolic production in an economic field that encompasses fashion, design, advertising, media, the arts, and popular music. In their role as both producers and consumers of stylized culture, and moreover in their urban lifestyles in cities that have been restructured around symbolic rather than manufactured goods, the new cultural intermediaries are a central link between the political economy of signification and postmodern culture in everyday life. As we will now witness, intermediaries working in the field of rock music were instrumental in first articulating a growing crisis within rock and then paving the way for punk to emerge in a style that incorporated many features of postmodern culture.

One of the most dramatic events of the end of the 1960s was the demise of the New Left and student radicalism. Antiwar action peaked in May 1970 with student strikes on a great number of campuses in the aftermath of the National Guard shootings at Kent State University. Yet in previous months the disarray within the New Left had become evident with the dissolution of SDS and the Weathermen's town house explosion. Particularly after Richard Nixon's election as president in 1968, the movements for peace and racial justice in the United States became targets of police violence and government counterinsurgency; these organizations' physical and economic resources were spent in these confrontations, with many groups imploding in an atmosphere of constant confrontation. But perhaps more important than the organizational devastation of the New Left was the demise of its vision, which was never thoroughly fully articulated but still pointed in the direction of a better world and expressed the confidence that young people could and would create social change. The outlook of the New Left had been deteriorating as it tried to strike a Faustian bargain with media and television visibility. As its revolutionary posturing and rhetoric of violence was amplified and blown up on screen, the New Left rapidly expanded beyond the capacities of its organizational and ideological infrastructure, quickly descending into vulgar sloganeering and confrontations with the police.[17]

In roughly this same time period, most hippies lost any interest they might have once had in the idea of turning on the rest of the country, and now saw the quest for growth and potential in strictly individualistic terms. The whole counterculture appeared to have exploded by the end of the 1960s, with the pieces blown in at least three different directions. One part of the hippie dream immediately incinerated under the growing influence of hard drugs and destructive behavior, which Altamont and the Manson murders somehow seemed to symbolize. A second fraction was pushed back to the countryside in search of community, nature, and health, while in an analogous change the founding fathers of folk rock— Bob Dylan, the Byrds, and the Grateful Dead—revisited country, folk, and country music in down-to-earth albums (*John Wesley Harding, Sweetheart of the Rodeo,* and *Workingman's Dead,* respectively) that substituted traditional sounds and iconography for psychedelic experimentation. Finally, the commercial apparatus of rock was propelled into a juggernaut that quickly became the dominant force in youth culture and the music industry, ensuring a long and profitable livelihood for rock music recordings and performances.

The demise of the New Left severed the link to those cultural intermediaries who had only begun to explore the power of rock music through the prism of radical politics, especially in the movement's underground press. Meanwhile, rock's continuing commercial successes expanded the strata of intermediaries more or less directly linked to the music industry, film, advertising, and fashion. Divorced from movements for social change and insulated within a massively profitable enterprise, there were no checks on rock music's inflated sense of self-importance, but also no hopes that it could help create a better world. Rock's sense of significance and potential turned exclusively toward the individual and the private, with the result that experimentation often descended into narcissism and self-indulgence. As rock's cultural intermediaries increasingly came from within the ranks of the music industry or were otherwise connected to some aspect of corporate media, they began to function less like critics and more like an echo chamber, as they had a vested interest in heaping praise on the latest thing.

A number of songwriters composed eulogies for the Sixties as they slumped into the 1970s. One of the most direct was issued by John Lennon in 1970 on his first solo album, a song called "God" in which he renounced Elvis, Dylan, and the Beatles alongside a host of religious beliefs and idols, finally declaring, "The dream is over / What can I say?" But there was a feeling that the Sixties were "over" before the decade had even ended, both among New Left intellectuals and rock critics bemoaning a sense of failed promise. For example, writing in December 1969, the same month as the disastrous Altamont Speedway Free Festival, Greil Marcus penned a review of the Rolling Stones' *Let It Bleed* for *Rolling Stone* magazine. Marcus wrote, "*Let It Bleed* is the last album from the Rolling Stones we'll see before the sixties, already gone really, become the seventies."[18] The notion that the Sixties were "already gone" could be heard in how the Rolling Stones' traditional bravado and arrogance had passed into themes of resignation and retreat: "Years kick in: it's a long way from 'Get Off My Cloud' to 'Gimme Shelter,' from '(I Can't Get No) Satisfaction' to 'You Can't Always Get What You Want.'"[19] The album's standout track, "Gimme Shelter," was hailed by Marcus as "the best melody they've ever found," but as "a song about fear" he also heard it as "a passageway straight into the next decade."[20]

A number of cultural intermediaries in the social movements and rock music culture had begun to express feelings of exhaustion and withdrawal. Some rock critics had begun to see rock's complexity and experimentalism as noxious pretension and rock audiences as increasingly sedate and self-absorbed. For example, writing what was ostensibly a review of the Stooges' *Fun House* in 1970, Lester Bangs lamented that so many of the rock stars of his time had "a mythic aura around them" such that it was impossible to imagine throwing a pie in their face.[21] He condemned "the whole pompous edifice of this supremely ridiculous rock 'n' roll industry, set up to grab bucks by conning youth and encouraging fantasies of a puissant 'youth culture.'"[22] Bangs also mocked how his generation had been reduced from a counterculture to a passive crowd of smug spectators, "a groovy, beautifully insular hip community."[23] Lennon, Marcus, and Bangs identified different root causes—the end of idealism, the commercialization of rock music and deification of rock stars, the complacency of audiences—but they came to the same conclusion: that rock could no longer matter in the way it once had.

Within the rock press, a group of the young rock critics, including Bangs as well as Greg Shaw and Dave Marsh, were in the process of developing a counteraesthetic called "punk."[24] Shaw had started a fanzine based in Los Angeles called *Who Put the Bomp* (later known simply as *Bomp!*) in which he celebrated the garage bands of the mid-1960s that predated the psychedelic movement and were therefore free of its pomposity. Although once a devotee of San Francisco's psychedelic rock, Shaw declared that "hippies are the squares of the '70s and the less they have to do with rock 'n' roll the better."[25] Bangs was one of the first to write for *Bomp!*, and here and elsewhere he was asserting an alternative set of aesthetic criteria for rock based on aggressiveness and loudness, minimalism, and defiant amateurism.[26] He commemorated bands that formed in the mid-1960s and had largely been forgotten as they were bypassed in the psychedelic era (e.g., the Troggs, the Seeds, the Count Five) but could now be retroactively situated within this developing counteraesthetic. Bangs wasn't alone, as rock critic and future Patti Smith Group guitarist Lenny Kaye was also assembling a collection of "lost classics" by bands from this era; when this compilation was released in 1972 with the title *Nuggets: Original Artyfacts from the First Psychedelic Era, 1965–1968*, the liner notes contained one of the earliest references to "punk rock."

In the many histories of punk that have appeared since, the garage rock bands archived in *Nuggets* are often given credit for influencing punk music and attitude, but the undisputed center of the punk rock canon is occupied by the Velvet Underground, the Stooges, and the MC5, with Jonathan Richman and the Modern Lovers sometimes receiving honorable mention. All these bands could be assimilated into the counteraesthetic that was being articulated by Bangs and some of rock's other cultural intermediaries in the early 1970s, though with some elements emphasized differently in each individual case. Bangs praised the Stooges' manic singer, Iggy Pop, for his confrontational antics that seemed to embody all the male adolescent angst that Bangs thought fundamental to rock 'n' roll. Just as important, Bangs praised the Stooges' assaulting yet primitive music, writing that "none of them have been playing their instruments for more than two or three years, but that's *good*—now they won't have to unlearn any of the stuff which ruins so many other promising young musicians."[27] Bangs, Marsh, and other critics also embraced the MC5, the Stooges' compatriots in Detroit, though less because of the band's association with the radical politics of John Sinclair's White Panther Party and more because of the sheer volume of their amplifiers and guitar noise, which was supplemented by high-energy performances and a generally working-class approach.

The counteraesthetic forming in the early 1970s was a reaction against rock's appeals to high culture, but this is not the same thing as saying it was wholly opposed to art. A case in point is the Velvet Underground, who maintained strong ties to the New York art scene but still inhabited the central position in this counteraesthetic and would come to be regarded by many as *the* founders of punk music. Bangs praised them because, like the Stooges, they "had the good sense to realize that whatever your capabilities, music with a simple base was the best."[28] The Velvet

Underground's association with Andy Warhol put them squarely in the "art rock" milieu, but they had a notoriously darker and grittier vision that was directly at odds with the brightly colored optimism of the folk rock and psychedelic bands on the West Coast. Mostly ignored or reviled in the late 1960s, the Velvet Underground were now viewed as ahead of the time in their lengthy yet simplistic and repetitive compositions of noise that dispensed with heady hallucinations of transcendence. Such dystopian clamor had become indicative of a structure of feeling that permeated society at large, as Ellen Willis wrote: "Though it's probable that only the anything-goes atmosphere of the sixties could have inspired a group like the Velvets, their music was prophetic of a leaner, meaner time."[29]

Pretty Vacant

It is always risky to generalize about entire scenes or assign labels to musical performers, but in relation to postmodern culture the New York bands of the 1970s can be categorized according to two styles or approaches. One category, including Patti Smith, Television, and the Talking Heads, personified postmodernism's interplays and skirmishes between art and pop, incorporating poetry and different elements of the musical and visual avant-garde. These performers brought an artistic sensibility to popular music, but they also served to establish an artistic status for music that could be distinguished from the popular in the notion of an "underground" distinct from mainstream rock. The second category was made famous by the New York Dolls, the Ramones, Blondie, and lesser-known bands like the Dictators, groups that veered more to the pop side of the art/pop spectrum yet still embodied postmodern styles of pastiche, irony, and intertextuality. The New York Dolls personified camp and an ironic style of amateurism through glam rock; the Ramones and the Dictators caricatured themselves as moronic products of junk food, shopping malls, and amphetamines; and Blondie recycled the image of the blonde bombshell and the sound of early 1960s girl groups.

From a sociological perspective, one of the most interesting things about this moment in musical history is how many people were thinking along similar lines across wide swaths of space. In the mid-1970s a protopunk scene had formed in Cleveland with the band Rocket From the Tombs and its offshoots Pere Ubu and the Dead Boys, and Radio Birdman and the Saints were also developing unique forms of postrock noise in Australia, as was Simply Saucer in Canada.[30] But of course it was the events in Britain during 1977 that moved punk into the spotlight of the news media and shaped its development as a distinct form of music, style, and subculture. Malcolm McLaren, the Sex Pistols' manager, imported punk's style from New York after a 1974 visit to the States (including a stint where he briefly managed the New York Dolls).[31] McLaren was struck by the Dolls' blatant amateurism and use of ironic distance, as well as the confrontational fashion and attitude of people in the New York scene like Richard Hell, and so upon returning to London in 1975 he and Vivienne Westwood redesigned their clothing boutique around this burgeoning punk style.

As a cultural intermediary, McLaren's role in the evolution of British punk was both political, in the sense that he was envisioning a youthful rebellion that could succeed those of the Sixties, and economic, insofar as he was an entrepreneur who would profit from peddling youthful rebellion as music and fashion. Influenced by the Situationist International, which provided the inspiration behind the French revolt of May 1968, McLaren's hope was to exploit the mass media and commercial culture in waging an assault on the society of the spectacle. McLaren and fellow Situationist Jaime Reid would later write, "The media was our helper and our lover and that in effect was the Sex Pistols' success . . . as today to control our media is to have the power of government, God or both."[32] The central events in this regard were the media scandals that followed the Sex Pistols' cursing on a television show in December 1976 and the release of the "God Save the Queen" single some six months later. These events occurred within a social context in which there was a widespread feeling that Britain was in a state of rapid decline, as economic and fiscal crises thrust the country into structural turmoil and provoked a resurgence of racism and xenophobia. In this milieu, the Sex Pistols and punks more generally appeared as monstrous symptoms of the end of civilization.

The evolution of British punk was a postmodern event in the sense that the mediated moral panic about the Sex Pistols and punk largely preceded the development of a full-fledged punk subculture, similar to how the musical aesthetic of punk had been articulated by critics in the rock media before something called punk music had come to exist. A number of punk bands had formed and there were some landmark performances and singles released in 1975–76, but 1977 was the year that punk hit the streets of London and became the new reference point for British youth culture, music, and fashion. Punk music and fashion was adopted by an incipient subculture of young people and began filtering out to a larger audience through the consumer culture and popular music. As in the United States but on a much larger scale, cultural intermediaries played a crucial role in articulating and arguing over the aesthetic and political significance of British punk. One group illuminated the affinities between punk and critical forms of modernist artistic revolt, epitomized by the Dadaists and Arthur Rimbaud, and an emergent postmodern aesthetic based on irony, pastiche, and simulation. The key institution that facilitated the cultural exchange between punk and art was the British art schools, where a great number of bands formed in the wake of punk's ascent.[33] These artistically inclined intermediaries, however, were rivaled by another group of writers, activists, and punks who viewed punk in more political terms as a collective response on the part of young people to Britain's social crisis. Sometimes these competing discourses within punk could mix together in a potent alliance, but more often they split the subculture into separate artistic and political factions.

Whereas the New York scene was fueled by the tensions between art and pop, argued music critic and sociologist Simon Frith, the British punk was divided between formalist and realist aesthetics and an analogous opposition between vanguard and populist sensibilities. Those in the realist and populist camps maintained that punk was and should continue to be the voice of working-class youth, or "dole queue rock" as some had called it. The raw amateurism and emotional immediacy of the music were thought to reflect the status of working-class youth in late-1970s Britain. Frith argued that this was a "realist" aesthetic because it judged music as a medium of true or false representations about an external reality, and is thus derived from broader theories that suggest "media images represent reality as if through a window or in a mirror."[34] He maintained that this aesthetic was connected to a populist sensibility expressed in punk's DIY ethic, which made amateurism and simplicity into virtues, because punk was imagined to be a new kind of folk music and the basis for a democratic community. The goals of aesthetic realism and popular participation made it imperative for punk to maintain its independence from the corporate music industry, because the industry threatened to turn punk into a commodity that no longer expressed the true frustrations of working-class youth and was disconnected from any sense of authentic community.

In 1977, the Clash were situated squarely in this camp, although the band's enthusiasts had to overlook the fact that some of the members had been art school students and their image of militant proletarian youth was symbolically constructed. The social crisis of the late 1970s lent an urgency to these claims about realism and populism, as punk became a battleground in the struggle for the hearts and minds of Britain's white working-class youth; antiracist punks aligned with leftist organizations opposed the racism of the National Front and some skinhead subcultures by creating Rock Against Racism. Beginning in late 1976, Rock Against Racism organized concerts that put punk, ska, and reggae performers on the same bill, and it also created an antiracist and antifascist magazine called *Temporary Hoarding*.[35] Realism and populism continued to figure into offshoots of punk like Oi!, where neofascist and quasi-socialist factions both laid claim to the voice of working-class youth and made constant appeals to solidarity in their conflicts centering on race and politics. Realism and populism also shaped the development of hardcore punk beyond Britain and into North America in the late 1970s and early 1980s, where the DIY ethic of commercial independence was endowed with an aura of authenticity and the act of selling out was condemned as the betrayal of a community.

On the other hand, those who articulated a formalist aesthetic within the punk vanguard had absorbed the lesson that "media images don't reflect or copy reality but construct it."[36] The considerable interchange between art schools and local music scenes shaped this approach to punk and the various forms of "postpunk" that continued developing through the mid-1980s.[37] Though some tried to claim that the Sex Pistols' nihilism was the true expression of working-class youth, their techniques of semiotic annihilation and spectacular moments of interruption can be seen more clearly as the instigating source for this deconstructive method. Musically, one of the earliest and most innovative groups to utilize this approach was Wire, whose explosively disjointed 1977 debut album *Pink Flag* was conceived as a "a piss-take of Rock music."[38] As a style of personal appearance, a method of media production, and a loosely political sensibility, punk and postpunk evolved when they came into dialogue with modernist and postmodernist ideas about signification, reification and commodity fetishism, self-reflexivity and intertextuality, and the cultural politics of subversion.

The realist/populist and formalist/vanguard approaches created considerable tension within British punk, and their cultural oppositions spilled over into the American scenes that developed afterward. In Britain the intense political conflicts of the late 1970s further separated these two camps, as the Rock Against Racism campaign made political demands on musicians that some of the more aesthetically motivated felt to be too constraining. But there are several places where the two approaches do intersect, particularly with how the do-it-yourself methods of cultural production mesh with the technique of "bricolage" whereby cultural producers utilize all the resources at their disposal in the creation of new meanings.[39] Indeed, the development of postpunk was facilitated by an extensive network of independent record labels, distributors, fanzines, and retail outlets.[40] While hardcore variants of realism have often stifled the creativity of punk music by insisting on minimalism and speed, the independent media generated through the DIY ethic have also enabled several periods of extraordinary innovation and diversity when "punk" was defined a method of production rather than a singular sound. Bands that came to punk from a formalist/vanguard perspective, like Gang of Four and the Mekons, were able to create music that contained trenchant political critiques, not necessarily by appealing to working-class experience but by disrupting cultural codes that link music to consumerism and ideology.

California Screaming

The historical facts surrounding the original punk scenes in Britain and New York are now well-known, and so the main themes and conflicts can be sketched in relation to their social context without rehashing all their details. The punk and hardcore scenes that arose in California have received less attention and are usually treated as a postscript to these predecessors, but the California scenes reshaped the field of punk subculture in ways that were distinct for their time and place. The punk scenes in Northern and Southern California exhibited considerable differences, which parallel the two regions' conflicting political cultures. The punk scenes in San Francisco and Berkeley, respective homelands of the counterculture and the New Left in the 1960s, had much stronger elements of leftist political activism. Los Angeles, on the other hand, was in many ways the capital city of postmodernity, owing to its economy of image and entertainment, de-centered suburban sprawl, and apparent lack of history or community.[41] The Southern California region, stretching from Los Angeles south through Orange County to San Diego, had also become a hub for the emerging form of conservatism that would catapult Ronald Reagan into the White House in 1980 and provide popular support for the undoing of the welfare state. In this setting, the Southern California punk scene and its hardcore successor exhibited nihilism and violence as even more dominant tendencies than they were in Britain or other parts of North America.

In Los Angeles, punk initially evolved through the "glitter rock" that had taken hold on Hollywood's Sunset Strip in the 1970s. Characterized by androgyny, decadence, and outrageous stylishness, glitter rock was imported from Britain, where it was known as glam rock, and influenced by recent L.A. transplants like David Bowie and Iggy Pop. Glitter rock created a Babylonian atmosphere within the Hollywood scene that contrasted with the easygoing sounds of folk and country rock that arose from nearby Laurel Canyon to conquer FM radio in the form of Crosby, Stills, and Nash; Joni Mitchell; and the Eagles. The two central figures in facilitating the transition from glitter rock to punk in the L.A. scene were the Anglophile DJ Rodney Bingenheimer and the producer and promoter Kim Fowley. Bingenheimer had established a club called Rodney's English Disco, which became the nucleus of the glitter scene as a hangout for touring rock bands and their groupies. After the English Disco closed, Bingenheimer was given his own radio program on KROQ beginning in 1976, after which he played a crucial role in introducing L.A. audiences to the newest punk and new wave music on his show, *Rodney on the Roq*. Meanwhile, Fowley, like his English counterpart Malcolm McLaren, had always been looking to exploit the latest trends in music and style. He helped assemble a band made up of teenage girls called the Runaways, which played on the Hollywood's image as a haven for sexually available and aggressive young women, and later would organize and promote some of the first punk shows in Los Angeles. A third individual engaged with the scene was Greg Shaw, who (as we've already seen) was instrumental in articulating punk's anti-aesthetic through his fanzine *Bomp!*, which then also became an independent record label.[42]

The infrastructure of a scene was therefore in place and ready to absorb punk, and there was also a preexisting demand for a depraved alternative to the city's established singer-songwriter country rock. As news of a punk movement reached Los Angeles, a cluster of fanzines began publication, including *Lobotomy*, *Flipside*, and *Slash*. In the appropriately simulated style of Los Angeles, the local punk media thus anticipated the development of an actual punk scene, as *Slash*'s chief writer, Claude Bessy, recalled: "We were pretending there was an L.A. scene when there was no scene whatsoever."[43] When bands did begin to form, they generally reproduced the stylistic heterogeneity of the original punk scenes: there was the vanguard art punk of the Weirdos and the Screamers, the Marxist punk of the Dils, the theatrical aggression and musical incompetence of the Germs, the urban bohemianism of X, and the so-called Mexican Ramones known as the Zeros. These groups constituted the L.A. scene, but fittingly a Hollywood movie would also influence how punk was understood and acted out: Cheech and Chong's *Up in Smoke*, filmed in 1977 just as the scene was being born. In the movie, after learning of a "Battle of the Bands" contest at the Roxy, Cheech persuades Chong that their band should perform despite the fact that they don't know any songs: "Besides, it's just punk rock, man. You don't have to know how to play, all you gotta do is just be a punk, man. We can do that." The link between punk and amateurism was thus solidified from the onset, not only inside the scene but also from the outside through mass media. Meanwhile, in "real" life, during the filming of *Up In Smoke* at the Roxy, the Germs recorded a live performance of "Forming," regarded by most as the first single of the L.A. punk scene.

By contrast, the San Francisco punk scene was more influenced by the city's enduring culture of bohemian lifestyles and political activism. The key fanzine of the San Francisco scene, *Search and Destroy*, was created by an employee of the independent bookstore-publisher City Lights with funds donated by Lawrence Ferlinghetti and Allen Ginsberg, and the main venue for punk shows, Mabuhay Gardens, was also located in the North Beach district immortalized by the Beats. Among the first cluster of local punk bands, the Avengers were formed by an art student named Penelope Houston and adopted a leftist political orientation, while Crime cultivated a juvenile delinquent image and the extravagant claim to be "San Francisco's first and only rock 'n' roll band." After forming in 1978, the Dead Kennedys added a political dimension to the scene not only with their music but also in establishing the independent record label Alternative Tentacles.[44]

By the end of the 1970s, however, many people were already talking about the "death of punk" and speculating about its mutation into something different. The more tame expressions of punk music and fashion were being packaged for mass consumption as "new wave." Meanwhile, its incendiary core, ignited by nihilism and the crisis of a particular historical moment, was rapidly burning out, and so the torch was passed to the next generation. The new music and subculture would be called "hardcore." Its partisans were younger than the original cohort of punks. They surfaced from the sprawling suburbs of California and beyond, not its urban bohemian enclaves. They were not particularly artsy or postmodern in their aesthetics, though they were certainly symptomatic of the crisis of meaninglessness and purposelessness resulting from the condition of postmodernity. Hardcore music was louder, faster, and angrier than its punk predecessors, and hardcore shows were frequently more violent and male dominated. Yet for all its stylistic homogeneity, hardcore represented even more divergent political possibilities than punk: in some circles it could be not simply nihilistic but shamelessly homophobic, misogynist, and racist, while others used the do-it-yourself ethic to mobilize resources into one of the very few social movements to challenge the Reagan agenda from a radical, multi-issue perspective.

The principle band of L.A. hardcore was Black Flag, who initially made their presence felt with the explosive single "Nervous Breakdown" in 1978. Black Flag formed in Hermosa Beach, and they developed an especially rabid following among young surfers and skateboarders from Southern California's beach towns, where hard drugs and violence were now rampant. Keith Morris, Black Flag's original singer and later a founding member of the Circle Jerks (he was eventually replaced in Black Flag by Henry Rollins after trying out other singers), represented the lifestyle of these drug-addled and sun-stroked casualties in his autobiographical song "Wasted": "I was so wasted / I was a hippie / I was a burnout / I was a dropout / I was out of my head / I was a surfer / I had a skateboard / I was so heavy, man, I lived on the Strand / I was so wasted." Most of Black Flag's songs, however, were written by the band's visionary guitarist and ham radio aficionado, Greg Ginn. If Morris was the hard-partying wasteoid, Ginn was the awkwardly tall and lanky social misfit more comfortable alone in his room, tinkering with his technology and plotting his revenge on the world. His songs are the emotional equivalent of a caged animal, with a surplus of pent-up rage and frustration that sounds like it might come bursting through your speakers at any moment: "I'm about to have a nervous breakdown / My head really hurts / If I don't find a way out of here / I'm going to go berserk." Ginn's brother, Raymond Pettibon, designed the cover art for "Nervous Breakdown" by drawing an adolescent boy cornered by an adult, fists clenched and ready to fight back.

As hardcore accelerated the tempo of punk music, it provoked more physically confrontational forms of dancing and response among its audience. This new form of "slamming" supplanted "pogoing" at hardcore shows. Black Flag's roadie, a formerly homeless teen named Mugger, recounted this evolution:

Black Flag's singer, Henry Rollins, dives into the crowd at a show in 1981. From *Get in the Van: On the Road with Black Flag.* Henry Rollins. Los Angeles: 2.13.61, 1994.

Pogoing, which started a few years earlier, was kids just jumping up and down, and if you fell, somebody picked you up. Slamming, which started around the hardcore scene, was kids smashing into each other full-on football style with nobody picking you up anymore. . . . A football-playing friend of mine said he would just go to the Fleetwood [a venue in Los Angeles' South Bay that regularly hosted hardcore shows] 'cause it was a football game to him. He didn't even care how the bands sounded or if the music was any good. He'd just go to show people who's tougher.[45]

Hardcore shows thus became more male dominated and individualistic in the competitive displays of "toughness" among audience members.

In a city defined by the movies, it was somehow appropriate that the L.A. punk scene and its nihilism would be solidified by its cinematic representation, Penelope Spheeris's documentary *The Decline of Western Civilization.* A recent graduate of UCLA's film school, Spheeris took to the L.A. scene in 1979–80 to not only document but also amplify its violence, drug abuse, and maliciousness, and indeed there was plenty there for her to put on film. Fear, Black Flag, and a disoriented Darby Crash of the Germs figured prominently in the film. The violence depicted had the effect of a self-fulfilling prophesy, further intensifying that trend in the L.A. scene as some who saw the film were attracted to punk as an outlet for their anger and aggression while the more artsy and less belligerent were often driven away. The violence was also considerably escalated by the actions of the Los Angeles Police Department, which reacted to the punk scene with techniques of repression once reserved for radical social movements, including its violent actions during notorious riot at the Elks Lodge in 1979 and a systematic campaign of harassment and surveillance directed at Black Flag. This too had the effect of driving the punk scene further into the suburbs, as several Hollywood clubs banned punk rock performances for fear of violence or trouble with the police.

Poster for Penelope Spheeris's documentary *The Decline of Western Civilization*. From *Lexicon Devil: The Fast Times and Short Life of Darby Crash and The Germs*. Brendan Mullen with Don Bolles and Adam Parfrey. Los Angeles: Feral House, 2002.

In the L.A. suburbs, nihilism begat a new sub-subculture of punk bands described as "brat-core" or "snot-core." The names of some of the seminal bands—the Dickies, the Circle Jerks, and the Adolescents—seem to say it all. These were groups of young men who flaunted their immaturity and idiocy while making high-speed but very melodic music, which might be best described as the sonic equivalent of being teased by an annoying child. This was "punk" in the juvenile sense of the word, and their songs were full-blown but fleeting temper tantrums against authority. The Adolescents personified this state of retardation in "No Way": "No class / No job / I'm just a victim of society / A slob / No ass, no head / I gotta go home and jack off instead." This sense of boredom and anomie had originally been expressed by the Ramones and the Buzzcocks, but it seemed especially relevant to punks growing up in the Southern California suburbs. The Adolescents were part of a circle of punk groups in the Orange County cities of Fullerton and Placentia that included Social Distortion and Agent Orange. Although nestled in the suburbs, the city of Fullerton in particular was beginning to experience downward mobility, and Social Distortion developed a uniquely working-class aesthetic in that social milieu. Further toward the coast, an even more violent punk scene developed among much more affluent youth in Huntington Beach who followed the bands T.S.O.L. [True Sounds of Liberty], the Vandals, and China White.

As a form of music, brat-core or snot-core was eventually mastered by the Descendents, who accelerated the harmonies of surf music while dumbing them down into fry-cook anthems like "My Dad Sucks," "I Like Food," and "I'm Not a Loser." The Replacements, who emerged from Minneapolis to become one of the very best rock bands of the 1980s, began their career with an extraordinary and thoroughly snotty album titled *Sorry Ma, Forgot to Take Out the Trash*. The Replacements' venerated singer-songwriter, Paul Westerberg, crafted poetic lyrics based on the banality of teenagers' suburban experiences, like falling in love with the girl who works at the convenience store or getting a headache from cheap pot. Although they would later branch out into a variety of musical styles, the Replacements maintained a bratty attitude that wavered between self-destructive and self-deprecating (encoded in their name, as if they were scab labor among musicians). Punk music was still dominated by this juvenile aesthetic when it resurfaced and enjoyed unprecedented commercial success beginning in the mid-1990s, reworked by California-based bands like Green Day and Blink-182 as the soundtrack for surfers, skaters, and snowboarders. The impudent yet catchy tunes of these bands led them to be designated as "pop punk."

In fact, brat-core or snot-core punk seemed to anticipate a larger trend in dumb and dumber American popular culture, where billions of dollars are now made from men who regress to adolescence on screen, over the airwaves, or in cartoon form. In the most generous interpretation, this is the latest manifestation of a long history of "carnivalesque" rebellion in popular culture, whose transgressions expose bourgeois society's repression of the body while longing for an imagined state of pre-Oedipal satisfaction.[46] The ignorance and infantilism of these idiot-heroes are depicted as symptoms of society's failures, much like the characters of gangster film or gangsta rap who introduce themselves as the monstrous consequences of pervasive greed and violence. To recall the Adolescents' lyrics in "No Way": "No class / No job / I'm just a victim of society / A slob."

Over the course of the 1990s, the cartoon TV shows *The Simpsons*, *Beavis and Butt-Head*, and *South Park* achieved massive success largely on the strength of prepubescent male characters depicted as willfully ignorant and defiant of authority. The cartoon medium greatly enhanced these shows' postmodern sensibility, enabling them to literally caricature their subjects (including other forms of popular culture, and even themselves) with great irony and reflexivity.[47] Marketers identified and subsequently targeted their legions of young male fans as "mooks" who seem infatuated with bodily functions, especially those emanating from the anus. The mook is not just antiauthority but antisocial, evading responsibility by playing dumb in the interest of resisting anything that could get in the way of the way of a good time. The man in the gray flannel suit, we might say, has been replaced by the boy in the backward baseball cap. The mook is a consuming machine yet prides himself on not being taken in, for he uses his cynicism as armor against anyone who might threaten the immediate gratification of his most primal self.

How are we to explain the (d)evolution in American popular culture from the punk to the mook? Judith Kegan Gardiner has theorized that the ubiquity of media and consumerism and the demise of the breadwinner ethic triggered a shift in the social character of masculinity from the "anally retentive" to the "anally expulsive." The law of the father appears increasingly ineffectual and laughable, but the new breed of adolescent male is now also confronted by what Gardiner terms a "more seductive, amorphous, and relentless . . . market of the mother."[48] Boys struggle to fulfill the masculine ideals of autonomy and impassivity as they are raised on a steady diet of corporate advertising and entertainment, perhaps best symbolized by the mother on *South Park* who is continually fattening up her already-obese son with "cheesy poofs" while he sits on the couch watching TV. If yesterday's masculine character was defined by bourgeois hoarding, entailing the (literal) internalization of authority in the course of Oedipal rebellion, today's "masculine anality," Gardiner writes, "is dedicated to fighting against taking things in by pushing things out. The inputs it expels are not merely food products and sexual threats but also advertising, adults, and their authority."[49] He enjoys making a mess, especially if he is confident that others will pick up after him. This generation's hero, to take another example from *South Park*, may well be "Mr. Hankey, the Christmas poo," that little piece of shit who crawls out of the toilet to ruin the annual U.S. orgy of consumerism by smearing himself all over the place.

Among the L.A. punk bands, it was Black Flag who articulated the condition of young people saturated with media and lulled into apathy and antisociality. Delivered in a satirical style, Black Flag's "TV Party" became an anthem for beer-guzzling couch potatoes by inviting listeners to sing and clap along with its chorus: "We've got / Nothing better to do / Than watch TV / And have a couple of brews / Don't talk about anything else / We don't want to know / We're dedicated to our favorite shows." Indeed, hardcore's furiously fast songs, typically delivered in less than two minutes, seemed to mimic the spasmodic flows of television, video games, and commercial amusements; it was the soundtrack for a generation raised on high-sugar diets and plagued by attention deficit disorders. "[The songs are] fast," Chuck Dubowski of Black Flag explained in *The Decline of Western Civilization*, "'cause that's the amount of energy we have, and they're short because that's how long our inspiration lasts."

California hardcore thus amplified its punk predecessor's sense of meaninglessness and purposelessness, frequently parodying that crisis without presenting an alternative sensibility. The subculture emerged at a time when California, particularly Southern California, was the epicenter of a major social transformation in the United States away from Fordism and toward a new political economy of laissez-faire capitalism, Sunbelt conservatism, and postmodern simulation. At roughly the same time that teenagers were forming punk bands in the garages of the Southern California suburbs, a social movement was gaining momentum among their parents at the grass roots (or perhaps we should say crabgrass roots) to repeal property taxes used for public education and social services. This movement culminated in the passage of Proposition 13 in 1978, which Mike Davis has called "an epochal event that helped end the New Deal era and pave the way for Reaganomics."[50] The tax revolt, coupled with a campaign against school busing, was the product of protracted right-wing mobilization in the Southern California suburbs, and its success would prove central to the conservative turn in American politics generally. Punk and hardcore promoted themselves as rebellion, but upon closer inspection we may find more similarities with, or at least symptoms of, this increasingly cynical and antisocial political culture.

Just a Minor Threat

Punk made a huge splash in the late 1970s in part because it seemed to symbolize a particular moment in history characterized by the death of idealism. But punk then imploded as quickly and thoroughly as one might expect a subculture founded on destruction and nihilism would do: some people died and many more bands broke up. Punk disappeared from the spotlight and left only a couple of traces in popular culture during the 1980s. The first was MTV, where the look (though not the sound) of the first wave of video artists, including Madonna, Cyndi Lauper, and Pat Benatar, owed an obvious debt to punk in their ripped and torn clothing and defiant posturing. Some of the original cohort of punk bands, such as Devo, the Talking Heads, Blondie, Billy Idol, and the Clash, also gained exposure on MTV. The second residue was in cyberpunk science fiction and movies like *Blade Runner* and *Repo Man*, where urban seediness, cold-blooded cyborgs, and reckless capitalism made up the dystopian vision of the 1980s.

Yet at the same time that the original punk imagery persisted in the postmodern culture of MTV and cyberpunk, the newest incarnation of punk subculture was actually turning toward an ethos of sincerity instead of spectacle, discipline instead of destruction, temperance instead of intoxication. In Washington, D.C., the band Minor Threat led a movement that identified itself as "straightedge" in rejecting drugs, alcohol, and promiscuous sex. Straightedge enlarged punk's revolt against rock into a movement against the whole hedonistic consumer lifestyle of sex, drugs, and rock 'n' roll. Sobriety and abstinence could now be revamped as acts of nonconformity. Straightedge linked itself to an even more intense version of the DIY ethic in which independence from commercialism, the music industry, and mainstream audiences was conferred with a sense of authenticity and even purity. As straightedge was a reaction to the culture of gluttony and instant gratification, the DIY ethic sought to establish a durable refuge from the fleeting and frivolous trends of popular music and youth culture.

The music and rage of this hardcore punk subculture was driven by a mission to expose hypocrisy and "sellouts" of all stripes. Minor Threat's singer, Ian MacKaye, was the first to articulate straightedge, and the band's music was punctuated by his accusatory vocal style, in which he often sounded like a drill sergeant berating his audience for their weaknesses and inconsistencies. For example, in "In My Eyes," one of Minor Threat's most powerful songs, MacKaye initially seems to be railing against an acquaintance for drinking, smoking, and giving into peer pressure, but it soon becomes evident that his sermon might apply to any number of emotional crutches or mindless acts of conformism, like finding religion or listening to Bachman-Turner Overdrive. As the music accelerates to impossible speeds, MacKaye bellows, "It's in my eyes / It's in my eyes / And it doesn't / Look that way to me." This is the voice of a young man who doesn't believe what he's seeing and whose self-righteous indignation is growing stronger by the minute. MacKaye is carrying on a dialogue with this imaginary acquaintance, shouting his responses with unbelievable ferocity:

> You tell me that nothing matters
> YOU'RE JUST FUCKING SCARED
> You tell me that I'm better
> YOU JUST HATE YOURSELF
> You tell me that I make no difference
> AT LEAST I'M FUCKING TRYING

The music stops momentarily and MacKaye reaches back to deliver one final denunciation: "WHAT THE FUCK HAVE *YOU* DONE?" MacKaye would eventually develop a leftist political ideology in his more mature years as a member of Fugazi, but in this song he's just a kid who can't really explain why he's so mad, and that just makes him madder. Most of all he seems to want something to matter. He wants to make a difference, but how, or for what, he has no idea. Everyone else seems to have been lulled into apathy or is hiding behind their cynicism, but at least he's fucking trying.

Although it later became a social movement of considerable size, the straightedge lifestyle was just the tip of the cultural iceberg. Less a coherent ideology than a nebulous structure of feeling, straightedge appealed to young people both in search of meaning and outraged by the fraudulence of their peers and their society in general. Something had to matter. The other legendary band in the D.C. hardcore scene was the Bad Brains, composed of four Rastafarian African Americans who became one of punk's most renowned live acts. Rastafarianism didn't catch on with punks the way that straightedge did, but the Bad Brains did share a common desire to link punk with an ethical way of being that differed sharply from the nihilistic forms that preceded them.

Straightedge quickly migrated beyond D.C. to become a movement all over the United States. Between 1983 and 1986 about 40 percent of punks identified themselves as straightedge in the annual polls conducted by *Flipside* magazine.[51] But the search for a principled alternative to nihilism went beyond straightedge to other variants hardcore built around concepts like positivity and unity. At about the same time that straightedge was starting, some punks in Southern California started the Better Youth Organization (BYO), which organized punk shows, put out records, and spread the message that drugs, alcohol, and violence were ruining the scene. In 1982 the Better Youth Organization planned a North American tour featuring the bands Youth Brigade and Social Distortion, which became the subject of a documentary film titled *Another State of Mind*. Depicting the nearly wholesome sight of these youngsters traveling across the continent in a broken-down school bus, *Another State of Mind* was like a do-it-yourself counterpoint to *The Decline of Western Civilization*. Straightedge and other forms of what would be called "positive punk" had the functional benefit of enabling a network of hardcore scenes to sprout and survive on the margins of American society during the 1980s, a time when there was no popular or commercial interest in punk. It also allowed this subculture to avoid the self-destructiveness and minimize the police repression that devastated the original punk movement. As someone who participated in the Southern California straightedge scene as an adolescent explained to me in an interview: "Everything was always kind of getting fucked up because of people drinking, and whenever shows would get closed down it was usually because there was underage drinking going on or people getting in fights because they were loaded. We just wanted to go to shows, at least me and my friends, we just wanted to go to shows and see bands play. We were into the music enough to where all the drinking and drugs kind of seemed like older things, like things you do after you're burned out."[52]

Do-it-yourself production meant that all it took was a handful of enthusiasts to get together and create a little scene in their hometown. There were punk shows at the American Legion hall in Boise, Idaho, the old Coca-Cola bottling plant in El Paso, Texas, and the YMCA in San Diego, California.[53] In Lawrence, Kansas, punk shows were regularly held in a cinder-block garage in a cornfield four miles outside town, appropriately named the Outhouse. Such "venues" were created when bands like Black Flag or the Dead Kennedys came through town on their cross-country tours and locals would scramble to find any available space to host a show. Local bands would have the opportunity to open the show, and thereafter the venue was usually established as a site for future performances. Widely circulated fanzines like *Maximumrocknroll* reported on these events in their "scene reports," which covered everywhere from midsized California suburbs to eastern European nations, thus solidifying the sense of an "imagined community."[54] Fanzines also provided an important economic service of promotion and publicity, as they regularly featured interviews with musicians, countless reviews of punk records, and cheap advertising for independent labels. Thus an infrastructure of media was being created that would allow this subculture to subsist throughout the 1980s and set the stage for its surprising advance into the mainstream during the 1990s (see ch. 4).

This faction of punks may have represented an about-face from their more nihilistic predecessors, but they were responding to the same crisis of meaning and affect in postmodern society. Do-it-yourselfers, straight-edgers, and nihilists alike had been left with scant opportunities to find creative fulfillment at their day jobs, no guidelines for transforming a culture of consumption into meaningful existence, and unable to participate in the spectacles of mass media as anything but spectators. Left with "nothing better to do than watch TV and have a couple of brews," one cluster of punk bands and personalities screamed that they were bored, flipped the bird to everyone around them, and broke up after their first album. They were as dramatic and spectacular as the rush of consumer culture, and they vanished just as quickly. On the other hand, those involved with straightedge and positive punk sought to take control over what they consumed, transformed passionate consumer tastes into a basis for cultural production, and created a scene they could call their own. Doing it themselves, they made the ephemeral world of consumption into grounds for durable identities and participatory community.

Straightedge would eventually develop into a social movement in its own right during the later part of the 1980s. For many adherents, it became linked with vegetarian or vegan lifestyles and concern for the environment and animal rights. Straightedge could also serve as an alternative model of masculinity in its resistance to alcoholism, physical abuse, and sexual conquest.[55] And yet straightedge and other forms of positive punk were imbued with a streak of what can only be called fundamentalism. Noah Levine, who was a so-called gutter punk on the streets of Santa Cruz, California, and became addicted to drugs and alcohol before joining the straightedge scene and later becoming a teacher of Buddhist meditation, described the movement's different factions: "In the Straight Edge scene there were actually two factions. One talked about unity in the punk scene and overcoming our differences through positivity, a lot of emphasis being put on brotherhood and a set of moral standards. The other was a harder and more violent sect that put energy into those who drank and used. This hard-line movement got its strength through feeling superior and separate from everyone and anyone who didn't believe what it believed."[56] All over the world, fundamentalism has resurged in recent decades in response to the hedonism of consumer culture and the globalization of American-dominated entertainment.[57] Like fundamentalism, straightedge strongly appeals to doctrinaire young men who think in binary categories and have little tolerance for ambiguity. Even if straightedge did represent an alternative model of masculinity in one sense, in another sense it replicated a long history in which masculinity has been defined as the exercise of self-control over pleasure and lust. Straightedgers spoke of "purifying" their bodies and utilized militaristic rhetoric about the need to maintain "discipline" and "vigilance" in the face of potential sources of "weakness."[58]

A similar fundamentalist discourse of purity and pollution was evident in DIY punk and its notions of anticommercial authenticity. Fundamentalists depend on mythologies about original moments of community and brotherhood that have been disrupted or betrayed by some outside enemy. For the various DIY and hardcore punk scenes, these alien forces were represented by "the media" and "the mainstream." All subcultures make distinctions between the genuine article and the Johnny-come-lately, but within these scenes this distinction became an end in itself. The scene had to be "defended" from sellouts and "poseurs" (bands that craved commercial success and spectators who only imitated "true" punks in their dress and demeanor, respectively).[59]

Throughout the 1980s, fanzines like *Maximumrocknroll* and *Flipside* were overwhelmingly concerned with defining what punk was and what punk was not, complaining about people who thought they were punk but really weren't, distinguishing between true originators and "trendy" followers who just "look cool," accusing certain bands of selling out, and so on. The discursive divide between independence and co-optation also echoed masculinist fears in which selling out is equated with castration, and mass culture is associated with stereotypically feminine qualities like passivity and vanity.[60]

Fundamentalist ideologies also influenced the style of hardcore music. The homogenous simplicity of hardcore rage ensured that it would remain outside the "mainstream" so long as it remained true to its style, for it was so abrasive and amateurish that it could not possibly be absorbed by the music industry or appreciated by mass audiences. Those who slowed down the tempos or included nonpunk influences were immediately under suspicion of "selling out" and betraying their fans and community. While in theory the DIY ethic was supposed to make music accessible to all, in practice the insistence on purity of form placed overwhelming limits on the possibilities for sonic experimentation. Former Dead Kennedys singer Jello Biafra would accuse *Maximumrocknroll* of "punk fundamentalism" when its editor, Tim Yohannon, pulled up the drawbridge by announcing that the fanzine would only review and accept advertising from what he called "raw punk." In 1994 Biafra had his leg broken at the Gilman Street Club in Berkeley by punks who, as they assaulted him, accused him of being a "rich rock star."

The do-it-yourself attempts to achieve commercial independence were torn between conflicting cultural traditions. In many ways, the DIY ethic of punk shares an affinity with the culture of folk music, which proposes that anyone can play music, that there should be minimal separation between musicians and audiences, and that lyricists should address important social issues. DIY also includes a more elitist reaction to the commodification of culture, however, akin to the mass culture critique of intellectuals who scorned commercial art and vilified those suspected of compromising themselves for success or profit.[61] Pierre Bourdieu has described this as a field of cultural production in which the logic of the market is reversed: artists accumulate symbolic capital by seeming to refrain from the pursuit of economic capital.[62] Both of these traditions condemned commercialism as part of a larger critique of industrial society: culture was debased by the principles of standardization and rationalization that fueled mass production on the assembly line and consumerism through the mass media. The mass culture critique views the popular arena as a source of mediocrity and fears that commercial culture is the main force that brings such mediocrity to the fore by appealing to the lowest common denominator. Meanwhile, folk music rebuked mass society from a more genuinely populist perspective, as it was intended to maximize participation, demystify the artist, and give recognition to ordinary people and places. Folk music also distinguished itself from commerce and mass culture, but it did so as part of a larger culture and social movement whose goal was to improve the lives of working people and restrain the domination of big business and the power elite.

Punk as Social Movement

The politics of punk have generally been assessed in terms of its symbolic gestures, as in Hebdige's interpretations of the meaning of style relative to the hegemonic culture of signs and language. But punk and its hardcore successor have also been connected with organized social movements, which have sought to create political change by more traditional means of protest, demonstration, and voting. For instance, the Dead Kennedys' Jello Biafra ran for mayor of San Francisco in the aftermath of the assassination of mayor George Moscone and city supervisor and gay rights activist Harvey Milk in November 1978. Biafra's campaign proposals combined the humorously absurd, such as the idea that businesspeople should be forced to wear clown suits, with the serious demands of the city's radicals, such as requiring elections for police officers. Biafra received over six thousand votes in the mayoral election of 1979, placing fourth overall.[63]

Maximumrocknroll also brought a strong leftist political orientation to the hardcore subculture after its founding in Berkeley in 1982. The fanzine helped politicize hardcore by including feature stories about issues pertaining to the nuclear arms race, U.S. policies in Central America and South Africa, sexism and violence against women, and the history of anarchism. Tim Yohannan and others who published *Maximumrocknroll* eventually established a volunteer-run, nonprofit, all-ages community center in Berkeley located at 924 Gilman Street, which held its first performance on New Year's Eve 1986. The founders of this Gilman Street project designed it to be an extension of the participatory and egalitarian spirit of the DIY ethic and accordingly refused to book performers associated with major labels.[64]

Between 1982 and 1984, some punks living in the San Francisco Bay Area came to political activism through their involvement in the peace and nuclear freeze movement, specifically with the direct actions of the Livermore Action Group (LAG) between 1982 and 1984. LAG organized

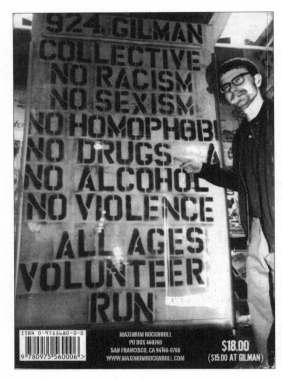

The collective, volunteer-run Gilman Street project in Berkeley, California. From *924 Gilman: The Story So Far . . .* Compiled by Brian Edge. San Francisco: Maximum Rocknroll, 2004.

blockades of the University of California's Livermore Labs, where nuclear weapons were being designed and developed. LAG included many veterans of Bay Area activism, and thus it was more hippie or pagan than punk in its cultural orientation.[65] During LAG actions, punks, who often formed their own affinity groups, utilized more confrontational as well as theatrical tactics, like staging "die-ins" in the streets and corporate lobbies of San Francisco's financial district. Punks then played a central role in the acts of civil disobedience and a "Rock Against Reagan" concert at the Democratic National Convention in San Francisco in 1984, where hundreds were arrested on the convention's final day.[66] The more aggressively defiant tactics used during these actions were clearly consistent with the confrontational style of punk music and fashion, though this did not necessarily sit well with older activists.[67]

The emergence of those who came to be known as "peace punks" in San Francisco reverberated with an upsurge of political activism in the hardcore scene in Washington, D.C. The protests of 1983–84 led to the formation of a punk-based social movement organization known as Positive Force, which was founded in Nevada through the band 7 Seconds but quickly established a strong presence in D.C.[68] Positive Force, D.C., as it came be known, expanded considerably as it linked itself to an especially vibrant scene centered around the steadfastly independent Dischord Records and innovative bands like Rites of Spring, Beefeater, and Fugazi. Punk and political activism developed symbiotically in the D.C. scene during the mid-1980s as the growing popularity of the local punk bands meant increasing visibility for Positive Force, while the demonstrations and organizing efforts of Positive Force and other activists had a politicizing effect on the bands and their audience.

The merger of punk music and political activism culminated in what participants called "Revolution Summer" in 1985, as local punks participated in regular protests against apartheid outside the South African embassy in Washington, D.C. The punks brought an element of novelty to these demonstrations in the form of "punk percussion protests," where they would pound on drums, trash cans, and buckets outside the embassy, thus mobilizing punk's noisemaking capacities for the purposes of political dissent. Meanwhile, Positive Force established links with a variety of grassroots organizations in the Washington, D.C., area, particularly abortion clinics and groups who provide assistance to the homeless, low-income people, battered women, and the elderly. Punk shows, particularly those by Fugazi, became the central means of Positive Force's ability to mobilize financial resources, as the organization claimed to have hosted nearly three hundred benefit concerts, which had raised $200,000 as of January 2000.[69]

Led by Fugazi, Dischord Records, and Positive Force, the Washington, D.C., scene set the example for do-it-yourself cultural production, commercial independence, and political activism that many others all over the United States would follow during the late 1980s and early 1990s. In San Diego, for instance, a politicized punk scene formed with an anarchist fanzine called *San Diego's Daily Impulse*. Published every two months by a collective of punks, students, and activists, this fanzine combined reviews of the latest punk concerts in San Diego with articles on everything from how to resist the draft to the history of the Haymarket strikes to reprints of Emma Goldman essays. The *Daily Impulse* also included a "Community Bulletin," which announced upcoming demonstrations or boycotts and provided contact information for local activist groups, periodicals, punk bands, and bookstores. On a more personal level, it also featured a regular column called "Dealing with Family Life," written by social workers who advised young people about how to cope with physical, emotional, and sexual abuse in their families.

An important figure in San Diego's political hardcore scene was Bob Beyerle, proprietor of the independent label Vinyl Communications and former candidate for mayor of the nearby city of Chula Vista. Beyerle was introduced to punk as a young man during the 1980s, and recalled that he was immediately attracted to its political message: "I liked the music, the whole kind of 'fuck you' thing. I was more into the social change aspect—if people hear this, they're going to think differently. And I still believe that."[70] He and some friends soon formed a band, Neighborhood Watch, and Beyerle created Vinyl Communications to distribute their music. At that time, Beyerle was also working in construction and learning to become a plumber, and he utilized those skills to build a rehearsal space and recording studio in the backyard of the house he was renting. Dozens of bands have since rehearsed, recorded, and even temporarily lived in this space, and Beyerle has also allowed it to be used by local political groups for organizing and fund-raising. For Beyerle, the do-it-yourself ethic embodied by Vinyl Communications, which released over 150 records during its tenure, is an extension of his commitment to a politics of democratic participation:

> I really like starting with something that isn't there and then turning it into something that people can hear. It's a form of communication. . . . Basically, I think a lot of it to me was like, "I think society will be better off if this stuff is out there." . . . I like to support people who are doing things that are a little more off the beaten path. . . . I just realized if we could just keep it honest and real down to earth and just put out people that a lot of people won't touch, if we can support people whose views most people don't want to hear, or haven't heard, at least we're making them available. . . . A lot of it is that it's friends and friends of friends, I like the people, I like some of the stuff they have to say, and so let's just do it. I don't love every song on every album, and anyone that runs a label and does has either put out less than five releases or is a liar. When you're supporting those people sometimes you just have to let them do their own thing, make their own mistakes. Sometimes it's worked out great. And I've learned to like a lot of styles of music.[71]

In 1990, Beyerle and some friends founded Tit Wrench, which he described as "part political party, part comedy troupe, and part band," taking

A 1986 issue of *San Diego's Daily Impulse*, an anarchist-punk newsletter (*above*).

Local punk rocker Bob Beyerle gets suited up to run for mayor of Chula Vista in 1991 (*left*).

their name from his experiences as a plumber: "I was always working on these real big houses that I couldn't buy or own. . . . The equivalent of my plumbing work in thousands of houses probably made between twenty and a hundred houses, yet I don't even own mine. I've plumbed million dollar homes. I just felt like people were breast-feeding on me on some level. I just felt like I'm like being milked. The rich sucking the tit of the working class."[72] That same year, Roger Hedgecock, a right-wing radio talk show host and former mayor of San Diego, began a campaign to "Light Up the Border," which involved having motorists shine their lights toward Mexico to "expose" those undocumented aliens purportedly entering the country. Sensing a racist campaign (which would eventually result in the passage of California's Proposition 187 in 1994), Bob and a friend felt compelled to act. They too drove down to the border that night, but rather than shine their lights toward Mexico they slowly passed in front of the other motorists and unveiled a larger banner reading, "GO BACK TO EUROPE!" They then wrote a song and collected newspaper clippings documenting the violence of border patrol agents for the release of Tit Wrench's "Go Back to Europe" seven-inch single.

In 1991 Beyerle undertook a full-fledged campaign to become mayor of his hometown of Chula Vista, located about 20 miles south of San Diego, near the Mexican border. Twenty-six years old and now working as a professional plumber, Beyerle presented himself to the largely blue-collar and Latino electorate of Chula Vista as the only working-class candidate. In an interview with *Maximumrocknroll* he stated: "I felt I am basically a working-class person and realized that there is a lot of class struggle in Chula Vista. I figured if attorneys, deputy district attorneys and financial consultants and other type of executive people, real estate developers and their friends had their candidates . . . why can't regular people have theirs?"[73] During the campaign, Beyerle attacked the incumbent city government's role in subsidizing the construction of a bayfront yacht club and a luxury hotel at a time when the majority of Chula Vista's citizens were suffering from fiscal cuts to public services. He also drew from his experiences in the punk scene to offer some alternative programs for dealing with Chula Vista's gang and drug problems: "You need to channel your rebellion into creative directions, rather than fight each other and fight your other gangs, which I think the police happen to enjoy. . . . You can channel your creativity a little more constructively and still say what you want without being violent about it or just going nowhere and then end up having to join the military and be disciplined rather than teaching yourself discipline."[74] Despite a lack of funds or the ability to take off work, Beyerle received 475 votes and finished fifth in a pool of 11 candidates.

In sum, the political activism surrounding punk and hardcore shares many similarities with what have been called "new social movements" mobilized around identity and lifestyle.[75] These examples demonstrate that punk's modes of resistance have not been limited to cultural provocation, however, for punks have also periodically engaged in what social movement scholars call "resource mobilization," which involves the strategic organization of dissent and political action.[76] The DIY ethic, especially as it involves the publication of fanzines, has facilitated this mobilization of resources in giving punks a space in which they can communicate and exchange ideas about political issues in a way that is not possible in the mainstream corporate media. In the case of Positive Force, it has also been a means of raising money and strengthening social movement organizations. The capacity of DIY cultural production to serve as the media of social movement organization will be revisited in chapter 4 when I discuss the mobilization of riot grrrl feminism.

If Reagan Played Disco

Punk came about in an age of social crisis, when there were no alternatives or utopian dreams to imagine a way out of this crisis. In retrospect we can see it as a transitional moment when capital broke from the concessions of Fordism, the political pendulum swung back to the right, and a climate of pessimism permeated popular culture. Punk embodied multiple possibilities for responding to these conditions. Many performers dramatized the cynicism of their times, some by artfully utilizing avantgarde postmodernism, others by personifying nihilism in a fashion that was only partly ironic. Some punks conceived brilliant protests against the new hegemony, and another faction sought to escape the superficiality and self-indulgence of commercial culture and created a network of little scenes in the hidden crevices of the United States.

Punk's indeterminate form sometimes facilitated extraordinary musical and political creativity. Perhaps the most shining example of all is the Minutemen, who formed in 1980 in San Pedro, California, the working-class home of Los Angeles Harbor and one of the busiest ports in the world. The Minutemen drew on their proletarian backgrounds and experiences in cultivating both a populist aesthetic and a class-conscious political critique of Reagan's America. In "This Ain't No Picnic," singer D. Boon hollers, "Working on the edge / Losing my self-respect / For a man who presides over me / The principles of his creed / Punch in punch out / Eight hours five days / Sweat pain and agony / On Friday I'll get paid." This class consciousness carried over into their denouncement of the Reagan administration's military interventions in El Salvador, Nicaragua, and Guatemala. "We know who is murdering the innocent," Boon charges in "Untitled Song for Latin America," "They are children playing with guns / They are children playing with countries / Mining harbors / Creating contras / . . . They bank their monies in this country / They steal from Indians / A colonial trait / That is much too old." And the Minutemen were all too aware that it would be working-class kids like them who would be called on to kill and die in these imperialist adventures. As they put it very succinctly in "The Only Minority": "They own the land / We work the land / We fight their wars / They think we're whores."

The Minutemen put a new spin on the do-it-yourself ethic with their proletarian populism. They developed a philosophy about recording, touring, and living that they called "econo." Doing it econo meant being as frugal as possible and maximizing the scarce resources at their disposal. Minimizing their recording and production costs, the Minutemen recorded and released about 200 songs in five years. They also created their own record label, New Alliance, which released the first album by the equally seminal Hüsker Dü, among others. But touring was their main calling, to the point where they even thought of their records as simple advertisements or "flyers" for their gigs (the opposite of what is usually done in the music industry, where tours are done to promote records). Indeed, they toured almost continuously, often while crammed into a van with Black Flag, hauling their own equipment and sleeping on people's floors. But they made enough money to keep going. Econo thriftiness gave the Minutemen access to a means of self-expression they otherwise would have lacked, because their music was too unorthodox to have any possibility of commercial success and they certainly didn't look like rock stars either, even by punk standards (Boon was quite overweight and unkempt, and as a scrawny young man, bassist Mike Watt has been said to resemble Jerry Lewis).[77]

The participatory ethos of punk and its disdain for mainstream rock's showy displays of virtuosity were the stimulus for Boon and Watt to start writing their own songs and speaking their minds. As Watt recalled it for me during an interview: "We graduated [from high school] in 1976, just when the [punk] scene starts. They were very inspiring, these guys were not afraid to start creating, no matter what their ability or anything. . . . What we saw in [punk] was open avenues to expression—gigs, records, write your own songs, talk about what's on your mind, try out new styles." He then explained that this newfound freedom to do it themselves encouraged the Minutemen to develop their sociopolitical critique through music: "With the punk rockers saying very outrageous shit, we thought, 'Well maybe we should say what's on our minds too.' . . . Our songs were slogans of what was on our minds."[78] Indeed, their song titles often read like slogans: "Dreams Are Free, Motherfucker," "The Roar of the Masses Could Be Farts," "Joe McCarthy's Ghost," and "Little Man with a Gun in His Hand."

The DIY ethic enabled the Minutemen to forge a unique sense of working-class identity at a time when that point of view appeared to be eroding and in a place (Greater Los Angeles) where it seemed to have never existed at all. They expressed their allegiance to "Pedro" in a way that rap musicians would do with their neighborhoods years later. Identifying with San Pedro set the Minutemen apart from the punk scenes that grew out of the glitz and glamour of Hollywood and the suburban sprawl of Orange County. At one time San Pedro had been a hotbed of labor radicalism, and in fact Upton Sinclair was arrested in San Pedro in 1923 for reading the U.S. Constitution in public during an IWW strike. When I interviewed Watt he was reflecting on his father's death and the unforeseen similarities between his life as a musician who had gone on over 40 tours and his father's occupation as a career navy man who did several tours in Vietnam. His father joined the navy to escape his suffocating hometown, and Watt was motivated to go on tour for similar reasons. Keeping a band going, he told me, was a lot like keeping a boat going. When I somewhat foolishly asked him when the Minutemen decided to write working-class songs, he replied: "We never really said, 'Let's write more working-class songs,' because, well, for one thing, we *were* working-class. . . . We were just talking about where we came from, where we were, and things we were facing in the day."[79]

For the Minutemen, punk was a method of creative production and self-expression rather a fixed genre of sound and style, and this philosophy empowered them to incorporate disparate sounds and influences. Within a few years, the Minutemen evolved into not only champions of the econo approach but also one of punk's most original and best musical acts. Although they included gems like the rollicking "If Reagan Played Disco" and the urgent "Paranoid Chant" (in which Boon repeatedly yells, "I keep thinking of World War Three"), their early songs (recorded in 1980–81) were merely fast and sparsely produced, and therefore often sounded redundant. By 1984, however, they had recorded a double album that is now widely hailed as a masterpiece, *Double Nickels on the Dime*, which included everything from funk to folk to free jazz. An astounding 43 tracks in all, *Double Nickels on the Dime* was a collection of song fragments that laid down a laid down a beat, a riff, and an idea and then quickly took a turn in a new direction. One critic described the sound as "dada with a groove."[80] The lyrics were perfectly suited to such fragmentation, often sounding like a stream-of-consciousness jumble that would add up to a powerful thought and sociopolitical critique. Tragically, in

December 1985, just as the Minutemen were hitting their stride, front man D. Boon was killed in an automobile accident in Arizona. Watt and drummer George Hurley later regrouped with longtime Minutemen fan Ed Crawford on vocals and guitar to form fIREHOSE.

The Minutemen have now accumulated quite a lot of critical acclaim, but mostly they were out of place in the 1980s hardcore punk scene. Watt recalled that their music "had an intensity like hardcore. . . . But if you ask the hardcore kids, they didn't know *what* the fuck we were."[81] The fundamentalist tendencies of hardcore achieved dominance and marginalized all other possibilities. Despite the rhetoric of anarchy and nonconformity, hardcore punks enforced a uniformity of sound and style in the 1980s by policing a firm boundary between themselves and the alleged poseurs and sellouts. But the DIY ethic lived on, eventually exceeding the fundamentalist limitations. The econo approach would both collide and correspond with the "New Economy" of the 1990s, and that story is told in chapter 4.

I sought out an interview with Mike Watt because he was not only a musical-political-artistic inspiration but also something of a hometown hero to me. I too had been raised in San Pedro, graduating from San Pedro High School in 1988, 12 years later than Watt. We met outside the San Pedro apartment where he still lives, and Watt immediately put me to work helping haul his gear. We drove up to a small practice space in his van (an Econoline, naturally) crammed with band equipment and stickers seeming to cover every inch of the upholstery. After our interview, we went out to get a couple of torpedo subs, and while we were eating we talked about the changes that had occurred in our hometown and on the docks. But it occurred to me that Watt and I had had very different experiences of San Pedro: if he and his buddies had been out doing it themselves, my friends and I spent our teenage years loitering around the South Bay and its beach towns, headbanging to thrash metal and getting wasted at the high point of Reagan's America. Although I was too embarrassed to tell him so, I had never even heard of the Minutemen until years after I had left San Pedro, as a graduate student studying sociology in the 1990s. By the time I was in high school, punk's thunder had been stolen by variants of heavy metal known as thrash or "speed metal," along with its "glam" and "hair band" rivals. Our story is told in chapter 3.

3

Hell Awaits

He who has been treated as the Devil recognizes the Devil when they meet.

—James Baldwin[1]

Long Beach, California, 1985: The English heavy metal band Iron Maiden performs four shows on consecutive nights at the Long Beach Arena and records their concerts for the release of a live album, *Live After Death*. A 14-year-old ninth grader at the time, I didn't go to any of the concerts. I was, however, immediately impressed by all the kids who showed up at my junior high school in the following days wearing Iron Maiden T-shirts depicting the band's mascot, Eddie, as a kind of Egyptian pharaoh on the front and a list of dates for the "World Slavery Tour" on the back. The heavy metal kids clearly stood out at my junior high school with their long hair and reputation for troublemaking, and they had carved out their own little space on school grounds that was relatively out of the sight of teachers and authorities. My years in junior high school had been very difficult, as I was a sickly and physically underdeveloped boy who was subject to a lot of bullying and harassment and didn't have much of a social life. I played baseball but had become increasingly disenchanted with the athletic crowd, as much of the bullying I experienced had come from jocks and other members of the more popular cliques at school. The heavy metal kids also picked on me when there was a group of them trying to impress one another, but when dealt with individually a lot of them seemed much nicer and friendlier. I was also becoming an angry and confused teenager, and something about the rebelliousness of the heavy metal look had begun to captivate me. So sometime shortly after those Iron Maiden concerts I simply decided that I was going to hang out in the heavy metal section of our school until they accepted me as one of their own.

As I began high school the following year, I fully immersed myself in the heavy metal subculture. Although social concerns had initiated my entry into the heavy metal crowd, I had come to enjoy the music of bands that I had seen on MTV, like Van Halen, Mötley Crüe, Ratt, and Twisted Sister. Entering high school gave me an opportunity to reinvent my identity, although some of those who remembered me from junior high taunted me with the label of "poseur." Before long I had made some new friends within the heavy metal crowd, and one of them made me a mixtape with what he said was the newest thing in metal music. The collection included the bands Exodus, Metallica, Venom, Slayer, Anthrax, Dark Angel, and Exciter, and the music was faster, angrier, and seemingly more evil than anything I had ever heard. I listened to that tape at least once a day for months and became a total convert of what my friend had introduced me to as "speed metal."

The rest of my high school years were consumed by heavy metal. I spent every penny I had on albums, T-shirts, and concert tickets. When I was still too young to drive, my mother kindly drove my friends and me to concerts at the Long Beach Arena, the L.A. Forum, and Irvine Meadows Amphitheater to see the likes of Dio, Kiss, and Iron Maiden, and she even more kindly agreed to drop us off outside the arena parking lot to save us the embarrassment of being seen driven by my mother to a heavy metal concert. As I grew older, however, I became a rabid partisan of the speed metal or "thrash" scene that had been inspired by Metallica and Slayer among others, and this brought me to smaller clubs like Fenders Ballroom in Long Beach. I grew my hair long in the back but kept it relatively short in the front, resulting in a hairstyle that is now known as a "mullet" and never fails to make me cringe when I look at old photographs, particularly those from the time when I was also trying to grow a bad teenage mustache. I also overhauled my wardrobe so that it almost exclusively consisted of T-shirts of metal bands, ripped blue jeans, long-sleeve flannels, and a sleeveless denim jacket that I adorned with the insignias of my favorite bands written in black marker. Notebooks and textbook covers became blank canvases for me to desecrate with the names of metal bands, pentagrams, and drawings of Eddie.

Heavy metal also completely reorganized my social life. Nearly all the friends I hung out with and the young women I pursued in high school listened to heavy metal music and dressed in heavy metal style. The majority of my free time was spent with other metalheads loitering on the Esplanade in Redondo Beach or waiting in liquor store parking lots for someone over 21 to buy beer for us, and always trying to avoid the police wherever we were. My engagement with heavy metal immersed me with a class of people that was very different from those I had known as a child. While my family was solidly middle class, most of the metalheads I hung out with had much more precarious backgrounds and appeared headed to quite perilous futures. Many I knew were from broken homes or were being abused by a member of their family. Some of my friends had dropped out or been kicked out of school, and a few were on their way to becoming teenage parents. It became very common for me to see people who were developing serious alcohol or drug problems, were angry or violent in a way that made it risky to hang out with them, or had contemplated or attempted suicide. This chapter will explore the sociological connections I perceived but did not understand during those years: the nexus between youth, downward socioeconomic mobility, and heavy metal subculture.

The Origins of Heavy Metal

The fusion between the Sixties counterculture and the U.S. middle and upper classes has garnered much attention in recent years.[2] Although fewer intellectuals have taken note, the counterculture also made its imprint on the lower classes of white America, with one result being heavy metal music and subculture. By the early 1970s, the counterculture had spread beyond college campuses and urban bohemian enclaves on the coasts to make its presence felt throughout every region of the United States. Although the utopian dreams of Woodstock Nation had fallen to the wayside, the symbols of countercultural rebellion—long hair, dope, and rock music, along with lessened inhibitions about sex, inherent suspicion of authority, and passive indifference to achievement—were actually more pervasive during the 1970s.[3] The counterculture fit into a working-class culture that had an ongoing tradition of rebelliousness and a deep mistrust of the middle-class ideology of meritocracy and deferred gratification. After all, the counterculture was partially rooted in working-class forms of rebellion that preceded the Sixties, such as outlaw biker gangs and images of juvenile delinquency in early rock 'n' roll and movies like *Rebel Without a Cause.*

These antecedent working-class subcultures, like the rockers in England and Hell's Angels in the United States, also brought to the counterculture their persistent elements of hypermasculinity and patriarchal gender roles, militarism and xenophobia, and fear of racial and sexual difference. These reactionary ideologies have been historically constructed and inculcated into the white working class as a means of securing a hegemonic coalition with the ruling class. This coalition has allowed the ruling class to secure economic and political power while white workers settle for mostly symbolic rewards, such as "whiteness."[4] The persona of the reactionary white worker was revived in media and popular culture beginning in the late 1960s, particularly in the images of the "hard hat" and "silent majority" that were mobilized as a backlash against the social movements for peace and equal rights.[5] Heavy metal developed from a collision between the counterculture and working-class culture in this historical moment. It emerged as a deeply contradictory subculture whose enthusiasts took pride in their rebelliousness but otherwise adhered to very conventional ideas about gender, race, and sexuality.[6] So whereas the more middle-class, post-hippie, New Age subcultures of the 1970s cultivated an aesthetic of naturalness and authenticity, the culture of heavy metal was replete with images of power, violence, and hedonism.

Heavy metal music originated during the early 1970s, its sound defined by Black Sabbath, Led Zeppelin, and Deep Purple.[7] Those bands built on the heaviest sounds of blues rock pioneered by the likes of Jimi Hendrix, Cream, and the Who, adding even more distortion to the guitars, darkening the lyrics and visual imagery, and punctuating the music with vocal wails and screams.[8] As sartorial style, heavy metal infused the hippie attire of long hair and blue jeans with the physical power embodied by the biker's leather fetish and macho posturing. Compared with the other genres that rock music splintered into during the early 1970s—southern rock, progressive rock, country rock, and so forth—heavy metal proudly identified itself as the loudest and the crudest. Heavy metal music is first and foremost defined by volume and distortion, fueled by the appropriately named power chords played on the guitar. Heavy metal also emerged at a time when rock music was becoming big business in radio airplay, concert performances, and record and musical instrument sales.[9] Radio stations often deemed the music too vulgar for airplay and record sales were modest as a result, but heavy metal bands were able to build a following among devout concertgoers. Heavy metal concerts were spectacles of power in which giant stacks of amplifiers were prominently displayed and elaborate light shows created an aura around the musical performers. Acts like Alice Cooper and Kiss capitalized on this audience by turning their shows into spectacles of blood, fire, smoke, and makeup, thus codifying heavy metal as not only a style of music but also a theater of fantasy and horror.

The popular success of heavy metal increased dramatically in the 1980s, and during this decade the genre split into different sounds and styles. The British bands Iron Maiden and Judas Priest and the solo acts of vocalists Ozzy Osbourne (iconic former front man of Black Sabbath) and Ronnie James Dio amassed large audiences through extensive touring while furthering heavy metal's association with occultism, mysticism, and mythology. A successive wave of American bands like Metallica, Slayer, Anthrax, and Megadeth mixed heavy metal with hardcore punk to create a new genre of "thrash" or "speed metal." At the other end of the spectrum, "glam metal" embodied showmanship and decadence; Van Halen, Mötley Crüe, Poison, and Guns N' Roses emerged from the Hollywood club circuit to reach extraordinary heights of celebrity and wealth. These musicians employed androgynous styles of appearance and, in a unique twist of gender performance, assumed the position of sex objects to be gazed at by an audience with a large female presence. Any gender anxieties that androgyny might have provoked were repressed by continuous affirmations of heterosexuality and masculinity, however, in which male performers purported to "kick ass" and take female groupies as their conquests.

A reciprocal yet complex relationship between heavy metal music and its young, predominantly working-class audience developed during these decades. Indeed, previous studies of heavy metal have concluded that its fans and performers, both in the United States and Britain, are disproportionately from working-class backgrounds.[10] Of course, not all metalheads are working class, but they are more commonplace as one descends down the socioeconomic hierarchy into the ranks of white society's uneducated and unskilled, especially among "at-risk" youth who find themselves in trouble with authority.[11] This is not to say that heavy metal represents a grassroots or authentic working-class culture, as the connection to its audience is mediated by music industry corporations and other powerful economic interests. Heavy metal achieved popularity because its dominant themes of power, alienation, and violence resonated with this audience, and in turn heavy metal performers fashioned their music and iconography to meet the expectations of their fans. For these reasons, although it is dangerous to equate heavy metal and working-class culture, it is also impossible to fully understand the music and subculture without a class analysis.

The connection with working-class audiences is also reinforced by heavy metal's status as among the most degraded of all forms of popular culture. From its inception, most rock journalists and academics have dismissed heavy metal as generic and oafish. These sentiments are generally shared by the public at large: a study using data from 1993 General Social Survey concluded that heavy metal was the most disliked of all genres of music.[12] But for many fans who already endure alienation and marginalization, society's rejection of heavy metal simply validates and intensifies their identification; in Deena Weinstein's words, they become "proud pariahs."[13] As social class is constituted through taste and consumption, heavy metal's condemnation of intellectualism and its infatuation with power and visceral pleasure are most likely to strike a chord with working-class audiences.

I Was Iron Man: Deindustrialization and Masculinity

Heavy metal emerged from the intersection of working-class culture and the counterculture amid deindustrialization during the 1970s and 1980s. Deindustrialization has contributed to the polarization of class structures, but it has also been experienced in gendered terms as a crisis of masculinity. The job losses and downward mobility caused by deindustrialization have emasculated working-class men by displacing the notion of the "breadwinner ethic" that was romanticized during the 1950s and 1960s.[14] Even for men who simply feared losing their job, the reality of being at the mercy of market forces contradicted the ideal that defines masculinity as a position of control. This insecurity has coincided with the increasing numbers of women in the workforce and the overall visibility of the feminist movement, which many men have interpreted as another threat to their privileged status in society. In recent decades these changes have provoked a backlash of "angry white males," directed at relatively powerless groups like racial minorities, women, immigrants, and gays, rather than corporations and the wealthy.[15]

The transition from a goods-producing to a service-based economy has also redefined work in a way that is threatening to previous conceptions of masculinity. The skills that service work demands and rewards, such as self-presentation, emotional labor, and customer service, have historically been defined as "women's work." Conversely, the conventional meanings of masculinity, especially among working-class men, have rested on attributes that are associated with the manufacturing economy, such as production, muscle, and the mastery of heavy machinery. Even if this was always something of a mythological ideal, it was a mythological ideal by which men measured and tested themselves. At the same time, the culture of consumerism and media saturation has ushered into men's lives the cycle of objectification and vanity once reserved for women. As everyday life is bombarded with a ceaseless flow of images, celebrities, and brand-name commodities, masculinity has been redefined to fit what Susan Faludi calls a "culture of ornament" (or the "new lad," as British and Australian media have dubbed him).[16] In this media-saturated culture: "Manhood is defined by youth and attractiveness, by money and aggression, by posture and swagger and 'props,' by the curled lip and petulant sulk and flexed biceps, by the glamour of the cover boy. . . . The aspects of this public 'femininity'—objectification, passivity, infantilization, pedestal-perching, and mirror-gazing—are the very ones that women have in modern times denounced as trivializing and humiliating qualities imposed on them by a misogynist culture. No wonder men are in such agony."[17]

The adolescent years are crucial in the formation of working-class masculinity, particularly as it is mediated by schooling, peer groups, and parent culture. Writing about British youth, Paul Willis described the ways in which nonconformist working-class boys become especially concerned with their performances of masculinity, which is expressed in a "shop-floor culture" of rebellion against school authorities and the educational process in general. In an economy where manufacturing jobs were still relatively plentiful, this socialization into working-class masculinity was somewhat functional, as the rebelliousness of working-class boys ensured their failure in the educational system and lack of social mobility, while their investment in masculinity prepared them to embrace a future of manual labor. But the consequences of deindustrialization have disrupted this link, and so heavy metal found its audience among the first generation of working-class youth and masculine rebels who didn't have a factory job waiting for them when they left school, and who would therefore constitute a surplus population subject to intensified processes of social control.[18]

The consequences of economic restructuring are dramatically evident in Donna Gaines's ethnography of heavy metal fans, or "metalheads," growing up in the suburb of Bergenfield, New Jersey, during the 1980s. Working-class families came to Bergenfield in the 1950s and 1960s, benefiting from rising incomes, reasonable housing costs, and an expanding school system. The situation was much different for the generation of metalheads that Gaines observed, however, as this suburban community became a site of renewed class divisions, which were especially prominent in the cliques of winners and losers formed among its teenagers. A large number of Bergenfield's metalheads were students at the local vocational and technical schools, so much so that it was dubbed "heavy metal high." Most had been tracked and filtered into this school because they weren't "college material," had gotten into some trouble, and were labeled emotionally disturbed or mentally disadvantaged. Much of their training had been rendered superfluous by deindustrialization, as Gaines describes the typical student who would graduate, "only to find out that your skills are obsolete, superficial, and the boss prefers people with more training, more experience, more training."[19] The jobs awaiting them after graduation were more likely to be in services and retail, where social skills and personal appearance are of paramount importance, thus putting metalheads, especially the self-described "dirtbags," at a disadvantage. With their opportunities for mobility restricted to military service or the microscopic chances of rock stardom, these young metalheads looked to the future like "animals before an earthquake."[20]

As a redundant population of declining economic value, the metalheads that Gaines observed were often being shuttled between institutions and diagnosed with various psychological and behavioral conditions. Some were warehoused at a place they called "the Rock," a facility for special education that housed a few of Gaines's subjects who had been diagnosed as "emotionally disturbed." The kids themselves saw the Rock as a passageway to incarceration, telling Gaines, "Well, from the Rock you go to Conklin. From Conklin you go to Jamesburg. From Jamesburg, you go to Rahway State Prison."[21] Gaines, a former social worker, explains that in the 1970s the juvenile justice system was "a punitive, patriarchal, authoritarian mess" that needed to be replaced with a more "humanistic" approach.[22] But in the 1980s, federal funds for social services had become increasingly scarce with the exception of the expanding and politically acceptable field of special education, thus providing well-intended service providers with an incentive to arbitrarily label troubled teens with the "emotionally disturbed" diagnosis. In effect, this redefined the "shopfloor culture" of working-class masculinity—fighting, talking back to authorities, not sitting still in the classroom, engaging in sabotage and pranks, and so forth—as pathologies in need of medical treatment.

The 1980s also witnessed an extraordinary growth in rehabilitation institutions and mental hospitals for teenagers who had been diagnosed with labels like conduct disorder (CD) or oppositional-defiant disorder (ODD). The number of young people confined in locked psychiatric wards more than doubled during the first half of the 1980s, from 16,735 in 1980 to over 36,000 in 1986.²³ This increase in institutionalization was closely linked to a resurgence in "moral panics" that saw heavy metal as a cause of drug use, suicide, and satanic worship.²⁴ In California, the Back in Control Center was founded with the idea that heavy metal was a cult and metal fans needed to be deprogrammed, or "de-metaled" as they put it, by confiscating all the child's music, posters, and clothing. A similar approach was taken against punk with the formation of an organization known as Parents of Punks. Meanwhile, the private psychiatric hospitals capitalized on the climate of fear by including CD and ODD in mental health treatment and often using terrifying images of teen suicide in their television commercials. With the typical 30-day stay at one of these private hospitals bringing in about $16,000 of insurance money, Mike Males wryly renamed the problem "Kid-with-Insurance-Disorder."²⁵ It is little wonder, then, that Suicidal Tendencies' "Institutionalized" and Metallica's "Welcome Home (Sanitarium)" became instant anthems within punk and heavy metal subcultures during the 1980s.

One of the musicians I interviewed ("Steve") had been placed in a mental hospital at the age of 17 under circumstances that exemplify these processes of social control. At the time, Steve was a self-proclaimed straightedge, pacifist fan of punk rock and speed metal. He had run away from home after what he described as a "wrestling match" with his step-father, an employee of the San Onofre, California, nuclear power facility, that ended when his stepfather pinned him to the ground, cut off Steve's long hair with a pair of household scissors, and then held the hair in front of his face while screaming, "You think you're a big man now?" After staying at some friends' houses for awhile, Steve agreed to meet in a neutral location with his mother, who said she was afraid he "just didn't fit into the family" and then asked her son if he would agree to check in to a nearby facility for psychiatric testing. He might have to stay overnight, but no longer, she promised. Steve agreed to go, thinking that he might actually have a problem. Upon arriving at the mental hospital, however, his fellow inmates informed him that, because he was under 18 years of age, he would have to stay a minimum of 30 days. A couple weeks passed before any "testing" was done, but Steve was soon released after his minimum-length stay produced no evidence that he was crazy ("I'm *fine*," he assured me). He returned home after being released but was promptly kicked out of the house by his stepfather. Having run out of places to stay, Steve told me that he ended up with a group of kids who would hang out at a shopping mall during the day and sleep in a ditch behind a graveyard at night.[26]

This remainder of this chapter will examine heavy metal within the social context of deindustrialization and the mediating experiences of class, gender, and youth. I begin with an analysis of the original heavy metal bands that emerged from Britain in the 1970s. Drawing on the Marxist concept of reification, I maintain that heavy metal's iconography has objectified socioeconomic sources of disempowerment in images of evil, chaos, and destruction beyond human control. In moving on to the American heavy metal of the 1980s, I argue that the symbolic response to social processes differs greatly within two different subgenres of heavy metal. In the faster and gloomier speed metal and thrash, power continues to be represented as an unstoppable force that overwhelms its victims, though in American thrash these forces were less often depicted as supernatural. In contrast, the glam metal scene centered on Hollywood's Sunset Strip celebrated wealth, hedonism, and "rags-to-riches" mythologies in its collective fantasy of escape from downward mobility. Glam metal musicians embodied ornamental masculinity in a most exaggerated way, as they adopted a feminine appearance and sexually objectified themselves, but did so as a means to the conventionally masculine ends of sexual conquest and playboy-style decadence. In its extreme image consciousness, vulgar materialism, and individualistic ideology, glam metal was a nearly perfect complement to Reagan's America.

The Unmaking of the English Working Class

In his monumental work *The Making of the English Working Class*, historian E.P. Thompson documented the formation of class consciousness and culture among the English proletariat in response to industrialization in the years between roughly 1780 and 1850. In some circles, the Jacobins of the French Revolution, Thomas Paine's *Rights of Man*, Robert Owen's vision of socialism, and Luddite destruction of machinery radicalized working-class culture. But English workers' responses to industrialization were not always overtly political. The same time period saw the dramatic rise of millenarian movements that prophesized apocalypse with reference to the book of Revelations, the most popular of which was Joanna Southcott's "cult of the poor." Although such movements may be easy to dismiss as paranoid fantasy, Thompson's historical analysis treated them as an important "sign of how men felt and hoped, loved and hated, and of how they preserved certain values in the very texture of their language."[27] These prophesies of impending doom took hold among people whose communities and traditions had been uprooted, and who found themselves de-skilled, impoverished, and threatened with sickness and starvation in England's overcrowded industrial cities. Thompson's social history demonstrates that class exploitation can have cultural consequences in which power and chaos are only indirectly confronted through fantasy and metaphor. Thus even the most bizarre and paranoid visions cannot be written off as mere "false consciousness."

Thompson wrote that this was "a time when men's psychic world was filled with violent images from hell-fire and Revelation, and their real world was filled with poverty and oppression."[28] He might just as easily have been referring, however, to the emergence of heavy metal in a time when deindustrialization was decimating many of these same factory towns in the 1970s. In Britain, the number of manufacturing jobs declined from 8 million in 1971 to 5.5 million in 1984.[29] The consequences of deindustrialization were especially harsh for large industrial cities, as London, Manchester, and Liverpool lost a disproportionate number of jobs and experienced a 15 to 20 percent decline in their populations between 1971 and 1981.[30] Some of the self-anointed mystics from the early nineteenth century described by Thompson bear a striking resemblance to the heavy metal doomsayers who surfaced from the declining industrial cities in the late twentieth century. Consider the Unitarian minister Ebenezer Aldred, a "dreamy and wild" man with "grey hair flowing down his shoulders" who "lived in a kind of solitude"; or "Zion" Ward, a crippled shoemaker who believed he was Christ but had also once been Satan during his lifetime.[31] Thompson reports that Ward's lectures calling for the overthrow of all clergy "drew enormous audiences" of up to 2,000 during the summer of 1831, until he was eventually found guilty of blasphemy and imprisoned for two years. His story thus parallels many heavy metal bands whose profane performances achieved massive popularity along with persecution from the powers that be. Like many heavy metal performers, Ward also gained a following among young people by preaching a message of sexual liberation and antinomianism (the belief that Christians are not obliged to obey moral law), holding that "if you love one another, go together at any time without any law or ceremony."[32]

We can thus detect a parallel between the ways that heavy metal and punk reacted to the social crises of the 1970s and 1980s and the millennial cults and radical social movements during the Industrial Revolution.

Operating as postmodern successors to the socialists and Luddites who raged against the machines of industrialization, punk directly and dramatically confronted the social system and its hegemonic culture. Not surprisingly, punk has received far more attention from radical intellectuals and activists. Heavy metal, on the other hand, dwells in a world of demons, monsters, and other forces of evil and destruction, and like millennial cults it has fulfilled its apocalyptic imaginations with biblical prophesies, from Black Sabbath's "War Pigs" to Iron Maiden's "The Number of the Beast" to Venom's "The Seven Gates of Hell." Because of a perceived lack of political engagement, as well as its low cultural status, heavy metal has received far less attention from scholars, despite album sales and concert attendance that suggest greater popularity than punk. And yet heavy metal may hold the keys to understanding the plight of working-class youth in the 1970s and 1980s, particularly their failure, inability, or refusal to confront the social inequalities and injustices stemming from deindustrialization.

In heavy metal, working-class consciousness in the context of deindustrialization is mediated by reification, which György Lukács defined as a metamorphosis in which "a relation between people takes on the character of a thing and thus acquires a 'phantom objectivity.'"[33] Under the capitalist mode of production, society's creations appear to have a life of their own, as if they are forces of nature and are therefore timeless and immutable. Lukács traced reification back to Marx's notion of commodity fetishism, in which exchange value reshapes social relations among people such that they "assume, in their eyes, the fantastic form of a relation between things."[34] Reification is therefore a consequence of capitalist societies in which people lose control over the production process and social relations are determined by economic forces that operate with mysterious objectivity, as suggested by the common metaphor of the "invisible hand" of the market. The products of human labor, as well as social activity in general, become alien to their producers and seem to acquire power over them. Lukács thus brilliantly reconstructed the young Marx's concern with alienation, and he was also influenced by Max Weber's theories of rationalization and bureaucracy as well as Georg Simmel's studies of money and exchange.[35] The common denominator among alienation, rationalization, and the money economy is the way people create social forces that then take on an objective form beyond their ability to control.

The devil and other symbols of evil materialize within this context as powers of destruction that cannot be comprehended or influenced, much less stopped, by ordinary human beings. They are an expression of the irony that society has become a victim of social forces, "like the sorcerer, who is no longer able to control the powers of the nether world whom he has called up by his spells," in the words of Marx and Engels that resemble the lyrics of a heavy metal song.[36] For example, in *The Devil and Commodity Fetishism*, the esteemed anthropologist Michael Taussig found peasants invoking the image of Satan to describe the economic transformations taking place in the sugar plantations of western Colombia and the tin mines of Bolivia, where peasants were being rapidly turned into proletarians in a manner strikingly similar to the making of the English working class described by E.P. Thompson. Over the course of Taussig's fieldwork, these communities saw their long-standing economies based on reciprocity and use value supplanted by capitalist processes of commodification and calculation, and in both places the workers invoked the devil as a metaphor for the havoc wreaked by this transformation. Colombian and Bolivian workers used the devil to represent capitalism in their folklore as "collective representations of a way of life losing its life" and symbols of "what it means to lose control over the means of production and be controlled by them."[37]

Heavy metal evolved from a social context that differed from the periods of industrialization chronicled by Thompson and Taussig; yet the loss of power among English and American working-class youth in the 1970s and 1980s was once again fueled by mystifying market forces that resulted in deindustrialization, downward economic mobility, and a crisis of masculinity. The devil was conjured again as a symbol of social processes that are absolute and overwhelming in their consequences yet invisible and impersonal in their origins. These ominous forces extend beyond the class system to include the dogs of war and the authorities of school, law, and family. The music and iconography of heavy metal speaks to a general sense of powerlessness among young people that pervades all aspects of their everyday lives. Heavy metal objectifies power into monsters and magical forces of evil in an act of reification that symbolizes a loss of control over all of society's institutions.

Reification was also apparent in other forms of popular culture that coincided with heavy metal's evolution during the 1970s. In Hollywood there was a revival of horror and disaster films in which social crisis was metaphorically represented by skyscrapers that catch fire, planes that crash into airports, and evil spirits who take possession of young girls. The causes of destruction were depicted as machines or demons, but equally important were their consequences of social disorder and an absence of authority. In the disaster genre, order is restored by men and the symbols of patriarchy, by heroes who represent the police or the church but act as lone rangers independent of any organization. Their enemies are pencil-necked peons of bureaucracy and government, emasculated men or ball-busting women who attempt to rein in the rugged individualist. Popular movies thus anticipated many of the changes in political culture that would occur in the 1980s: the fear of disorder and change; the desire for an authoritarian male leader; the exaltation of individualism and evasion of social responsibility; the association of liberalism with effeminacy; and nostalgia for the symbols of tradition and patriarchy. The movies of the 1970s depicted a society in crisis and a void waiting to be filled.[38]

Reification is not only evident in the way that heavy metal subculture demonizes the powerful and dominant, but also in the instances where it tries to harness supernatural forces as sources of resistance and empowerment. Although various adult authorities and media have wildly exaggerated the extent of devil worship in heavy metal, it is also clear that some metal fans and performers have indeed experimented with the occult in an attempt to gain magical powers or get revenge on authorities or peers. For instance, while Black Sabbath usually portrayed Satan and the supernatural as forces of destruction, in "The Wizard" they contrastingly fantasized about magical forms of resistance against demonic evil. Aleister Crowley, the notorious English occultist and drug enthusiast, has occupied a role analogous to "The Wizard" in heavy metal lore, from Led Zeppelin guitarist Jimmy Page's purchase of his estate to Ozzy Osbourne's "Mr. Crowley" to Iron Maiden's "Moonchild." Heavy metal's search for mystical sources of empowerment speaks to a profound sense of disempowerment in the social world, for it can only imagine fantastic and otherworldly methods of resistance to power. Reification thus operates in a dual sense, both in the way that heavy metal depicts oppressive authorities as evil spirits and in its fantasies about resistance derived from magical energies. In either case, the imagery of heavy metal expresses a mystification of power relations—a general sense of confusion about how social power subjugates young people and the working class, and how exploited peoples can take power and resist their exploiters.

The notion that heavy metal's devils, monsters, and evil spirits are actually metaphors for social power contradicts the prevailing view of heavy metal as escapist fantasy. Like the millennial movements of the Industrial Revolution, its apocalyptic imagery is a cultural response to socioeconomic disruption and injustice. The reification of class consciousness in heavy metal, however, poses the same problem that it did for Lukács and his successors in the Frankfurt School: if capitalism appears to be natural, timeless, and operating with a life of its own, how is it possible to imagine social change? Indeed, the cultural politics of heavy metal are typically antiauthoritarian yet libertarian. Its symbolism is ripe with opposition to individuals and institutions that exercise power visibly and directly, but the same ideology of libertarianism is complicit with economic forces that are often more destructive in their consequences but are largely invisible or apparently inevitable.

Three forms of reification can be found in heavy metal music and subculture: the representation of power as demonic or supernatural; the displacement of power into ancient mythology and history; and the fetishism of commodities and spectacles that signify power. Each of these forms of reified power will now be discussed in association with the seminal British heavy metal bands Black Sabbath, Iron Maiden, and Judas Priest. As is well-known, each of these bands emerged from working-class communities in industrial cities during the peak of deindustrialization and urban decline in the late 1960s and 1970s: Black Sabbath and Judas Priest from Birmingham, and Iron Maiden from East London.

Black Sabbath and Satan

Black Sabbath solidified the partnership between heavy metal and demonology. Musically, as Robert Walser observed, they "took the emphasis on the occult even further [than other heavy metal bands], using dissonance, heavy riffs, and the mysterious whine of vocalist Ozzy Osbourne to evoke overtones of gothic horror."[39] Black Sabbath established the distinctively evil sound of heavy metal with the use of the diminished fifth, otherwise known as the "tritone," that in the Middle Ages was condemned as the sound of Satan and eventually earned the name *diabolus in musica* ("the devil in music").[40] On Black Sabbath's self-titled debut album, Satan appears as a force of destruction to be feared, not a deity to be worshipped. On the terrifying song "Black Sabbath," Osbourne sings from the perspective of someone being chased by Satan, screaming, "Oh no, no, please God help me," as bells ring ominously alongside the guitar drone; by the time the song reaches its climax, everyone in the song is running to escape Satan. In "N.I.B.," the devil is a manipulator who steals people's souls and takes psychological control over their whole person. These two

sides of power—a force of violent annihilation on some occasions, an om-
nipotent master of personal deception and control in others—characterize
Satan's appearances in most other Black Sabbath songs. These are primarily songs about power, whether it is power over an entire community of
people or total control over one individual.

The paradigmatic example of how Satan and black magic symbolize
the social powers that create war, poverty, and injustice is "War Pigs," in
which the architects of war are portrayed as witches, sorcerers, and evil
minds. Recorded in 1970, "War Pigs" begins with the sound of air raid
sirens and Tony Iommi's distinctively heavy but slow guitar sludge, and as
the music's tempo increases Osbourne charges that politicians start wars
"just for fun" but leave poor people to do the fighting, treating them like
"pawns in a chess game." As the song comes to a close, it is Judgment Day,
God is taking vengeance, and the warmongers are on their knees begging
for mercy. Satan appears in the song's last line, laughing and spreading his
wings, perhaps knowing that although his minions have been destroyed,
he will live on to create more episodes of destruction in the future. "War
Pigs" is a powerful antiwar song, but again it reifies warfare by portraying
it as a conflict between supernatural forces in which divine intervention is
the only hope for peace.

Satan had made previous appearances in the history of popular music
before heavy metal, but his meaning in earlier genres was somewhat different. In the blues, the devil periodically materialized as a "trickster" with
whom someone like Robert Johnson, according to blues legend, could sell
his soul in exchange for extraordinary powers on the guitar. This image
has its roots in West African folklore, as George Lipsitz has written: "The
trickster figure at the crossroads—often interpreted in the romantic tradition as the devil—is really Eshu-Elegbara (Legba, Elebgba, Esu), not the
incarnation of evil, but an unpredictable deity with the power to make
things happen, a god described . . . as 'the ultimate master of potentiality.'"[41] In the blues, Satan is often encountered at the crossroads, a symbolic place where decisions must be made and multiple possibilities arise.
He is not the force of unequivocal evil and destruction he is in Black Sabbath songs, but rather a spirit with the ability to make things happen and
instill people with creative powers.

In 1968 the Rolling Stones recorded "Sympathy for the Devil" amid a
worldwide youth revolt. In this song, the devil "introduces" himself as a
figure who has presided over other revolutionary and apocalyptic moments in history. He is to be feared and respected but is not a figure of

unambiguous evil, for he also personifies the specter of change that entranced millions of youths all over the world in 1968. In Marshall Berman's reading, the devil in this song is akin to the one Goethe created in *Faust*, in which experimentation and annihilation are irrevocably bound together in modernity's spirit of creative destruction.[42] "Sympathy for the Devil" urges the Sixties generation to know who they're dealing with—to guess his name and the nature of his game—but it doesn't caution them to stay away. The Rolling Stones had summoned the devil the previous year in *Their Satanic Majesty's Request*, but the results were notoriously disastrous, as they levitated him into a cosmic, psychedelic imitation of the Beatles' *Sgt. Pepper's Lonely Hearts Club Band*. Satan was better suited for 1968, the cataclysmic year when the impossible was demanded and the forces of law and order responded by laying young souls to waste.

"War Pigs" demonstrates how supernatural powers can be used to signify social forces, but it is a significant departure from blues songs in which devil-like figures appear as a "master of potentiality" or the Faustian spirit of "Sympathy for the Devil." As with punk, it is an expression of the loss of confidence in social change among rebellious youth in the aftermath of the Sixties. In 1967 Abbie Hoffman, Jerry Rubin, and the Yippies organized an antiwar action in which they fantasized that supernatural spirits might be conjured to serve peace; they costumed themselves as witches and humorously performed a ritual to levitate the Pentagon and exorcise its evil spirits. This sense of possibility had largely evaporated by 1970. In "War Pigs," it is God, not the antiwar movement, who brings the war machine to justice, and even then Satan just laughs, spreads his wings, and presumably lives on to fight another day.

Iron Maiden, Mythology, and History

Iron Maiden also dwelled in demonic imagery but further expanded the scope of images of power borrowed from history and mythology. The band originally formed in London's East End, where working-class subcultures of skinheads and mods had previously emerged from neighborhoods razed by urban redevelopment.[43] Iron Maiden initially cultivated an urban, street-tough image that drew from the punk movement that surrounded them in the late 1970s. Their mascot, Eddie, a zombie-like creature who appeared on albums, T-shirts, and merchandise as a kind of "undead Mickey Mouse," was conceived by Derek Riggs to embody "the idea that the youth of the day was being wasted by society."[44] Eddie appeared against a background of urban slums on early album covers and singles, and he even became a subject of controversy when he was depicted knifing prime minister Margaret Thatcher on the cover of Iron Maiden's second single, "Sanctuary." So although Iron Maiden's music was always distinguishable as heavy metal, its imagery of urban decay, political violence, and "wasted youth" was initially quite similar to punk's depiction of social chaos.

From the band's self-titled debut album, "Running Free" exemplifies the early Iron Maiden aesthetic, where power appears in more socially realist forms, if only as something to be escaped. The song introduces a protagonist who resembles so many of Iron Maiden's fans who were young, broke, and had nothing to do. He soon finds himself in jail, as the single's cover art depicts a young longhair trapped in an alley and running from some ghoulish-looking monsters. The song's triumphant moment is certainly its chorus, one of the great heavy metal sing-alongs, which prompts its audience to collectively affirm, "I'm running free, yeah / I'm running free." "Running Free" became a staple of Iron Maiden's concerts, and the sound of thousands of young misfits singing along with this chorus, as recorded in the concert album *Live After Death*, speaks volumes about heavy metal's escapist inclinations.

Iron Maiden's representations of power were thus more direct and realistic in their early years, locating themselves and Eddie in the decaying urban environment of late-1970s London, escaping if not resisting authority and the law. Over the course of the 1980s, however, Iron Maiden's representation of power and authority became less direct, as the band delved into an eclectic (some would say incongruous) mixture of symbols drawn from mythology, literature, history, and occultism. Various songs were inspired by, among other elements, the book of Revelations, Greek mythology, Viking conquerors, Egyptian pharaohs, and Japanese samurais, as well as science fiction, romantic poetry, World War II battles, and legendary historical figures. For subsequent albums and tours Eddie was costumed as a British soldier, a lobotomized prisoner, an Egyptian pharaoh and a mummy, and a futuristic cyborg. Iron Maiden's imagery was abstracted from its social context, and abstraction reified those images of power by making them appear to have a life of their own. As Robert Walser explained in his analysis of Iron Maiden's mysticism: "Christianity, alchemy, myth, astrology, the mystique of vanished Egyptian dynasties: all are available in the modern world as sources of power and mystery. Such eclectic constructions of power, which might usefully be called postmodern, are possible *only because* they are not perceived as tied to strict historic contexts."[45] Whereas Iron Maiden initially confronted forms of power and authority literally, in this phase they did so from the distance of history and fantasy.

The band's selectively appropriated histories and mythologies of conquest, slaughter, and slavery depicted the powers that be as overwhelming and irresistible. Iron Maiden eventually released a concept album titled *Seventh Son of a Seventh Son*, whose songs loosely fit together in a story of fate, power, and the struggle between good and evil. The album plays on the mythology that boys who are the seventh son of a father who is himself a seventh son are born with special powers of clairvoyance. Those powers are also a curse, however, as the seventh son cannot control them and is tormented by visions and nightmares. Over the course of the album, the child comes to understand his visions only to see that his village is bound for destruction. He tries to warn the other villagers, but they ignore him. In fact, when the village is finally destroyed they blame the seventh son, believing that he has brought a curse on them. The boy realizes that the future has already been written and cannot be changed, and as the album comes to an end we are told that "only the good die young" and "all the evil seem to live forever." Here again, although *Seventh Son of a Seventh Son* dwells in fantasy and magic, it is not difficult to see how this is a story tailor-made for those who feel helplessly doomed by authorities in the real world. The seventh son can see his community's imminent destruction but is powerless to do anything about it, and no one is listening to him anyway. When disaster strikes, he is turned into a scapegoat in much the same way that rebellious young people and youth culture have been demonized throughout recent history.

Judas Priest, Spectacle, and Commodity Fetishism

If Black Sabbath and Iron Maiden established heavy metal's association with occultism and mythology, Judas Priest was largely responsible for defining its style, specifically in their fetish for leather and motorcycles. In the early 1980s, Judas Priest led the way in establishing heavy metal as a unique style of its own as they dropped their earthy hippie look and adopted a more fetishistic style dominated by leather, studs, and spikes. Singer Rob Halford cultivated this look while shopping in London's clothing stores catering to sadomasochistic tastes and lifestyles. Halford remained a closeted gay man throughout the peak of Judas Priest's career and up until the late 1990s, and when he did come out some wondered how he was able to maintain such an exalted place in "the most Neanderthal-posing rock genre in music" and consistently "[fill] arenas with nasty beer-drinking, head-banging hetero boys."[46] While there are certainly strong elements of homophobia in heavy metal subculture, it also exhibits a lot of latent homoeroticism and, especially outside of its glam metal variations, largely excludes all things feminine.[47] In short, Judas Priest defined heavy metal with a masculine style in which masculinity is realized by the exhibition of power and domination, which are channeled through fetishized commodities like leather and motorcycles.

Judas Priest represented reified forms of power through commodity fetishism, and their performances can be usefully described as a "spectacle" in the sense that Guy Debord meant it, further elaborating on Marx's notion of the commodity. Debord revisited Marx's concept of commodity fetishism in developing his theory of the spectacular society in the mid-twentieth century. The spectacle is also an outgrowth of Marx's critique of religious illusion, in which religion is not merely the "opiate of the masses" but the objectification of social relations and power, a force that then appears to seize power over the people who created it. Judas Priest concerts were spectacles in the sense of a social interaction between performer and audiences that is about the exhibition of power, and where power is mediated by things like motorcycles, macho fashion, machines, and earsplitting music. The band's sadomasochistic style was complemented by Halford's piercing vocals, the Harley-Davidson motorcycles he would ride on stage, and the dueling rhythm guitars and giant stacks of amplifiers. The way that these commodities seem to magically embody power is analogous to how gods or idols (or, in this case, rock stars) are endowed with extraordinary qualities by the people who worship them. Debord observed: "The spectacle is the material reconstruction of the religious illusion. Spectacular technology has not dispelled the religious clouds where men had placed their own powers detached from themselves; it has only tied them to an earthly base."[48]

Judas Priest endowed the spectacle with competing possibilities for both oppressive power and empowering resistance, just as we have said that the reification of power more generally haunts heavy metal's fantasies of both exploitation and empowerment. In "Electric Eye," one of their most beloved songs, Halford sings from the perspective of a machine of surveillance. The electric eye is the spectacle as reified power in the sense of Foucault's panopticon, a machine with a life of its own that is irresistible because it is watching all the time and able to penetrate into private lives, while those who are being watched cannot know if and when the machine is watching. Meanwhile, in the music and Halford's vocals, as Walser elucidated, "the eye's persona is split: the first stanza is official and public, marked by Halford with measured, middle-range singing and by added chorus and reverb that suggest spatial power and social legitimacy."[49]

The video for "Electric Eye," however, reveals the other dimension of the spectacle, which involves religious illusion in the social interaction between performer/commodity and audience/consumer. Filmed at a Judas Priest concert, the video begins with blue lights illuminating what looks to be some sort of machine on stage. Thousands of fans scream in anticipation and throw their hands up in the famous metal/devil salute, and the machine explodes as the guitar riff reaches its triumphant moment, with pyrotechnics and fireworks shooting in every direction. Then a new, larger robot begins to arise, and Halford comes on stage to join his bandmates. The robot's mechanical arms lift him up as he begins to sing the opening lines, thus literally positioning him "up in space" and "looking down on" us, his fans. The fans scream for Halford as the robot lifts him, and they keep screaming when he points back to acknowledge them.

The video for "Electric Eye" thus depicts the spectacle of the Judas Priest concert not simply as a technological force of inhuman power but also as a source of ecstasy for its audience. This aspect of the Judas Priest concert reveals it to be a spectacle in the sense of a religious ceremony, one that may be profane in many ways and tied to "an earthly base," as Debord put it, but is still shrouded in mystical imagery and the worship of idols that continues to resemble "the religious clouds where men had placed their own powers detached from themselves."[50] The ceremonial or ritualistic elements of Judas Priest concerts—humorously captured in the short cult film *Heavy Metal Parking Lot*—depict how the collective power of the audience is transferred to the God-like performer, who in turn wields the power to induce his worshippers into a state of religious (if intoxicated) frenzy.

In other instances, however, these sources of empowerment have been channeled not only for religious ecstasy but also for political resistance against the spectacle itself, as in the early promotional video for "Breaking the Law," where Judas Priest use their guitars and the volume of their music to rob a bank and overpower the bank tellers and customers. One of the first images we see in this video is a surveillance camera in a bank, and the next shot shows a security guard asleep at his job in front of the camera. Next we see Halford riding in a car and singing the blues of a newly unemployed drifter. As the video progresses, the formerly sleeping security guard is transformed into a rocker overcome by the urge to play air guitar. Meanwhile, Judas Priest's guitarists have terrified the tellers and customers by pointing their instruments at them menacingly while Halford sings, and they escape after using their guitars to open the bank vault (in a moment of pure self-promotion, however, they only take a gold record of their own album). "Breaking the Law" is therefore a fantasy of resistance in which heavy metal music overpowers the surveillance machine and the capitalists it serves, in part by the sheer power of the music itself but also by converting the worker who supervises the financial system into a headbanger.

The Metal Militia

Heavy metal and punk emerged as antagonistic and seemingly incompatible subcultures, but in the 1980s they began moving closer to each other. For example, Black Flag, the kings of California hardcore, were growing out their hair and composing longer songs using thicker guitar riffs. The metal-punk crossover was also embodied by the biker band Motörhead and the horror-punk spectacle of both the Damned and the Misfits. Suicidal Tendencies, Dirty Rotten Imbeciles, and Corrosion of Conformity were among a number of bands who had started out playing hardcore punk but began to incorporate more metal music over the course of the 1980s. In cities like San Francisco and New York, the audiences for metal and punk had also been forced to coexist during the 1980s as gentrification shrunk the number of clubs and venues available for musical performance.[51] For years, punks and metalheads had been embroiled in a bitter and frequently violent rivalry: punks routinely dismissed metalheads as politically apathetic wasteoids, while in turn metalheads accused punks of being self-righteous and puritanical. As a result, the metal-punk crossover met with a lot of resistance, especially on the part of politically oriented punks.

In its intersection with punk, the thrash metal subculture represented a significant departure from the form of heavy metal that originated in Britain during the 1970s. Thrash metal adopted punk's veneration of authenticity, distinguishing between insiders and "poseurs," minimizing distance between fans and musicians, and maintaining an underground scene through independent record labels. Influenced by punk, thrash bands abandoned the fantasy and mysticism that defined heavy metal acts like Iron Maiden and Dio and began to write songs about real-world injustices like environmental destruction and political corruption. As I will argue, however, thrash metal bands continued to represent these forms of power as reified forces of destruction. Though they were ostensibly more "political" topics, ecological ruin and nuclear annihilation simply replaced Satan and the book of Revelations as objectified sources of obliteration.

As a style of music, thrash metal merged heavy metal's volume with punk's speed. If heavy metal's thunderous volume produced an atmosphere of gloom and doom, speed created the feeling of an out-of-control world changing too fast. During live performances, the speed in thrash metal intensified the slam pits that originated with punk, where mostly male spectators would form a fast-moving circle in front of the stage, flailing their arms and legs while periodically slamming into one another. As in the initial punk scene, the thrash subculture's ethos stated that anyone knocked down in the pit should be helped up in a communitarian spirit, but increasingly the reality was that it was every boy for himself. Periodically, a spectator would climb to the front of the stage, revel in his 15 nanoseconds in the spotlight with the band, and then try to escape the beefy bouncers policing the stage and dive back into crowd. Thus the meanings and contradictions of this subculture were on full display in the rituals of the thrash show—the push to go faster without getting anywhere, the spirit of community, the threat of violence, and the pleasures of evading authority. The pit served as an apt metaphor for disenfranchised youths running in circles and getting nowhere, and it also mirrored the conflicts of working-class masculinity built with one part solidarity and one part aggression.

The most popular and successful band to emerge from this thrash scene, and American heavy metal in general, is Metallica. The band's principal founder, Lars Ulrich, was the son of a professional tennis player whose family moved from Denmark to Los Angeles when Ulrich was 16 so that he could pursue a professional tennis career of his own. Metallica was formed in 1981 when Ulrich placed an advertisement in the *Recycler*—a classifieds-only newspaper that has mediated the formation of countless rock bands in the Los Angeles area—that was answered by James Hetfield, the son of a truck driver and opera singer who were strict practitioners of Christian Science. Ulrich in particular had been influenced by a cluster of British bands that had been collectively dubbed the "new wave of British heavy metal," which included Iron Maiden along with many other more

The mosh pit during a thrash show (*above*). From *Waiting for the Sun: Strange Days, Weird Scenes, and the Sound of Los Angeles.* Barney Hoskyns. New York: St. Martin's, 1996.

Flyer for "Thrashfest 1987" in San Diego (*left*).

obscure groups. Metallica's first recorded song was released in 1982 on a compilation album called *Metal Massacre* organized by Brian Slagel, the Los Angeles–based publisher of a fanzine called the *New Heavy Metal Revue* and founder of the independent label Metal Blade Records.

There was a burgeoning heavy metal scene that was rapidly supplanting punk on Hollywood's Sunset Strip, but it was a more image-conscious glam scene and Metallica did not have a place. Ulrich and Hetfield were courting a new bassist they had seen at the Whisky a Go Go, a hippieish iconoclast named Cliff Burton with a uniquely distorted sound, and Burton insisted that he would join Metallica only if the band agreed to relocate to San Francisco. The crossover thrash scene had just begun to develop in the Bay Area, with the bands Exodus and Blind Illusion having already formed and a throng of new bands, including Death Angel, Possessed, Lääz Rockit, Legacy (later renamed Testament), Heathen, Forbidden, Vio-lence, Attitude Adjustment, Faith No More, and Defiance, that would all form in the first half of the 1980s. The names of these bands—Exodus, Death Angel, Possessed, Testament, and so forth—illustrate the biblically violent preoccupations of the thrash scene. Most of the local thrash shows were held in the city of San Francisco, particularly at a club called the Stone, but a large number of the scene's fans and musicians hailed from the East Bay's industrial cities of Oakland, Hayward, and San Leandro, whose blue-collar neighborhoods experienced explosive population growth during and shortly after World War II. Thus thrash metal found its most devout supporters in a generation of young people whose working-class parents had benefited from the social democracy of postwar Fordism but who were facing precarious futures in a new postindustrial economy.

Early in their career, Metallica songs drew on heavy metal's most dependable sources of inspiration: the books of Exodus and Revelations. They renamed one of their earliest guitar epics "The Four Horsemen," and on their second album, *Ride the Lightning*, they wrote a song based on the ten plagues from Exodus called "Creeping Death." But beginning on *Ride the Lightning*, they also began to tackle social issues, from nuclear war ("Fight Fire with Fire") to the death penalty ("Ride the Lightning") to the Spanish Civil War ("For Whom the Bell Tolls") to suicidal despair ("Fade to Black"). Their next album, *Master of Puppets*, continued to depict ominous yet unnamed forces of power wielding total control over helpless human subjects. On the title track, it is unclear who the puppeteer "pulling the strings" is, but the consistent message is that people are slaves to objectified powers, be they money, religion, drugs, family, or government. In general, the lyrics of *Master of Puppets* describe the consequences of alienation and oppression as people are powerless to resist the institutions that control them. For instance, "Welcome Home (Sanitarium)" conveys the thoughts of someone caged in a mental institution, while "Disposable Heroes" concerns a young soldier who is ordered to fight and die alone on the front lines.

Metallica's political critique continued with their next album, . . . *And Justice for All*, whose cover art and title track depicted the justice system being corrupted by money. The album's opening track, "Blackened," described environmental destruction, and the band reached new heights of popularity with their song and video for "One," inspired by Dalton Trumbo's antiwar novel *Johnny Got His Gun*. Indeed, Metallica's songs lambasted a wide range of authorities and institutions. But regardless of the specific target of criticism, one consistent message was repeated over and over again: there are overwhelming powers out to get you, they will control and destroy you, and there's nothing you can do about it. In this sense, although Metallica's songs progressed from the supernatural and the biblical to the social and political, there was considerable continuity in the way they portrayed power in reified terms as unstoppable and inescapable. In Metallica's world, power is corrupt but resistance is futile.

Following Metallica's lead, other thrash bands began to incorporate social criticism in their songs. It is impossible to know how audiences received and understood those messages, but the available evidence suggests some deep contradictions in the political consciousness of metal fans. Based on his interviews with heavy metal fans in which politics was one of a number of topics discussed, sociologist Jeffrey Arnett concluded: "Generally their positions on these issues are not best characterized as liberal or conservative, but rather as libertarian, in the sense of wishing to have as few restrictions or sanctions as possible on their behavior."[52] Indeed, libertarianism is an ideology that perfectly complements the reification of class consciousness, for it opposes those institutions that exercise power visibly and directly, yet it complies with economic forces that are often more destructive in their consequences but are largely invisible or appear to be natural and inevitable. The metalheads Arnett interviewed were opposed to government interventions in issues of abortion, gun control, the censorship of music and other media, and the criminalization of marijuana and pornography. This made them vocal opponents of the fundamentalist Christian faction of the New Right. But the same ideology of individual freedom and skepticism of government regulation could be used to manufacture a consensus for economic policies that greatly benefited corporations and the wealthy to the detriment of working-class people. While the impact of these policies might be clearly evident in unemployment and poverty, the reification of "the economy" could just as easily lead people to blame job loss on immigration or affirmative action.

Metallica is the most commercially successful band to have emerged from the thrash scene, but a great number of arguably more devoted fans identified with the genre's most extreme band, Slayer. At the dawn of the thrash scene, Slayer's music was the fastest and also the most brutal, with lyrics and visual imagery that went several steps further in depicting horrifying scenarios of violence. Formed in 1981 in Southern California's Huntington Beach, Slayer got their start playing covers of Iron Maiden and Judas Priest songs while incorporating an almost cartoonish image of satanism in their stage shows and personal appearance. In time, they shed most of these references to otherworldly forces of evil and replaced them with true-life accounts of warfare, serial killers, the Holocaust, and generalized violence of the most malicious and sadistic sort. While Slayer continues to attack the hypocrisies of Christianity, its narratives and imagery of violence are presented in matter-of-fact detail that portrays them as inescapable parts of life. These lyrical and visual themes are matched by music that sometimes maintains a blistering pace but somehow seems to sound even more sinister and ominous when it slows down. Perhaps the most outstanding element of the music is the terrorizing grain of the voice unleashed by singer Tom Araya, who shouts every word with commanding urgency and periodically lets loose a scream that can be heard either as the anguished wail of a torture victim or the howling delight of a sadistic torturer.

Slayer's signature song, "Angel of Death," is about the Nazi doctor who conducted experiments on human subjects at Auschwitz, Josef Mengele. "Angel of Death" takes off as one of Araya's most unholy screams twists into a menacing growl, and then Mengele's butchering is described in harrowing yet detached detail, with the listener positioned as victim. In the wake of this and several other songs about Nazis and the Holocaust, Slayer came to be accused of harboring fascist, racist, or neo-Nazi sympathies. The band has consistently denied these charges, but some white supremacists and neo-Nazis in North America and Europe have nonetheless gravitated toward the group's music. In other instances, however, Slayer's songs depict the reality of what happens on the battlefield with such gruesome frankness while lashing out against religion and government that they can be interpreted to fit an antiwar and antiauthority perspective. Because they summon the horrors of society without moral judgment, Slayer's music is subject to very different interpretations by its audience. But while the content of their ideological message is unclear, the more consistent and pronounced feature is a structure of feeling fueled by anger. The ferocity of Slayer's music thrives on this anger, which arises from alienation, but when it is unleashed in indiscriminate fashion in the absence of other feelings to affirm, Slayer's music embodies the danger of disempowerment fueling deeply sadistic impulses. So, on the one hand, Slayer's anti-Christian diatribes have made them an enemy of the religious right for more than two decades. But on the other hand their anger can still veer in a politically rightward direction, like in the song "Dittohead," whose title refers to fans of Rush Limbaugh and whose lyrics express the same litany of complaints that are commonly heard on his radio show.

Anger and alienation are persistent structures of feeling in thrash metal, but they can translate into radically different political possibilities. Cynicism, another prominent structure of feeling, represents an analogous spectrum of prospects and contradictions. The most indicative expression of cynicism within the thrash genre is Megadeth's song and accompanying video for "Peace Sells," from their 1986 album *Peace Sells . . . But Who's Buying*? The song begins with front man (and former Metallica guitarist) Dave Mustaine providing some sarcastic answers to questions that might typically be posed to a headbanger like him: "What do you mean 'I don't believe in God?' / I talk to him every day / What do you mean 'I don't support your system?' / I go to court when I have to," and so on. In the video we see Megadeth's performance periodically interrupted by flashing images of crowds and demonstrators, religious icons, the Statue of Liberty, and the various dead presidents on the face of U.S. currency. In the chorus Mustaine sings, "If there's a new way / I'll be the first in line / But it better work this time." Meanwhile, in the video the preamble to the U.S. Constitution burns while metalheads mosh and bang their heads. The video is momentarily disrupted as we are shown a young male with long hair watching the video on TV when his father (played by Jello Biafra of Dead Kennedys fame) bursts into the room: "What is this garbage you're watching? I want to watch the news!" He changes the channel with a flick of the remote but the young headbanger (who we see outfitted in a Slayer T-shirt) responds, "This is the news," and promptly changes it back. The song builds to its climactic moment with Mustaine repeatedly shouting,

"Peace sells, but who's buying?" In the video we see more fast-moving images of missiles, riot police, and alternating dollar signs and peace signs superimposed over flags from nations all over the world.

Among all the thrash bands of their time, Mustaine and Megadeth have consistently delivered the most political lyrics on a range of topics from the military-industrial complex to censorship to environmental degradation to ethnic civil war. Their name is a misspelling of a term used by a RAND Corporation military strategist amid the cold war to describe one million deaths in the event of thermonuclear war. But "Peace Sells" is also symptomatic of a profound cynicism about alternatives and social change, for the implication is that peace has been tried before but didn't "work." The seemingly indiscriminate flashing of ephemeral images and symbols in the video—riot police, religious icons, peace signs, dollar signs—suggest that these have all become equally superficial and empty signifiers detached from any referential significance. The social world is a fragmented and incoherent mess, while peace has become just another commodity to be bought and sold, or in this case sold but not bought.

Among the "big four" bands of thrash music, Anthrax articulated the most politically progressive stance, especially on race relations. The first band to mix metal and rap music in the 1980s, soon thereafter Anthrax embarked on a tour with Public Enemy after collaborating with them on a remake of the militant rap group's "Bring the Noise." At the peak of their success, Anthrax employed a lead singer who was partly Native American and recorded a song called "Indians" that condemned the theft of native people's land and the oppressive conditions of Indian reservations. But once again contradictions and divergent possibilities arise, for how does one explain the fact that Anthrax's founding members, Scott Ian and Charlie Benante, were also involved in a side project called Stormtroopers of Death (S.O.D.) that released an album called *Speak English or Die* in 1985? The title track succinctly replicates the xenophobic drivel that has captured the imagination of the American right: "You come into this country / You can't get real jobs / Boats and boats and boats of you / Go home you fuckin' slobs." And then there is the sadly prophetic "Fuck the Middle East": "Fuck the Middle East / There's too many problems / They just get in the way / We sure could live without them / They hijack our planes / They raise our oil prices / We'll kill them all and have a ball / And end their fucking crisis."

Confronted with controversy upon releasing an album expressing such blatantly racist sentiments, the members of S.O.D. and Anthrax tried to defend themselves by arguing that the songs were intended to be satirical and provocative. But in listening to Billy Milano, the singer for S.O.D. but not a member of Anthrax, this defense loses much of its credibility. Milano, it turns out, grew up in the same Bergen County where Donna Gaines had conducted her research, and although he identified as a skinhead punk, Milano was also a graduate of one of the vocational high schools that enrolled so many of the area's young metalheads. As Gaines interviewed him, Milano expressed many of the antiauthoritarian attitudes that circulated within the thrash subculture, particularly against parents, the media, and authorities who refused to listen to the alienated teenagers of Bergenfield and simply saddled them with deviant labels. But then Milano's anger and class resentment quickly turned into racial scapegoating and victimization in the same manner that has recruited so many other white working-class people into the ranks of the American right. Among other things, he told Gaines, "If I make a hundred dollars a week I would never get [a new apartment], because I'm white. Free college because they're black, because they're too stupid to want to go out and earn it," and "What I'm saying is why are we worrying about these other countries, about people who don't want to help themselves?"[53] Milano thus exemplifies the affective and ideological paradoxes we have seen throughout this chapter, as he perceives that people like him are being exploited but then misrecognizes the source of this exploitation, as if the white working class can't get ahead because black people are getting a free ride and the American government is too busy helping other people all over the world.

Hell Ain't No Bad Place to Be

A radically different strain of heavy metal emerged and also reached its zenith during the 1980s, and once again the key to its meaning could be found in the devil and his underworld. Beginning with Kiss' "Hotter than Hell"; AC/DC's "Highway to Hell," "Sin City," and "Hell Ain't No Bad Place to Be"; and Van Halen's "Running with the Devil," Satan arose as the gatekeeper to a hedonistic lifestyle of sex, drugs, and rock 'n' roll. This devil isn't presiding over war and destruction, as in the music of Black Sabbath or Slayer. Instead, he is hosting a party for young musicians to snort coke, trash hotels, and gang bang their groupies. His Faustian bargain is not the promise of a youth-led revolution offered in "Sympathy for the Devil" in 1968; as the political winds shifted, the devil's new offer recruited young men to sell their souls for short-lived celebrity and decadence at the price of burnout, addiction, and death, or at the very least a rapid descent into obscurity and cultural ridicule.

The theatricality of what would become known as "glam metal" was originated by Alice Cooper and Kiss, who wore makeup, designed elaborate stage shows, and created comic book alter egos. They lived up to these larger-than-life personas not only on stage but also off, cultivating reputations for reckless abandon and unlimited hedonism. Kiss also parlayed those comic book personas into a vast merchandising empire, stamping their likeness on lunch boxes, pinball machines, dolls, and T-shirts. In the 1970s there was also the artier version of what was known as glam rock in Britain and glitter rock in the United States, epitomized by David Bowie, Lou Reed, T. Rex, the New York Dolls, Suzi Quatro, Queen, and the Sweet. These performers were more closely associated with the increasing visibility of homosexuality, bisexuality, and androgynous performance in the 1970s.[54] By contrast, the glam metal scene of the 1980s was much more conventionally heterosexual and utilized androgyny as a means of spectacular entertainment rather than postmodern irony.

In the 1980s, the Sunset Strip became the setting for this glam metal scene founded on spectacle, decadence, and image, as it linked heavy metal's transgression and rebellion with Hollywood's surrounding culture of celebrity and glamour. Sunset Boulevard had been a hub for Los Angeles's folk-rock and counterculture scene in the mid-1960s, and it was the setting for violent clashes between hippies and police that inspired the Buffalo Springfield's 1966 song "For What It's Worth."[55] In the 1970s, Rodney's English Disco, the Rainbow Bar and Grill, and the Continental Hyatt House (more commonly known as the Continental "Riot" House) hosted a decadent atmosphere when bands like Led Zeppelin came to town. The punk scene briefly took up residence on the Sunset Strip in the late 1970s until the fear of violence caused several of the nightclubs to ban punk performers. By the end of the 1970s, the glam metal scene was emerging from a mixture of heavy metal, glitter rock, and punk. The trailblazing band in the Hollywood glam metal scene was Van Halen, who brought the amazing virtuosity of guitarist Eddie Van Halen together with the showmanship of singer David Lee Roth. But in the following years, the Hollywood scene produced fewer Eddie Van Halens (as most of the innovative guitarists gravitated toward the thrash scene) and more blond bombshell David Lee Roth clones with self-styled reputations for unlimited indulgence. In "Running with the Devil," the first song on their debut album, Van Halen summoned Satan to set the tone for a culture of hedonism and instant gratification, with Roth singing that he "lives life like there's no tomorrow" and "at a pace that kills."

The rise of MTV in the early 1980s raised the stakes and quickened the pace for stardom. Video and visual imagery had always been important aspects of rock music, but MTV made it even more important for bands to put their creative energies into their appearance. The cable network exposed mass audiences to the heavier rock bands who usually couldn't get radio airplay, and it had the power to launch them into overnight stardom much more quickly than could touring. In the first half of the 1980s, MTV launched Van Halen and Def Leppard into a new stratosphere of success, along with L.A.-based Quiet Riot, Ratt, and Mötley Crüe and New York's bikers-in-drag Twisted Sister.

The wealth and decadence of the rock 'n' roll lifestyle, now more visible than ever, enticed a new cohort of would-be rock stars. While thrash and its preceding forms of heavy metal lashed out in anger at disempowerment, glam metal celebrated the possibility of using music to achieve upward mobility in a new twist on the Horatio Alger story. Hollywood was soon swarmed by hundreds of musicians, who would typically pay to play at the clubs on the Sunset Strip on any given night. Penelope Spheeris captured this scene in her documentary *The Decline of Western Civilization, Part II*, which features a procession of would-be rock stars alongside the already famous. This experience is represented in Guns N' Roses' video for "Welcome to the Jungle," where we see a country bumpkin version of singer Axl Rose, who in real life came to Los Angeles from Indiana, as he gets off a bus with a stalk of wheat in his mouth. The exciting yet cruel streets of Hollywood then confront Rose, just as the song itself describes the city as an amoral capitalist game of survival where everyone and everything is for sale. He sees an image of himself on television being tortured, à la *A Clockwork Orange*, and in the next scene he is on stage performing in his glam metal getup of teased hair and tight leather pants. "Welcome to the Jungle" thus depicts the journey made by so many musicians who found themselves in a ruthless city of mercenaries scrambling to be the next image on TV. As suggested by the video's scenes of torture and the lyrical warning that "You can taste the bright lights / But you won't get them for free," as well as the eventual self-destruction of Guns N' Roses themselves, even the few who became kings of the jungle would pay a heavy price.[56]

Against a backdrop of deindustrialization, glam metal presented the fantasy that one could transcend social class through music. This is in stark contrast to other forms of heavy metal in which young people are hopelessly victimized by overwhelming forces of power and evil. For instance, in the late 1980s New Jersey native Jon Bon Jovi emerged as glam's answer to Bruce Springsteen, albeit with more hairspray. In the song "Livin' on a Prayer," Bon Jovi portrays the struggles of a Tommy and Gina, a young working-class couple who are "down on their luck." Tommy "used to work on the docks" but now has "his six string in hock," while Gina "works the diner all day" and "brings home her pay for love." The song's chorus optimistically affirms that the couple will make it with the power of love, but just as important as the lyrics is the fact that the actual music also departs from the darker sounds of heavy metal toward an uplifting tone. In Walser's musicological analysis, the song's chord progression of C-D-G gives it a cheerful sound that is lacking in heavy metal, which usually relies on C-D-E progressions that evoke "gloominess, paranoia, and rebellion."[57] This is a striking example of the differences between glam metal and its heavy metal cousins, differences that are simultaneously sonic and sociological: whereas the latter suggests that there is simply no way out, glam metal promises survival and even prosperity, personified by Jon Bon Jovi's own storied rise from the Jersey Shore. With this fantasy of working-class transcendence, Bon Jovi would reach a mass audience that was inaccessible to other heavy metal and thrash bands at the time. "Livin' on a Prayer" was the biggest hit on an album, *Slippery When Wet*, that would sell 14 million copies, making it one of the best-selling albums in history.

For glam rockers, the path to upward mobility was in the performance of an extreme version of what Faludi called "ornamental masculinity." On the Sunset Strip, male musicians would take the stage dolled up in makeup, teased hair, and feminine clothing, looking not unlike the thousands of female strippers, sex workers, and fashion models that populate the Greater Los Angeles area. Mötley Crüe bassist Nikki Sixx has thus described the band as "four male degenerates dressed like female sluts."[58] The androgyny of glam rockers was the perhaps the most radical signal of the ways that masculinity was being redefined by appearance and accessories in a media-saturated, consumer-driven society. As Faludi argues, the work of objectification and ornamentation was traditionally reserved for women and gay men but now increasingly encompasses heterosexual men's lives, reaching its fullest expression in the image of the "metrosexual."[59] Looking like drag queens with musical instruments, glam metal performers transgressed the boundaries between masculine and feminine, but in doing so they were simply a more exaggerated reflection of changes taking place throughout popular culture.

Glam metal's appropriations of femininity, however, stopped at the level of appearance. Beneath the mascara and spandex, glam metal generally conformed to the rebel masculinity and outright misogyny that has characterized rock music since its inception, and frequently it pushed the envelope of sexism even further. Songwriters frequently portrayed women as deserving of "degradation, violation, and even violence" and "voluntarily degrading themselves in order to please men."[60] In other instances, glam metal songs represented women as evil temptresses who threaten their male victims by seducing them to surrender self-control. These depictions complement each other in a textbook case of misogyny, as women's sexuality presents a danger to the masculine imperative of self-control and is therefore desirable only if it can be subdued into passivity. Far from initiating a challenge to traditional gender roles, glam metal performers often cultivated reputations for violence and sexual conquest to defend their masculinity from the questions that might have been provoked by their androgynous appearance. Michael Monroe, the singer for Hanoi Rocks, once said, "I always use the girls' bathroom because whenever I use the guys' room, I get into a fight because someone calls me a fag for putting makeup on in the mirror."[61]

Drawing on psychoanalytic theory, the feminist film scholar E. Ann Kaplan wrote that glam metal's misogynist androgyny suggests, "If I possess the feminine myself . . . then I no longer need to satisfy the desire for woman *outside* myself, thus avoiding the terror of so doing."[62] While glam metal's attempt to take possession of femininity is clearly evident, Kaplan's ahistorical notions of gender fail to situate that act of possession within a particular social context. Glam metal performers turned their bodies into objects of sexual desire in the same way that models, actresses, strippers, and porn stars in L.A. did because they recognized what was needed to "make it" in a postmodern society where looks and MTV-made images had become everything. In short, they appropriated the previously "feminine" capacity to objectify one's body and transform it into exchange value; but only these superficial dimensions of the feminine were possessed, while others were aggressively rejected. Whereas women's sexual objectification comes at the price of passivity, glam rockers parlayed the power of their ornamental masculinity into control over women, as demonstrated by the swarms of female groupies who surrounded these bands.

While embodying feminine qualities of vanity and exhibition, glam rockers also continued the revolt from the "breadwinner ethic" of masculinity by financially depending on women while they struggled with their musical careers. One journalist who covered the scene recalled: "That's how a lot of bands made it in the early days, at least in L.A. . . . . There were enough women that wanted to hang out with rock stars, knowing they could be the next big thing. . . . You can't believe it—those guys just got over. Women would buy them clothes, take them out to dinner, and buy them drinks and drugs."[63] Before achieving massive success as the L.A. scene's most feminine-looking band, Poison purportedly had a list on the wall of their apartment of women not allowed to come over unless they did some housework or brought food.[64] A joke circulated in Hollywood: "What does a stripper do with her asshole before going to work? Drop him off at rehearsal."[65]

In Barbara Ehrenreich's terms, some men have engaged in a revolt against the breadwinner ethic (that they should work a conventional job to support a family), as they have attempted to escape the responsibilities of manhood while preserving its privileges, especially in the realms of sexual dominance and financial wealth. Ehrenreich viewed the *Playboy* lifestyle and the Beat movement as two different sides of the male revolt: the former counseled that men should keep their jobs but use their earnings to indulge, while the latter advocated quitting the rat race and going on the road, at least as long as they could find women to put them up during their adventures.[66] Rock 'n' roll has also embodied this revolt against domesticity and day jobs since the 1950s. Glam rockers were able to escape work through their financial dependence on women, and they sought to personify the *Playboy* lifestyle of wealth, consumption, and sexual conquest. Thus, if glam metal represented a class fantasy in a context of downward mobility, it also epitomized a male fantasy in which men could reap the fruits of women's sexual objectification, not only by learning to imitate it in their own performances but also by living off women's earnings in the interim before "making it." Before Guns N' Roses became famous, lead guitarist Slash recalled, "At this point in time, there were many strippers in our midst. All I can say is God bless them all. Many a band before us has had this connection. . . . They were generous and thought we were cute or dark, mysterious musicians, or just lost puppies that they had to tend to and found attractive."[67]

Contrary to Kaplan's interpretation, the men of glam metal may have taken symbolic possession of femininity but they certainly did not free themselves from dependence on actual women. They needed women for financial support while struggling to make it, and to become successful musicians they depended on a largely female audience. In this sense, glam metal was unlike other genres of thrash and heavy metal, which had an overwhelmingly male[66] fan base. Indeed, the existence of a sizable female audience for glam metal made it much more economically lucrative than its heavy metal and thrash cousins. While it is difficult to know exactly what kind of meanings and pleasures female audiences derived from these bands and their music, they can be situated within a longer history in which young women have made male musicians the objects of their sexual desire. From Sinatra to Elvis to the Beatles to the more recent in-carnations of "boy bands" like the Backstreet Boys, *NSYNC, and the Jo-nas Brothers, young female fans have wept, screamed, and nearly rioted in the presence of their male musical idols. Journalists and casual observers have typically believed that these male performers wield extraordinary power over their "teenybopper" audiences, which causes them to go into a physical frenzy. Some feminist scholars, however, have alternatively pro-posed that musicians are objects rather than simply subjects of female pleasure, or in other words that female audiences use their idols to ac-tively construct their desire rather than being passively manipulated by them.[68] For many young women, the musical performer may be just as much an object of identification as of desire, as they (similar to male fans) crave the creativity, power, and independence that musicians embody. Af-ter all, teen and preteen girls have also begun to idolize female performers (Madonna, the Spice Girls, Britney Spears, Miley Cyrus, etc.) who fash-ion themselves as sex objects and yet appear to derive power and control from their position.

Susan Fast, who has conducted a musicological study of Led Zeppelin, has described her youthful attraction to the band in terms that reflect this duality of desire, one stemming not only from sexual attraction but also from the fantasy of possessing their creative powers: "When I fantasized about knowing [singer Robert] Plant and the rest of the band, two ele-ments were always inextricably bound together: I was a musician of equal stature to them—as talented and commercially successful—and I was also beautiful and sexy and loved by them for that reason as well. In other words, my fantasy involved being powerful and attractive, and respected for both characteristics. I did not quite want to be Robert Plant, rather I wanted to be just like him in terms of his ability to sing and his success in practicing his art."[69] Fast conducted a survey of 323 Led Zeppelin fans, and the data collected from her 76 female respondents seems to corrobo-rate her experience:

While the majority of the women acknowledge that they are sexually attracted to the band members and find the music sexy, they tend to want to point out that there is more to their attachment than this, or that questions of gender and sexuality cannot be separated from the rest of the experience of the band, from the "power" and "emotion" of the music (which is in some cases equated with something they describe as elemental or "primal" that operates at a "deeper" level than the sexual), from the energy it gives to them and how they can experience the songs on various levels (and from my own experience, I would say that these can be experienced simultaneously).[70]

While glam metal bands mostly personified a bad boy image of rebellion with overtones of misogyny, their biggest commercial successes typically came from so-called power ballads, songs that expressed emotional vulnerability in affirming love for a woman or the regret of losing one. These songs clearly targeted a female audience with a sound that was gentler, vocals that were sung from the heart, and lyrics that suggested the rebel could change his ways and settle down. The quintessential glam metal power ballads are Kiss' "Beth" and Mötley Crüe's "Home Sweet Home," odes to the virtues of domesticity after a long night of band practice or months on the road. Guns N' Roses, arguably the genre's most sexist band, scored its biggest hit with "Sweet Child O' Mine," in which Axl Rose sings about his girlfriend as a source of refuge from the heartless jungle of modernity. For all their bad boy posturing, glam metal musicians obviously needed supportive women in their lives, and they needed a female audience to achieve stratospheric record sales. Again, this was in stark contrast to previous forms of heavy metal and especially thrash, where references to women, love, and even sex were conspicuous by their absence.

Heavy Metal in a Micro/Soft Society

The ascent of heavy metal coincided with the decline of heavy industry. Heavy metal found an audience among young people who felt disempowered and marginalized by society and looked to their futures with a sense of dread. Their parents' generation had benefited from the social democratic aspects of Fordism, which enabled them to move to the suburbs and maintain a middle-class lifestyle. But economic restructuring and neoliberal policies prompted a "great U-turn" that widened social inequalities and fueled downward mobility.[71] Young people who rebelled against authority, dabbled in delinquent behavior, and were eventually filtered out of the educational system had once been able to fall back on manufacturing jobs that promised a tedious life but a secure standard of living; to paraphrase Paul Willis, this was how working-class kids got working-class jobs.[72] But what happened when the working-class jobs left town? Young people were left with low-wage, nonunion, instantly disposable jobs that would leave them unable to reproduce their parents' standard of living. The crisis was especially acute for young men, who found fewer outlets to prove their shopfloor masculinity as they drifted between service and retail jobs.

The music and iconography of heavy metal reflected the reification of these youths' class consciousness—they knew they were screwed, but it was hard to articulate why. The young and alienated can implicate power when it is exercised directly, like when schools discipline them, parents abuse them, police bust them, or the government tries to censor their music. But deindustrialization, globalization, outsourcing, and automation are not so easily represented—they just seem to happen. In heavy metal, ominous yet anonymous forces of destruction overwhelm their victims, taking the shape of inhuman, supernatural, or mythological beings whose wrath is unstoppable. And so heavy metal is a cry of protest against power, but the reification of those sources of power leaves no guarantees about whether its anger will go in a progressive or reactionary direction. The influence of hardcore punk led many thrash bands to confront social injustice more directly than their ethereal predecessors had. But alienation could also be mobilized for more sadistic purposes in the absence of an effective labor movement to raise consciousness about capitalism and globalization, and in the presence of a strong conservative movement that encouraged working-class people to blame their economic woes on immigration, welfare, and affirmative action.

Those in the glam metal scene faced the same series of problems but adopted a different solution. They embraced the one-in-a-million chance at stardom, not exactly upward mobility but rather a lottery of total success or total failure played by those with nothing to lose. Their main asset was the ability to embody the ornamental model of masculinity that was rapidly supplanting the industrial one as American society had become saturated with media and consumerism. Their main ambition was to fashion themselves as sexual objects to become dominant sexual subjects, or in other words to look like strippers but live like playboys. While their rebellious identities depended on the idea that they were offensive to the powers that be, these performers actually seemed more complementary to the Reagan/Bush era's cutthroat capitalism, postmodern simulation, and conspicuous consumption.

Heavy metal continued to evolve and splinter into further subgenres after the 1980s: death metal, black metal, nu metal, rap metal, and so forth. But in the early 1990s it was culturally displaced and exposed to ridicule when alternative rock and Seattle-based grunge suddenly moved into the center of rock mainstream, articulating a different set of values based on sincerity and simplicity and a revolt against excess and hedonism. We follow that story in the next chapter.

4

Young, Gifted, and Slack

I'm working / But I'm not working for you / Slack motherfucker.
—Superchunk, "Slack Motherfucker"

Everybody loves us / Everybody loves our town / It's so overblown
—Mudhoney, "Overblown"

In late 1991 and early 1992, Nirvana hijacked the airwaves with "Smells Like Teen Spirit." When their album *Nevermind* passed Michael Jackson's *Dangerous* on its way to the number one spot on the *Billboard* charts at the beginning of 1992, many people perceived that a significant shift in music and popular culture was underway. This shift was largely unanticipated because there had been few commercial successes within "alternative" music to date, and thus insiders at DGC, Nirvana's record label, were modestly hoping that *Nevermind* might become a gold record (sell 500,000 units) if management worked hard and the band toured extensively for a full year.[1] To everyone's surprise, *Nevermind* would go gold after only one month as Nirvana's music, along with the general persona of Kurt Cobain, seemed to resonate with large numbers of young people. "Smells Like Teen Spirit," with its opaque lyrics about apathy and angst, was quickly hailed as the anthem for a youthful demographic that were in the process of being christened as "Generation X."

Nirvana's success represented a major breakthrough for the kind of music that had been performed in local music scenes in college towns and bohemian enclaves across the United States during the previous decade. Indeed, many of these communities would be dramatically transformed after Nirvana entered the spotlight, as those in the corporate music industry came to believe that alternative music could be commercially lucrative after all, and so major-label representatives began to comb the local nightclubs in various cities in search of the next big thing. Nirvana themselves had emerged from the Pacific Northwestern scenes in Seattle and Olympia, Washington, each of which had their own infrastructure of independent record labels, zines, and college radio that developed in the DIY spirit of punk. The scene in Olympia, where Nirvana's Kurt Cobain and Krist Novoselic were living at the time that "Smells Like Teen Spirit" was conceived, maintained a virulently anticorporate stance and a budding style of "riot grrrl" feminism, both of which were nurtured by its links with the hardcore movement in Washington, D.C. Of course, Nirvana would be more commonly associated with the Seattle "grunge" scene, where there was a deeper connection to more mainstream forms of hard rock and heavy metal, and from which not only Nirvana but also Pearl Jam, Soundgarden, and Alice in Chains came to represent a new wave of alternative music that would suddenly become big business.

"Smells Like Teen Spirit" was in several ways the culmination of the socially outraged yet cynically resigned structure of feeling we followed throughout the preceding two chapters. The song's title originated in Kurt Cobain's relations with the members of Bikini Kill, the most celebrated of the feminist riot grrrl bands in Olympia. Cobain and Bikini Kill singer Kathleen Hanna had gone on a graffiti spree, spray painting revolutionary, feminist, and pro-gay slogans in the streets of Olympia, and when they returned to Cobain's apartment Hanna spray painted the words, "Kurt smells like teen spirit." Cobain had been dating Bikini Kill's drummer, Tobi Vail, and Hanna was apparently suggesting that he smelled like the deodorant she wore. But Cobain wasn't aware that Teen Spirit was a brand name, perhaps because he said he never wore deodorant, and instead he believed those words had something to do with the ideas about teen revolution that he and Hanna had been discussing.[2] And so "Smells Like Teen Spirit" was written as a response to the ideas circulating in the Olympia scene and beyond regarding anticorporate DIY punk, feminist and queer politics, and straightedge and vegan lifestyles. Cobain found those ideals seductive but ultimately naïve, and "Smells Like Teen Spirit" was fueled by the conflicted nature of his response. "The entire song is made up of contradictory ideas," Cobain once explained. "It's just making fun of the thought of having a revolution. But it's a nice thought."[3] Cobain believed a revolution may have been necessary but was simply impossible in light of his peers' consumer-induced apathy ("Here we are now / Entertain us"), which he also identified in his own confusion and ineffectuality ("I feel stupid / And contagious"). From the song's opening lyric, which is "Load up on *guns* / and bring your friends" but can also be heard as "load up on *drugs* / and bring your friends," "Smells Like Teen Spirit" captured the ambivalence of a singer who could never decide if he wanted to take up arms or just go get wasted.[4]

Of course, the lyrics of "Smells Like Teen Spirit" and many other Nirvana songs were mostly incomprehensible, so much so that MTV aired the music video with subtitles for a brief time during the peak of its popularity. The more dramatic register of the crisis of affect was Kurt Cobain's grain of the voice. Within the course of a single song, Cobain's voice would lurch between a range of emotional states, from the enraged screams of someone trying to articulate the source of his anger; to the gentle, even fragile, whispers of someone desperate for some sign of honesty; to the whining and wailing of someone who simply wants everyone to leave him alone; to the mumbles and murmurs of someone who has been defeated and demoralized. Indeed, Cobain believed this schizophrenia of affect characterized many people in his generation, and perhaps this too explained part of Nirvana's widespread adoration: "I'm such a nihilistic jerk half the time and other times I'm so vulnerable and sincere. That's pretty much how every song comes out. It's like a mixture of both of them. That's how most people my age are. They're sarcastic one minute and caring the next."[5]

Surveying the terrain of alternative rock music in the early 1990s, one could hear many other compelling voices vacillating between exhausted monotone and outraged incoherence: the blood-curdling screams of the Pixies' Black Francis (an important influence on Cobain); the lethargic indifference of J Mascis from Dinosaur Jr.; the smart-ass sarcasm of Stephen Malkmus from Pavement; the confessional mutterings of Sebadoh's Lou Barlow; and the adolescent whine of Billy Corgan of the Smashing Pumpkins. The use of inexpensive low-fidelity and four-track recordings was becoming a genre of its own known as "lo-fi," with artists like Guided By Voices, the Grifters, and Will Oldham making an aesthetic virtue out of poor equipment and technical "flaws" like distortion and background noise. Such recordings constructed a sense of authenticity and sincerity in their willingness to expose the listener to their conditions of production, which were typically low-budget studios located in the homes of the musicians themselves. Some musicians, like Smog, Sebadoh, and Liz Phair, complemented their lo-fi sound with highly personalized and emotionally revealing lyrics, while others like Pavement and Guided By Voices utilized an extremely fragmented songwriting style in which the lyrics were more like a collection of non sequiturs and a great number of fractional "songs" would bleed into another over the course of an album.

As heavy metal might have been heard as the music of disempowered and emasculated proletarian youth, these various forms of indie and alternative rock represented something like the sound of the middle class in a stage of decline and resignation. While Kurt Cobain's biography attests to the fact that alternative rock was not limited to middle-class youth any more than heavy metal was exclusively working class, the music's basis in college radio and college towns, the entrepreneurialism of its DIY ethic, and its aesthetic attachment to romantic anticommercialism and self-referential irony all served to position the genre firmly within the cultural prerogatives of the middle class. As noted in chapter 1, the decline of the American middle class has been particularly acute among its young people, whose experience of relative deprivation has been fueled by the discrepancy between increasing expectations and constricting opportunities. The structure of feeling personified by so many of these bands from the 1990s cannot be understood apart from the qualitative consequences of downward mobility, particularly the rising rates of anxiety, depression, loneliness, and the cynical belief that "there's no point in trying."[6]

During the 1980s, alternative music and its localized scenes were both culturally and commercially marginal. Prominent bands like Hüsker Dü and the Replacements failed to augment their underground following into mainstream recognition after signing major-label contracts, and even the more radio-friendly R.E.M. didn't achieve success until late in the decade. In the early 1990s, however, the "alternative" moved into the center, beginning with the Lollapalooza festivals and the Seattle grunge scene. With its disheveled look, unpolished sound, and ethos of austerity and authenticity, alternative rock came to be seen as not only the latest style of music and fashion but also a repudiation of the superficiality and shameless materialism of the preceding decade. Grunge and alternative were touted as low budget and unhyped, sensitive and antimacho, socially conscious and morally outraged—in short, the antithesis of the Eighties' excess and greed. The ascendance of Nirvana and other bands that personified modesty and sincerity almost instantly rendered the glam metal scene in Hollywood laughably anachronistic. The spotlight in Los Angeles shifted toward bands like Jane's Addiction, the Red Hot Chili Peppers, and Fishbone, all of whom had distanced themselves from the Sunset Strip and took a more electric approach that mixed hard rock music with funk, ska, or psychedelia. Many observers associated the unrefined aesthetic of alternative rock with a generation that had grown up in the shadow of the baby boomers, would be the first generation to experience a lower standard of living than their parents, and had developed an ironic style of consuming popular culture as a consequence of prolonged exposure to media and advertising. Moreover, in the 1990s alternative music and lifestyles could be more easily utilized in new strategies of youth-oriented marketing and emergent forms of capitalism that gainfully incorporated difference, authenticity, and even rebellion.

Post-Fordist Capitalism and Alternative Culture in the 1990s

A number of intellectuals writing from a wide range of political perspectives have recently argued that there has been a confluence between contemporary capitalism and bohemian lifestyles, a process that may have begun long ago but appeared to come to full fruition during the 1990s. David Brooks trumpeted the emergence of "bobos," or bourgeois bohemians, who have merged the bourgeoisie's stress on individual achievement with the bohemian spirit of transgression and pseudospiritual self-discovery.[7] For Richard Florida, the 1990s witnessed the growing economic power of the "creative class," as he demonstrated that economic growth was greater in cities with larger numbers of well-educated musicians, artists, and gay people, who value diversity and tolerance.[8] From a more critical standpoint, Thomas Frank and his colleagues at the *Baffler* lampooned the ways in which capital cloaked itself in the rhetoric of rebellion and revolution. At the same time, they browbeat would-be bohemians who imagined themselves to be warriors against yesterday's culture of conformity when in actuality they were little more than carriers of today's ideology of consumer individualism.[9] Frank and the *Baffler* condemned contemporary capitalism, while Brooks and Florida were mostly celebratory, but otherwise their analyses dovetailed closely with one another, as all maintained that the long-standing barrier between capital and counterculture had collapsed once and for all. Each of these authors could also agree that the "cultural contradictions of capitalism" identified by Daniel Bell in the 1970s had been resolved. Bell's fear that the Protestant work ethic was eroding in ways that would ultimately lead to the downfall of capitalism was supplanted by renewed faith in the consumer culture's capacity to maintain an uncontested hegemony.[10]

In short, it is not the case that bohemia suddenly changed, but instead that the transformations of capitalism have made innovation and

subversion more valuable than ever while bringing workers and consumers of all stripes closer to the lifestyles traditionally associated with bohemia. The most important change has been the heightened role of culture
in economic production, which multiplies the value of the hip and the
cool in everything from leisure-time experiences to new communications
technologies to brand-name images.[11] In a post-Fordist economy, the role
of the city shifts from a center of manufacturing to a site for the production of cool, with bohemian subcultures often taking root in the same
derelict neighborhoods and abandoned buildings that had once been the
nucleus of industry. Within the consumer culture, the change in emphasis from mass markets to niche markets idealizes individual differences
and idiosyncratic tastes while disparaging conformity and mass culture.
Meanwhile, the reorganization of the workplace resulting from strategies
of flexible accumulation have devalued the organization man and intensified the competition for creative minds that can "think outside the box"
and live with insecurity and risk in what has become a "free agent nation."[12] All these changes are consequences of the exhaustion of Fordism
and the restructuring of capitalism catalyzed by the crisis of the 1970s, but
one could argue that they did not become fully evident until the development of the New Economy in the 1990s. The Eighties style of capitalism
primarily thrived on acquisition and hedonism, but in the 1990s capital
found ways to profit from creativity and authenticity as well.

Both the celebratory analyses of Brooks and Florida and the negative
assessments of Frank and other critics share the functionalist assumption
that the market has successfully provided an antidote for the symptoms
that capital itself creates. After all, while high-tech start-ups and the creative class were grabbing all the headlines, the 1990s also witnessed the
more familiar process of corporate concentration, as Wal-Mart lowballed
thousands of mom-and-pop stores out of business and a Starbucks seemed
to pop up on every corner. This was especially true of the culture industry,
where the 1996 Telecommunications Act gave corporations carte blanche
to expand their holdings and develop into horizontally integrated conglomerates with untold opportunities for cross-promotion.[13] So while it
is true that there was an unprecedented ideological consensus about free
markets during the 1990s, this was still a decade of conflict, not between
capital and labor but between two forms of capitalism we might refer to as
"corporate" and "creative." Creative capitalism developed as a remedy for
the alienation engendered by corporate capitalism, as it promised meaningful work for those repelled by the nine-to-five tedium of the office,

exotic and quirky consumer goods for those fed up with the standardized fare of mass culture, and postindustrial playgrounds of diversity and deviance for those bored by the notorious homogeneity of the suburbs.[14]

Nonetheless, there are many questions that must be raised about how wage labor and the commodity form place intrinsic structural limitations on creative capitalism. For instance, how can employees be truly creative and autonomous if they are working within capitalist enterprises that must eventually attend to the bottom line of profit and exercise at least some degree of control over the production process? Times of economic expansion, like the dot-com boom of the late 1990s, can surely accommodate a certain amount of freedom in the workplace, but times of economic contraction are another matter, a fact that employees at hip startups were rudely awakened to when the bubble inevitably burst.[15] In the realm of consumption, capital's ability to offer an unending smorgasbord of goods and experiences to meet seemingly every conceivable human need or desire is indisputable. But when these needs or desires are social or experiential in nature—the need to forge a sense of identity or belong to a community, or the desire to experience something "real"—just how much fulfillment can commodities really provide? Finally, postindustrial cities have shown a remarkable ability to remake themselves as centers of cultural production and hip consumerism, but they also suffer from the ironies of gentrification, in which bohemian flavor increases a neighborhood's desirability for more affluent young professionals to the point where rents increase dramatically. When this happens, the artists, musicians, and hip businesses that made the neighborhood "cool" in the first place can no longer afford to stay there.

Grunge and alternative subcultures were thrust into the center of these transformations of capitalism in the 1990s. The various local scenes scattered across the American landscape had arisen in opposition to corporate capitalism, as the DIY ethic sought to establish at least some degree of autonomy from the culture industry. But after sitting on the sidelines for more than a decade, they became a central component in a developing form of creative capitalism that valorized its sincerity of expression and idiosyncrasy of style, especially when it came to marketing to Generation X. And yet this was not a smooth or happy process, at least for the hip insiders of alternative subcultures who grumbled about bands who "sold out," media conglomerates that sought to exploit their local scenes, and Johnny-come-lately poseurs who imitated their style. Many of these complaints rested on well-worn arguments about the incompatibility of art and commerce while also sharing similarities with the critiques of "recuperation" and "incorporation" proposed by radical thinkers during and after the Sixties.[16] These notions of anticommercial authenticity, however, proved to be increasingly outmoded in a post-Fordist economy, as it became more and more difficult to maintain the familiar opposition between bohemia, on the one hand, and mass culture, rationalized workplaces, and state bureaucracy. I will argue that this narrative about commercialization and co-optation falls apart when held to closer scrutiny, for in fact grunge had already been codified and commodified prior to Nirvana's breakthrough, not least by the Seattle-based independent label that gave Nirvana its start, Sub Pop Records.

Shiftless in Seattle

A unique local music scene that mixed punk and heavy metal had been developing in Seattle years before anyone had heard of Nirvana. Whereas in larger cities there had been intense and frequently violent rivalries between punk and heavy metal subcultures, in Seattle there was more overlap, perhaps because their numbers were too small to maintain this sort of social boundary. As one longtime participant explained, "It seems like everywhere else punk and metal were such diametric opposites, and there were fights between metal heads and punk rockers. But in Seattle they kind of coexisted all peacefully. There were a lot of punk rockers and metal heads and hippies, and there were a lot of punk rock hippies and metal punk rockers. Everyone lived together, everyone jammed together, everyone hung out and went to the same shows and had the same record collections."[17] As a consequence of this social intermingling, a sonic and stylistic hybrid evolved in Seattle during the late 1980s that was unlike that of other subcultures. "Grunge" seemed to be an apt descriptor of the fuzzy guitar riffs and slow, sludgy tempos favored by many of the bands in this scene. Likewise, "grunge" also described the prevailing subcultural style in which a sweaty, unkempt look superimposed punk and metal attitude on the flannel and blue jeans fashion of the Pacific Northwest proletariat.

The spectrum of musical styles made by mixing punk and metal was embodied in the three most prominent bands in the Seattle scene of the late 1980s: Mudhoney, Soundgarden, and Mother Love Bone. Mudhoney maintained the most direct lineage to punk, utilizing a heavily distorted guitar sound and a self-deprecating image that gave them an air of drunken amateurism. Soundgarden bypassed the recent history of punk and metal in returning to the pioneering sound of Black Sabbath and the Stooges, setting the thick, sluggish guitar of Kim Thayil against the astonishing vocal range of Chris Cornell. Mother Love Bone was a Northwestern cousin of the glam metal bands who ruled Hollywood in the 1980s. After Mother Love Bone's singer died from a heroin overdose, founding members Jeff Ament and Stone Gossard would go on to form Pearl Jam, recruiting a San Diego surfer named Eddie Vedder to be the singer and grunging up their sound and image in the process. As a sign of the extensive crossover between punk and metal in the Seattle scene, Ament and Gossard had originally played with Mudhoney's Mark Arm and Steve Turner in a band called Green River. As a sign of the ultimate incompatibility between punk and metal, Green River disbanded because Turner and Arm not only disliked Ament and Gossard's penchant for metal music but also distrusted their aspirations for commercial success.[18]

The hub of the Seattle scene at this time was Sub Pop Records, established by Bruce Pavitt and Jonathan Poneman in 1986. The label grew out of a zine that Pavitt created to print reviews and distribute compilation tapes of underground rock bands from across the United States, and throughout Sub Pop's tenure he primarily served as the creative visionary while Poneman handled the business and legal issues. Although Sub Pop evolved from the DIY spirit of punk and hardcore, it was quite distinct from the staunchly independent Dischord Records or K Records, their neighbors in Olympia. Sub Pop was more ambitious than other labels, but because that was socially unacceptable in the independent rock world, they engaged in what might be called ironic capitalism. For example, Sub Pop's motto was "World Domination" and their records would sometimes be printed with messages like "We're ripping you off big time." Such hyperbole provided the ironic distance that allowed Pavitt and Poneman to be capitalists while seeming to lampoon capitalism. But there was indeed a shrewd business strategy behind Sub Pop that focused on creating a brand identity for itself, taking a cue from Motown and other labels, rather than promoting individual bands that were by definition unknown commodities and varying in talent. For instance, Poneman and Pavitt created the Sub Pop Singles Club in which subscribers were sent a new record every month, a gimmick that guaranteed sales in an inherently unstable market but also simulated the mystique craved by hip consumers who want to believe they are privy to a secret unavailable to the mainstream. And although Sub Pop touted creative freedom for its musicians in the same way that other independent labels did, it did establish a distinctive grunge sound in large part by consistently employing the services of one particular record producer, Jack Endino.[19]

Beyond the music, Sub Pop also effectively promoted their relationship to the Seattle scene and the sense of participatory community that appeared to be flourishing within it. Their primary asset in this regard was the photography of Charles Peterson, who would go to shows and photograph not just the bands but also the audience in the same frame. These photos helped create the "scene" by reconstructing the social relations that are typically abstracted in the commodity form, as Pavitt said that Sub Pop wanted to "[advertise] the fact that there's a community here—it's not just this industry that's manufacturing bands, it's a happening scene where people are feeding off each other."[20] For disaffected young consumers, Peterson's photographs on Sub Pop records made the Seattle scene look like the real deal and promised that they could be part of it too. The images were often blurry and captured people in motion, thus creating the impression that something was happening and you were somehow there to see it. And although Peterson used black-and-white film largely out of necessity (because it was much cheaper to reproduce), this too was consistent with an image of authenticity and played into the idea that the Seattle scene was something different from the glossy and overhyped mainstream.[21]

At this time, Sub Pop began producing T-shirts with the word "Loser" printed on the back of them. "Loser" would become an ironic badge of identity for many young people who had experienced low status in their peer cultures as teenagers and then found themselves on the losing end of the job market as twenty-somethings. Sub Pop's Bruce Pavitt could identify with this experience of downward mobility and service employment, recalling that "throughout the eighties when I was working at all these shitty jobs, I was really, really angry. I was, like, 'I have a college degree, and the guy next to me, he's incredibly talented, and he has a college degree too, and we're both chopping carrots!'"[22] This subculture's magical solution to these social problems, to put it in the terms of the Birmingham School, was to use irony to invert the social hierarchies of winners and losers created by the markets of peer relations and employment prospects. A few years later, Beck would score a breakout hit with a song called "Loser," delivered in his deadpan white-boy rap style and featuring the chorus, "I'm a loser, baby / So why don't you kill me?"

Thus Sub Pop constructed many of what would eventually become the early 1990s clichés about grunge and, by extension, Generation X,

A Charles Peterson photograph of Kurt Cobain in the arms of his audience. From *Screaming Life: A Chronicle of the Seattle Music Scene*. Photography by Charles Peterson, essay by Michael Azerrad. New York: HarperCollins, 1995.

Fabricating the lumberjack image for a TAD video. From *Screaming Life: A Chronicle of the Seattle Music Scene*. Photography by Charles Peterson, essay by Michael Azerrad. New York: HarperCollins, 1995.

alternative music, "slackers," and so forth: the fry-cook loser as existential hero; the authenticity of the scene as local community; and the ironic simulation of regional proletarian fashion. This complicates if not wholly contradicts the narrative that was often heard about grunge after Nirvana broke, a story that mourns an underground scene's discovery and absorption into mainstream popular culture. Sub Pop represented creative capitalism practiced by an independent label, but it was still about manufacturing and selling an image along with a sound while offering an implicit promise to fulfill the customer's quest for identity and longing for community. For instance, Sub Pop's promotional strategies included flying the British music journalist Everett True to Seattle in 1989 and giving him a guided tour of the scene. True returned to England and raved about Mudhoney and other Seattle bands in ways that played on British stereotypes about working-class American "rednecks," an image that Sub Pop clearly had a hand in constructing but which did not accurately describe these musicians, many of whom had gone to college and in real life were more like geeks than lumberjacks.[23] Such incongruity was especially evident in their marketing of TAD, whose burly front man was touted as "the butcher from Idaho" when in actuality he had been a music student at the University of Idaho; in one of Charles Peterson's photos he is shown wielding a chainsaw but later admitted that he had never used one before that shoot. Sub Pop's fabrication of backwoods authenticity was also applied to their dealings with Nirvana, as Pavitt once explained that he saw them as "the whole real genuine working class—I hate to use the phrase 'white trash'— something not contrived that had a more grassroots or populist feel."[24]

There's a Riot Goin' On

When Kurt Cobain was hanging out in Olympia, he was involved but not totally immersed in a local punk scene that had been developing for more than a decade in the Washington State capital, home to only 40,000 people and located about 60 miles southwest of Seattle. The hub of this scene was Evergreen State College, an experimental liberal arts school founded in the late 1960s and the host of community radio station KAOS. In 1977 KAOS had instituted a policy in which 80 percent of the music they played had to be from records with independent distribution outside the six major companies that dominated the music industry at that time.[25] Students involved with KAOS regularly published reviews of independent music, and these writings eventually evolved into *Option* magazine, a central medium for underground scenes nationwide in the late 1980s and most of the 1990s.[26] Bruce Pavitt had also started the zine that became the basis for the Sub Pop record label while he was a student at Evergreen State. The Olympia scene thus drew inspiration from the anticorporate politics and grassroots cultural production of the wider hardcore subculture, particularly the scene in Washington, D.C. The hardcore community in the nation's capital was especially eye-opening to Calvin Johnson, an Evergreen State student who cofounded the label K Records in 1983 and around the same time emerged as the locally idolized front man of the group Beat Happening. Johnson played a leading role in helping to create a scene that joined an allegiance to straightedge living with faith in the revolutionary potential of youthful innocence. Local hipsters were known to go so far as to host tea parties and pie bakes in what was surely an affected but also partially sincere expression of nostalgia for the naïveté of childhood play and small-town community.[27] In a sharp expression of his skepticism about both their shows of asceticism and Johnson's cultish power, Kurt Cobain referred to these young people in Olympia as "Calvinists."[28]

On the eve of Nirvana's breakthrough, the major development in Olympia was the budding riot grrrl movement, which mixed punk's DIY methods of cultural production with feminist politics and a provocative sense of style. In August 1991 Calvin Johnson and K Records organized a music festival called the International Pop Underground Convention, whose promotional poster began with the words: "As the corporate ogre expands its creeping influence on the minds of industrialized youth, the time has come for the International Rockers of the World to convene in celebration of our grand independence."[29] The first night of the festival was reserved for all-female performances, which the organizers called "Love Rock Revolution Girl Style Now" or simply "Girls' Night." Whereas the Seattle grunge scene was quite macho and a little homoerotic in its rituals of mostly male youth bonding in mosh pits awash with sweat and beer, the Olympia scene was more friendly to female performers and disdainful of violent or hedonistic forms of masculinity. The Beat Happening had a female member, Heather Lewis, who played an integral role as one of the band's three rotating singers, guitarists, and drummers, and Calvin Johnson's performances both on- and offstage were anything but macho. The Washington, D.C., scene also played a significant role in fostering riot grrrl, as Ian MacKaye produced the first Bikini Kill record and Positive Force organized several fund-raisers for abortion clinics and self-defense training that included Fugazi and Bikini Kill on the same bill.[30]

Riot grrrl coalesced as a social movement with an innovative approach to DIY cultural production (especially zines) to mobilize resources for feminist consciousness-raising and self-expression. Tobi Vail had played in one of Calvin Johnson's earlier bands and was a DJ at KAOS, and she then began publishing a feminist-themed zine called *Jigsaw* that got the attention of Kathleen Hanna and led to the formation of Bikini Kill and their collaboration on a new zine called *Riot Grrrl*. Likewise, the pioneering group Bratmobile formed when Molly Neuman and Allison Wolfe, publishers of the feminist zine *Girl Germs*, joined forces with Erin Smith, who wrote a zine devoted to 1970s pop culture called *Teenage Gang Debs*.[31]

Riot grrrl brought a sense of urgency to zine publishing, as young women used zines to write about their own experiences and communicate with a network of others regarding the social and personal problems they faced. In her content analysis of female-authored zines, Kristen Schlit categorized five consistent topics in riot grrrl zines: sexuality, sexual abuse, self-destructive behaviors, sexual harassment, and puberty.[32] Riot grrrl zines thus addressed many of the issues that were also being identified around the same time in a landmark study by the American Association of University Women, which found that girls experience a severe decline in self-esteem as they enter adolescence and are imperiled by the risk of depression, eating disorders, and various forms of self-destructive behavior.[33] Zine publishing offered a unique opportunity for young women to respond to these issues, giving them an outlet to write about their own experiences, anonymously if they chose, while at the same time introducing them to a network of others with whom they could communicate. In providing a badly needed medium of self-expression and the ability to safely converse with others who share similar problems, these zines provide young women "with a network that prevents them from thinking they're insane," as K Records cofounder Candice Pedersen once put it.[34] Zines enabled young women to develop political consciousness alongside personal confidence in a way similar to the consciousness-raising groups of feminism's second wave, as communication brings the realization that seemingly personal problems are widely shared, have sociopolitical roots, and therefore can be changed through collective action.[35]

While claiming feminist identities for themselves, these women (most of whom were college age) appropriated the label and image of "girl" in ironic fashion, replacing its vowel with a triple-*r* roar. The life stage of preadolescence was exalted as a carefree time of friendship among girls, a time before boys are discovered and girls compete for their attention, a time before anxieties about one's body begin to multiply and a girl's self-esteem plummets. In matters of fashion and style, this semi-ironic attachment to girlhood was expressed through the use of barrettes, knee socks, pony tails, and lunch boxes among young women. Likewise, riot grrrl zines were often crammed with girlish imagery, and they extended the role of adolescent females as consumers of media and celebrity with a sense of irony. These feminist zines grew out of punk's DIY ethic, but their look and feel was shaped by what Angela McRobbie and Jenny Garber called the "bedroom culture" that develops as a consequence of adolescent girls' restricted access to public space.[36] In popular culture, girls' voices have typically been restricted to the fan worship of teen idols and movie stars, and so passionate adulation serves as a conduit for girls to express their own desire and pleasure (see the discussion of female Led Zeppelin fans in chapter 3).[37] The riot grrrl zines parodied but also borrowed from these teen magazines in the process of creating media that were more participatory and democratic. As Simon Reynolds and Joy Press have put it, "Riot Grrrl radicalised the teenage pen-pal and fanzine network in which girls had used teenybop idols as a pretext to write about their own desires and fantasies."[38]

The riot grrrl subculture took independent media in new directions with their innovative use of zines as a forum for community outreach and political communication. For example, many zines tried to expose the links between commercial objectification and girls' body image, presenting statistics about eating disorders and self-esteem with complementary illustrations that debunked or parodied media representations of beauty, sexuality, and femininity. But they were also effective in helping with more personal problems, like when young women would recount episodes of rape or molestation, thus giving the victimized an opportunity to safely confront her experience while providing readers with a story that may speak to them and remind them that they are not alone. There was also a connection with the queer identities represented by the zine *Homocore* and the lesbian punk bands Team Dresch and Tribe 8, which sought to break the silence and shame that so often surrounds youth and homosexuality. The significance of riot grrrl as a means of both personal empowerment and political mobilization was articulated to me by Jenny, a 20-year-old self-proclaimed feminist and riot grrrl enthusiast I interviewed in 1995: "If I didn't have that musical outlet, I'd be pretty depressed—I'd pretty much have no reason for living. Just listening to music empowers me to make a difference. . . . With female punk it's good because with all the zines that were coming out, a lot of it was about abuse and girls speaking about their abuse and not being afraid and taking measures so that it won't ever happen again. So I think that empowerment is definitely there for change."[39]

It was equally empowering for young women to get together and take the stage with their own musical instruments. Although punk and alternative rock had made some strides toward gender equality, masculinity remained hegemonic in its style of performance, imagery, and social networks, while women were still typically relegated to the sidelines as girlfriends and spectators. Girls are generally discouraged from playing rock music instruments when they are young, and those who do perform are more likely to be judged for their sex appeal while their competence as musicians is subject to closer scrutiny.[40] In general, riot grrrl bands performed music that was much like that of original punk and hardcore in that it was sometimes out of sync but always urgent and visceral, challenging masculinist notions of expertise while unleashing intense emotion and physical sensation. Perhaps its most salient feature was the screaming vocals appropriated from masculine noise rock but given a new urgency by riot grrrl singers. In the context of songs about sexual violence, the shouts and shrieks embodied the rage and resistance of young women: the refusal to remain silent and the demand to be heard. But for young women who were discovering the power of creating music, the scream also expressed an experience of pleasure, a discovery of community, and an assertion of sexual autonomy. "Taken together," Joanne Gottlieb and Gayle Wald wrote of the double meaning behind these riot grrrl screams, "they suggest not just that women are angry, but that there's pleasure in their performances of anger, or even just pleasure in performance."[41]

The performances and vocal style of Bikini Kill's Kathleen Hanna in many ways defined the confrontationally juvenile methods of riot grrrl in its early years. Hanna could shriek to the heavens, but she did it with a mall-rat accent, and in many songs it sounds like she's teasing her audience, her voice seething with sarcasm as she condemns the whole of our society with the conceit of a know-it-all teenager. Bikini Kill's first song on their first record, "Double Dare Ya," begins with the sounds of a band getting ready to take the stage. There's a bunch of noise and Hanna asks, "Is that supposed to be doing that?" Does this band know what they're doing? Is this their first gig? Hanna apologizes and awkwardly announces that they're going to start now. But then she incredibly reaches into some newfound reservoir of confidence to announce, at the top of her lungs and without a trace of self-consciousness, "We're Bikini Kill and we want Revolution Girl Style Now!" The drums and bass kick in with almost comic simplicity, the guitar screeches into a crude riff, and Hanna sings, "Hey girlfriend / I got a proposition / Goes something like this," while the music stumbles into high speed. This is punk rock in its most fundamental state, the sound of a band who knows they can't play and doesn't care, a band who's taken the stage whether you want them there or not, because they've got something to say and some noise to make. It's the sound of anger and resistance, but it's also the sound of joy emanating from young people who've just discovered that the rules don't matter and unlimited opportunities abound.

In the hands of Bikini Kill, punk became an instrument of empowerment for young women to create and communicate with one another using a do-it-yourself approach and exhibiting total disregard for their lack of experience. In "Double Dare Ya" Hanna is challenging and pestering her sisters to stand up for themselves—to "do what you want," "be who you will," and "cry right out loud"—by double daring and even triple daring them in the language of schoolchildren, thus exemplifying riot grrrl's volatile mixture of girlhood and feminism. Onstage, Hanna emboldened the female youth in her audience and often confronted the young males who came to confront her and Bikini Kill, thus carrying on the enduring punk style of performers who provoke their audiences but now directing the argument toward feminism. Hanna made it known that she had once worked as a stripper and frequently performed dressed as a schoolgirl or with words like "slut" or "whore" scrawled in Magic Marker across her belly, thus putting a feminist spin on the classic punk practices of contradiction, provocation, and irony.

Discovering the Purple-Haired People

Seattle's grunge scene in particular, but also its riot grrrl subculture, were thrust into the spotlight's glare for a fleeting moment in the early 1990s. As their development was reaching its peak, the marketing and entertainment worlds were searching for new methods of selling to young people. Advertisers suspected that this demographic was savvy enough to see through their machinations, and so they began to adopt two strategies for trying to reach young consumers, one utilizing self-conscious irony and the other drawing on the authenticity of alternative culture and its opposition to the processed goods of capital. It is unclear just how effective these marketing strategies were, however, as many young people were

Kathleen Hanna of Bikini Kill in 1994. From *The Encyclopedia of Punk*. Brian Cogan. New York: Sterling, 2008.

indeed savvy enough to see through this newest strain of advertising and quickly became resentful of the way they were categorized as a generation. Media attention and increased commercialization did accelerate the demise of many local indie scenes, however, as the move from alternative to mainstream provoked a collective identity crisis among those who suddenly found their music and style being consumed by the masses.

At a 1992 meeting of the Magazine Publishers Association, Karen Ritchie, executive vice president and director of media relations at McCann-Erickson, warned her audience with dramatic flair that they would need to find new methods for marketing to an upcoming demographic of young people they knew little about. "Face it: boomers are getting old," she told the magazine publishers, many of whom were undoubtedly baby boomers themselves, and all of whom made their living from entertaining or marketing to the baby boom generation in a variety of ways.⁴² Ritchie cautioned that the 18–29-year-olds of Generation X were turning away from traditional media like magazines and television that were focused on the life circumstances and collective memories of baby boomers at middle age. She confessed that those youths, whom she referred to as "the purple-haired people," were largely a mystery to her, and she admonished her audience of media purveyors that they didn't know anything about them either. The only thing that was obvious to Ritchie was the skepticism and cynicism with which Generation X viewed conventional media and advertising, which spelled doom for her industry. She speculated that young people were too savvy at decoding media to be reached by traditional forms of marketing—or, in other words, that they saw through the insincere and manipulative messages of the commercial media because they had grown up saturated with it.

Ritchie articulated the hunches and fears about Generation X shared by many within the media and advertising worlds.⁴³ She would later publish a book as her ideas about marketing to Generation X gained influence, and here again Ritchie warned of the difficulties in advertising to disaffected young people with strong bullshit detectors. "Generation X doesn't dislike advertising," she wrote. "They dislike *hype*. They dislike overstatement, self-importance, hypocrisy, and the assumption that *anyone* would want to be disturbed at home by a salesman on the telephone."⁴⁴ In short, advertisers were in a mess of their own making, and so they would have to find a new way to represent their products as honest and organic or, failing that, fess up to their own dishonesty and artificiality with a knowing smirk. Ritchie concluded, "One thing is clear: the more advertising clings to the 'newest, biggest, baddest' model that dominates today, the less successful we will be in convincing Generation X that advertising is an honest and reliable source of information."⁴⁵

To this day, a lack of legitimacy continues to haunt advertisers in their efforts to effectively market to young people. In the second half of the 1990s, commercials for the soft drink Sprite would take the lead in establishing a new style of youth-oriented advertising that seems to poke fun at advertising itself, employing the slogan "Image is nothing" and laying bare the reality that celebrities endorse products only because they are paid to do so. Such marketing strategies seek to align the commodity with the hip cynicism of youth culture, but they also have their limits insofar as it is easy to recognize that they are still a form of advertising, no matter how self-reflexive they may appear.[46] More recently, there has been a turn to "peer-to-peer" or "viral" forms of marketing that capitalize on the social relationships among young people, particularly their status hierarchies. Utilizing ethnographic methods of research, marketers have learned that young people may not trust advertisers but they do look up to the cool kids at school or in the neighborhood, and so these marketers go to extraordinary lengths to entice this elite to consume and display their products.[47]

In the early 1990s, however, the authenticity crisis of advertising provoked by the emergence of Generation X was experienced as new and original. Ritchie may have been the first or at least the loudest to sound alarm bells within the advertising world, but the national media had begun to profile the twenty-something generation a full two years before her speech about Generation X. *Time* was the first to examine the new cohort in a cover story published in July 1990, and articles in *BusinessWeek*, the *Atlantic Monthly*, and the *New Republic* soon followed. Like Ritchie, David M. Gross and Sophfronia Scott in *Time* depicted twenty-somethings as antimaterialists on a quest for authenticity: "They would rather hike in the Himalayas than climb a corporate ladder," the opening lines of the story read.[48] Drawing on what would become a familiar trope in later portrayals of Generation X, the *Time* story constructed twenty-somethings in opposition to their baby boomer predecessors, who were represented in terms of narcissism, self-indulgence, and permissiveness (which were said to have followed baby boomers in their alleged transformation from hippies to yuppies). By contrast, twenty-somethings were portrayed as more concerned about family, the environment, and local community; dedicated to noble professions like teaching and social work; and committed to a pragmatic approach to fixing social problems. *Time* thus established the template for the ensuing characterizations of Generation X's supposed preference for all things sincere and small-scale, which could then be translated to consumer preferences and leisure pursuits: "They sneer at Range Rovers, Rolexes and red suspenders. What they hold dear are family life, local activism, national parks, penny loafers and mountain bikes."[49]

Although hiking in the Himalayas failed to become the latest fad and penny loafers were soon surpassed by Doc Martens as the trendiest footwear, in several other respects the *Time* story on twenty-somethings was significant for cementing some familiar ideas about the people who would later be called Generation X. In the *Time* story it is most clearly evident that the discourse about young people is really about baby boomers them-selves, with twenty-somethings simply being defined as the Other of baby boomers' famous hedonism and permissiveness. This symbolic opposi-tion to the narcissism and self-indulgence widely associated with the baby boomers would continue to be implied whenever Generation X was por-trayed as victims of divorce or as disillusioned with revolutionary ideal-ism. This portrayal of the earnestness of young people in distinction from the Sixties had also begun to emerge in other contexts during the early 1990s. For example, as a protest movement was growing against the Gulf War of 1991, the *Washington Post* set out to profile a new generation of student activists whom they described as "rather clean-cut" and therefore "in the process of inventing the image of student anti-war protesters all over again."[50] After describing the young activists' painstaking efforts at politeness and reporting that "there isn't so much as a whiff of reefer," the *Post* concluded, "Abbie Hoffman would have been bored silly."[51]

The stereotypes of Generation X and "slackers" thus took shape in the image of disillusioned young people with an ironically cynical relation-ship to commercial entertainment and an ongoing cultural resentment of baby boomers. The taste for sincerity and modesty that the *Time* cover story on twenty-somethings originally identified could serve as the flip side of such disillusionment, and the various elements of alternative mu-sic and style would be employed by the culture industry in a seemingly desperate attempt to restore their credibility. The rebelliousness of this al-ternative culture was recognized as a valuable commodity, but in repack-aging the music and style for mass consumption the culture industry still managed to liquidate some of their more subversive elements. The term "slacker," for example, came to be associated with young people who are unmotivated or just downright lazy, but this is not exactly its meaning in either Richard Linklater's 1991 film *Slacker* or Superchunk's indie rock anthem "Slack Motherfucker." In both works, slacking is a way of life that developed out of DIY punk's refusal of wage labor and careerism, not for the sake of laziness but in favor of cultural production and control over creative work. In Linklater's *Slacker*, one character proclaims, "Every com-modity you produce is a piece of your own death," and another makes the fine distinction that "withdrawing in disgust is not the same as apathy." Likewise, "Slack Motherfucker" (quoted in the epigraph) was written in the DIY spirit that is anything but unmotivated, as members of Superc-hunk would eventually create their own label, Merge Records, and play an important part in building the indie music scene in Chapel Hill, North

Carolina. As slacking came to be redefined in the mainstream media as simple laziness, it served to recuperate the economic crisis provoked by downward mobility. It suggested that if young people failed to get ahead it was because they were unwilling to work and expected too much, as the business literature on Generation X sometimes argued.

Various musicians, artists, and writers led a backlash against the whole notion of Generation X, which we will examine below. Yet to question the accuracy of these characterizations was also beside the point, because they were shaped by the consumer culture from the beginning and immediately took on a life of their own within all the organs of the culture industry, which sought to market its wares to young people. Meanwhile, as Nirvana was exploding into stardom in late 1991, the attention to grunge and the Seattle scene dovetailed with both the emerging caricature of Generation X and new strategies of marketing to twenty-somethings, thus further reinforcing the image of angst-ridden youth. In 1992, undoubtedly the year of grunge, Nirvana was at the top of the charts, Pearl Jam and Soundgarden played an integral role in taking the summer Lollapalooza festivals to greater levels of popularity, and Pearl Jam's debut album, *Ten*, finished the year as one of *Billboard*'s best-selling albums. That year also saw the release of Cameron Crowe's film *Singles*, a romantic comedy about people in their twenties set in Seattle with the grunge music scene in the background. *Singles* included cameos from local musicians and a soundtrack laden with grunge bands, including Mudhoney's mockery of the commercialization of Seattle, "Overblown" (quoted in the epigraph). Grunge's climax and most absurd moment of appropriation seemed to arrive when fashion designer Marc Jacobs took flannel shirts, wool ski caps, Doc Martens boots, and stylishly dirty hair to the runways of Manhattan and made them the centerpieces of Perry Ellis's 1992 spring collection.[52]

Marketers quickly tried to latch on to the popularity of grunge with advertisements that were widely scorned by the young people at whom they were directed. There was, for instance, the infamous television commercial in which a scruffy young man compared the 1993 Subaru Impreza to punk rock. Former Black Flag singer and hardcore punk icon Henry Rollins appeared advertising a hooded T-shirt in a Gap billboard ad. Bud Dry also had the nerve to advertise itself as "the alternative beer" with pictures of sweaty stage divers and shirtless singers in a style derivative of Charles Peterson's photography. FM radio rock stations were quickly reformatted to make alternative rock a focal point, and MTV launched a new program of music videos called *Alternative Nation*, hosted by the

Henry Rollins, former Black Flag singer, in a Gap billboard ad. From *The Encyclopedia of Punk*. Brian Cogan. New York: Sterling, 2008.

spunky and bespectacled VJ Kennedy. More diffusely, movies and television shows began to include characters based on variations of Generation X clichés, most notably in *Friends'* portrayal of postcollege lifestyles in a hip New York neighborhood. The youthful taste for pictures of (hyper) reality also fueled the success of MTV's *The Real World*.

The culture industry was successful in making Seattle the new capital of the music world and putting flannel shirts in department stores across the United States. But the attempts to use the authenticity of alternative culture as an advertising ploy failed disastrously, largely for the same reasons that led advertisers to fear "media-savvy" youth in the first place. Young people still felt they were being manipulated, and a backlash against the very mention of "Generation X" or "grunge" was born the instant they became buzzwords.[53] When the *New York Times* was working on its story about the "success" of grunge in the fashion world, a former Sub Pop employee named Megan Jasper pulled off the now-legendary prank of providing the reporter with a fake glossary of grunge slang, which the *Times* then dutifully reprinted as truth. Like many others inside the subculture, Jasper was angry and annoyed at the perceived commodification of the grunge scene, which the *Times* story on fashion exemplified. The "lexicon of grunge" she fabricated included ridiculously cumbersome terms like "swingin' on the flippity-flop" to describe hanging out and "bloated, big bag of blotation" as code for being drunk.

As music industry and mainstream media interest in the Seattle grunge scene peaked, there was also a growing fascination with the riot grrrl movement that had begun in Olympia. Some of the media coverage was curious and generally positive, like that of the teen magazine *Sassy*, which printed the addresses of several riot grrrl zines that were subsequently deluged with mail from young female readers. Many participants felt that articles in the likes of *Newsweek*, the *Washington Post*, and most of the music press, however, sensationalized the sexuality of riot grrrl style while trivializing their feminist politics, and moreover that they positioned the members of Bikini Kill as "leaders" of what was supposed to be a nonhierarchical social movement.[54] This led a number of women who identified as riot grrrls to call for a "media blackout" whereby activists and musicians, including Bikini Kill, refused to be interviewed or photographed by mainstream media outlets. The media blackout garnered some controversy, however, among those who believed that riot grrrls needed to work with the mass media to have any hope of building a mass movement. For instance, the otherwise sympathetic journalist Lorraine Ali called it "dead-end elitism": it seemed that many within riot grrrl were more interested in preserving a sense of purity and authenticity than in spreading their message, much like their male counterparts in the hardcore scene.[55]

The Making and Unmaking of Subcultural Capital

The terms "grunge," "Generation X," and "alternative" largely disappeared from popular discourse not long after media and advertising outlets gave them currency. They were discredited by the demographic they were supposed to appeal to because young people could easily recognize them as calculated marketing pitches. Around the same time, "Alternative to what?" became a battle cry among young people who wouldn't have minded being called "alternative" a few years ago, but who now found the word odorous, reeking of market research and stagnant clichés. As FM radio was reformatted, a crop of new "alternative" bands emerged, looking and sounding like they had been assembled with different parts—guttural vocals, shaggy locks, gloomy imagery, and torn clothing—taken from the various Seattle bands.

Why did the attempts to market to Generation X using subcultural authenticity ultimately fail, and why did they incur such a backlash among their target audience? In her study of the British club cultures of dance music, Sarah Thornton used the term "subcultural capital" to describe the hierarchical distinction between high-status insiders and imposters, and comparable processes were observed in an ethnographic study of punk subcultures' distinction between "real punks" and "pretenders."[56] The concept of subcultural capital is of course derived from Pierre Bourdieu's analysis of how privileged classes reproduce their power through what they claim is their superior taste and consumption.[57] "Subcultural capital" is different, however, because it accumulates and circulates among young people who feel themselves to be outcasts in society and who invest their identities in the traditions of bohemia and rebellion. Subcultural capital is therefore compensatory, allowing people who are outsiders in all other aspects of society to feel superior because they are hip or cool. One must have a discriminating ear for the right sound and eye for the right look (or, perhaps most important, an ear for the wrong sound and an eye for the wrong look).

Subcultural capital has become a valuable commodity in marketing to those who want to seem versed in the latest thing, or at least don't want to be caught dead behind the times. The value of subcultural capital, however, can also fluctuate wildly, and just as it can be accumulated, it is also in constant danger of being liquidated by the media and corporations that seek to capitalize on it. Although many cultural studies scholars maintain that the boundaries between subculture and mass culture are more fluid than rigid, subcultural insiders do not see it this way.[58] When music and style they believe to be "underground" are commercialized and become available to a mass market, they experience a sense of alienation because they no longer own or control the culture they have produced, and because their expressions of rebellion are now consumed by the "mainstream" audience that they oppose. By definition, subcultural capital is a scarce commodity that can only belong to a minority. The threat of the media, fashion, and advertising industries is that they will cause inflation after leaking inside information to the majority. Hipsters believe that the music and the subculture no longer belong to them when anyone can hear Nirvana on the radio or buy grunge clothing in a department store. For certain, many people experience feelings of validation when large numbers of people suddenly take notice of something they like, but this satisfaction is typically kept under wraps. They are more likely to complain about the fact that now they must share their culture with an undifferentiated mass of consumers who represent the dreaded mainstream society.

Insiders and innovators do have a few methods for defending their subcultural capital when it is threatened by the inflation that results from commercial exposure. One involves accusing musicians of "selling out" when they achieve commercial success and a larger audience. Indeed, there is a built-in antagonism between musicians, who may be able to improve their financial status or simply want to change their sound, and their die-hard fans, who want the band to stick to their original aesthetic so that they can maintain their exclusive claim to them. Subcultural capital can also be defended or even augmented by claiming to have "been there and done that" before the masses caught on: for example, one saw a particular band in a small club before anyone else had heard of them or had a tattoo years before they started appearing on movie stars. When the media liquidates subcultural capital by bringing the alternative to the mainstream, insiders defend their status by claiming that they were there first and distinguishing themselves from all the Johnny-come-latelys.

Thornton and Bourdieu's ideas about various forms of cultural capital were developed to understand the hierarchies of distinction within social groups, but they can be further extended in examining how subcultural capital can be exchanged into financial capital by media and culture industries who seek to profit from their images of authenticity and rebellion. The commodification of styles, cultures, and differences is essential to contemporary capitalism. When conglomerates—especially the large ones that hipsters vilify as "corporations"—are seen to put their stamp on them, however, hip culture and music immediately begin to lose their value as subcultural capital. Capitalism thus exploits, destroys, and finally makes waste of subcultural capital in much the same way that it does with so many other resources, cultures, and people. The faddishness of the subculture expires quickly, as grunge did in the early 1990s, and the insiders and originators feel they have to move on to something else, and so the music and style is rapidly liquidated of its value as "cool" and prepared for its final resting place in a museum of dead styles. The ironic thing is that

this form of commercialization is so much more effective as a form of social control than the labeling and punishment of rebellious youth subcultures. Quite often, stigmatization and moral panics have made deviance
more enticing and alluring to many young people who were already looking for a way to express their discontent. But rebellion seems to lose its
vitality once it becomes a packaged commodity available to the masses, as
corporate capitalism destroys these hip and edgy resources in the process
of trying to profit from them. This form of social control dissolves rather
than reinforces the boundaries between the deviant and the normal, and
thus mainstream culture is increasingly saturated with images of deviance
that no longer seem shocking or provocative.[59]

In its more corporate form, alternative rock took shape with a spectrum of styles that spanned from the harder-sounding bands with a traditionally masculine approach to classic rock and heavy metal to the quirk-
ier and seemingly more intellectual groups with a softer sound and image that could be identified as "college rock." The harder of the alternative
rock groups were generally more macho than the original Seattle bands
and expressed little of the feminist consciousness articulated by Kurt Cobain or Eddie Vedder. The mainstreaming of alternative rock, along with
the diffuse influence of riot grrrl, did create many new opportunities for
female performers in popular music. Though not linked with the movement in Olympia, groups like L7, Babes in Toyland, and especially Hole
(led by Kurt Cobain's wife, Courtney Love) benefited from the vogue for
loud guitars, screeching vocals, and confrontational female personalities.
At more pop end of the spectrum, Alanis Morissette, Fiona Apple, and
Tori Amos delved into personal experiences related to sexual abuse or affirmed independence in ways that may have been sonically gentler than
the riot grrrl bands but were otherwise comparable; regardless of the style,
these topics had largely been unexplored by women in pop music until
this time. But as they were filtered through the worlds of celebrity and
commerce, the feminist messages in women's music became predictably
more individualistic and oriented toward the personal, but not collective,
empowerment of girls; moreover, this empowerment was largely conceptualized in terms of the hegemonic roles of consumption and sexuality.
Both the influence and the dilution of riot grrrl's feminist practices of
empowerment for female youth were staggeringly conspicuous when the
Spice Girls took the world by storm in 1997 with the slogan "Girl Power."

In the music world, riot grrrl's biggest direct impact was the emergence
of Sleater-Kinney, a three-woman group that Greil Marcus hailed as the

Corin Tucker of Sleater-Kinney, screaming her head off. From *We Owe You Nothing: Punk Planet: The Collected Interviews*. Edited by Daniel Sinker. New York: Akashic, 2001.

country's best rock band in a 2001 *Time* magazine article.[60] The band's founding members, Corin Tucker and Carrie Brownstein, both attended Evergreen State College in Olympia during the 1990s, and Tucker's first group, Heavens to Betsy, performed during "Girls' Night" at the International Pop Underground Convention in 1991. Sleater-Kinney formed in 1994, and they began to come into their own musically with the release of *Call the Doctor* in 1996. The title track and first song on the album finds Tucker singing, "They want to socialize you / They want to purify you / They want to dignify and analyze and terrorize you." She is singing to an audience subjected to an endless process of social control, much like what Foucault described as a microphysics of power, in which the subject is analyzed, terrorized, purified, and even dignified through control over their bodies and health.[61] "Call the doctor! Call the doctor! Call the doctor!"— Tucker ratchets up the intensity of the situation with her gigantic voice, but what we can't know is if it is really in the patient's best interest to be in the hands of a doctor and the medical establishment. The second half of *Call the Doctor* opens with "I Wanna Be Yr Joey Ramone," which became a sort of anthem for Sleater-Kinney's ambivalent aspirations to be the champions of the new punk rock world coupled with their misgivings about assimilating into a game that is rigged from the start.

Sleater-Kinney solidified their position at the top of the indie rock world with their 1997 breakthrough, *Dig Me Out*, and they continued to lead the maturation of riot grrrl by performing at the inaugural Ladyfest concert in Olympia in 2000. A musical and arts festival for female performers, Ladyfest is now an international, nonprofit event in which annual concerts are organized autonomously throughout Europe and North America.[62] And yet there was a continuing sense that riot grrrl had been co-opted and pushed aside in the process of commercializing young women's desires for empowerment. This was articulated in Sleater-Kinney's "#1 Must Have," a song that was written in reaction to the rapes of young women at Woodstock 1999 but simultaneously addressed a number of key issues related to consumerism, co-optation, women's body image, and rock's gender politics. Tucker sings, "I wish we could write something more than the next marketing bid," but by the end of the song she seems to have discovered a new level of determination and defiance. As the music picks up speed, Tucker tells us to get off our asses because "Culture is what we make it / Yes it is," and the song comes to a furious culmination with her repeatedly yelling, "Now is the time to invent."

In Search of the Next Seattle

After Nirvana and the other Seattle-based grunge bands had become commercial sensations, the major labels began scouring various regional scenes that had been in the making for several years but had been previously perceived as unprofitable. During this time, it seemed that a significant change in musical tastes had occurred and all bets were off about what would sell and what wouldn't, and so the major labels took a relatively indiscriminate approach to buying up budding talent. The search for the next Seattle thus led record companies to the bohemian enclaves in Washington, D.C., Chicago, and Portland, Oregon, and college towns like Athens, Georgia, and Chapel Hill, North Carolina. For instance, in Lawrence, Kansas, a small college town home to the University of Kansas with a population of 80,000, a Kansas City TV news station produced a feature story titled, "Lawrence: It's Not Just Grunge," shortly after the Lawrence-based band Paw became the subject of a major-label bidding war and finally signed a lucrative deal with A&M Records. In previous decades, the emergence of youthful subcultures centered on rebellious music and style had usually been greeted with a mixture of curious bewilderment and hostile condemnation, but in these times, places like Lawrence were promoting their local music scenes almost as a form of civic boosterism. Indeed, regardless of whether this was consciously understood at the time, cities did in fact have a material interest in nurturing their music scenes, as Richard Florida would later prove that their economic fortunes had become linked to the presence of creative types like musicians.

San Diego was another place where the local music scene became a focus of major-label interest and media hype, and I will draw from my ethnographic research there during the 1990s to present a case study of the consequences of such commercialization. The San Diego music scene had largely developed out of hardcore punk, and by the early 1990s there was an extensive network of local bands, independent labels, and fanzines. The major record companies signed seven San Diego bands in a short period of time, and there were numerous stories published in the national and regional media that speculated that the San Diego scene was "the next big thing." But like all the other next Seattles, the hype never materialized into real success, the bands never got famous, and they were eventually dropped by the major labels. I was interviewing musicians and other participants in the San Diego scene shortly after this time, and although commercialization was not the primary focus of my study, I would always ask interviewees what they thought about this "next Seattle" issue. I interviewed several of the musicians who got major-label contracts and asked about their experiences, such as the differences between recording for a major versus an independent.

The music scene in San Diego had a violent history dating back to the popularity of hardcore and thrash metal during the 1980s. The violence, largely fueled by alcohol and methamphetamines, was so pervasive that at shows, "you could watch fights all night and be entertained. Pay six bucks and watch guys beat the hell out of one another," as one long-time participant put it.[63] The main concert promoter during this time was Tim Mays, who had begun organizing shows in 1979 and opened a venue for punk rock shows in pregentrified downtown San Diego shortly thereafter, but the club was forced to close due to constant harassment from the police. Mays continued to promote hardcore and thrash shows in the San Diego area during the 1980s but never found a permanent home, in part because

Tim Mays show featuring Hüsker Dü, the Minutemen, the Meat Puppets, and Saccharine Trust (*left*).
Tim Mays show featuring Black Flag and the Minutemen (*right*).

Regulars gather outside the Casbah circa 1993. From the interior CD case of *Musica del Diablo: Live from the Casbah*. Live Casbah Music, 1993.

of persistent problems with police and the city, but also because of the destructive behavior of those who attended his shows.

His shows began to be frequented by a group calling themselves the San Diego Skinheads, some of whom were associated with Tom Metzger and his organization, White Aryan Resistance. The numbers of skinheads never amounted to more than a minority at any time, but they came to punk shows with the intention of starting as many fights and inflicting as much harm as they could. There were also large-scale acts of destruction, however, involving much of the rest of the audience, with the final straw coming when fans destroyed the first three rows of a run-down theater during a Red Hot Chili Peppers concert. Mays was determined to get out of the music business at that point: "I was sick of it. . . . The violence, plus running out of spaces to do shows in. I went through every hall that I could find. You know, you'd go out there and scour and try and 'Oh, I got a new place,' and do a few shows and the neighbors would get pissed off at the owner of the hall. It was a constant moving process. I'd say I went through eight different places in five years."[64]

By 1989 Tim Mays had been out of the business of promoting concerts in the San Diego area for three years. He and some friends had recently opened a bar, and Mays took a job in a department store to help pay the bills while the business struggled. A small club near the airport in downtown San Diego became available, and Mays and one of his partners snatched it up. They called their club the Casbah, but in light of the problems faced in previous years, they had no intention of hosting the sort of punk and thrash shows with which Mays had become associated. Live music was only performed two or three nights a week, mostly featuring rhythm and blues and roots music, along with the occasional rockabilly or swing band. The Casbah even had an espresso machine. Those days of tranquil conversation and low amplifier volume, however, were clearly numbered. The problem was that the kids just wouldn't go away, and they had no other space in which to congregate: "There were no places where young people could really go on a nightly basis and just hang out with their friends," Mays recalled. A generation of punks and headbangers who had cut their teeth at Mays' shows during the 1980s were becoming serious musicians and forming bands that constituted the nucleus of an emerging San Diego music scene. At that time, however, there were still no reliable venues where such bands could play, and thus it wasn't long before they started looking in Mays's direction. "We opened the doors and that's what happened," Mays said. "It took on a life of its own."[65]

A music scene quickly coalesced at the Casbah during the first few years of the 1990s. The range of alternative rock performed there varied from the more conventionally grunge (e.g., the crunching guitar riffs and catchy pop melodies of the band fluf) to wildly experimental (the spastically fragmented Truman's Water) to cyborg-style prog rock (Three Mile Pilot) to quirky lo-fi (Heavy Vegetable). At the center of the San Diego scene was John Reis, front man for the retro garage group Rocket From the Crypt and guitarist for the abrasively loud Drive Like Jehu. With a number of interesting and innovative bands in town, Headhunter/Cargo Records, a small label formerly based in Montreal, established operations in San Diego and began releasing full-length CDs in 1991. The scene also inspired the formation of a number of local zines, including the horror-and-humor themed *Genetic Disorder* created by Larry Harmon.

In the spring of 1992, a local punk rock fan and entrepreneur named Gary Hustwit returned from the annual South by Southwest Music and Media Conference in Austin, Texas, with thoughts of organizing a similar type of seminar in San Diego, one that could bring exposure to its newly thriving music scene and swelling numbers of alternative rock bands. South by Southwest is a music festival and industry seminar that grew out of the postpunk and alternative rock community in Austin, and it features four nights of live music in scores of local nightclubs along with three days of panel discussions with people in the music business as well as those hoping to make it in the music business.[66] The New Music Seminar had been organized with a similar purpose in New York City in 1980, but there was no such equivalent on the West Coast. Hustwit thought to himself, "Hey, why don't we do something like this in San Diego? We'll put on our own music seminar, we'll get a bunch of bands to play here. The original intent was just to get attention for the bands and the scene. At that time, there were so many great bands and Cargo was the only label doing anything."[67] Hustwit thought he might attract representatives from major labels, but more realistically he wanted the attention of the underground communities and independent labels dispersed across North America. Through the panel discussions, Hustwit also hoped that musicians could learn how to do it themselves: how to create their own record label; how to copyright music; how to have records, cassettes, or CDs manufactured; how to find a regional distributor for their music; how to get publicity from the music press and college radio; and how to book their own tours. Hustwit had recently authored a book, *Releasing an Independent Record*, which offered tips for starting a record label along with a massive directory of independent distributors, manufacturers, publishers, and retail outlets in virtually every state of the union.[68] In San Diego many people still assumed that aspiring musicians should move to Los Angeles and try to get the attention of major labels, but Hustwit was intent on showing that musicians could stay and build a career for themselves through independent networks and their local scene.

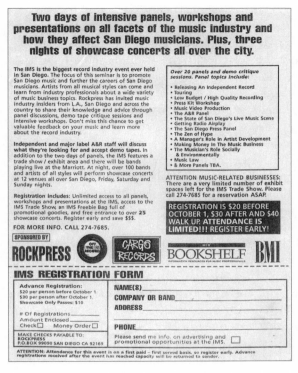

Two days of intensive panels, workshops and presentations on all facets of the music industry and how they affect San Diego musicians. Plus, three nights of showcase concerts all over the city.

The IMS is the biggest record industry event ever held in San Diego. The focus of this seminar is to promote San Diego music and further the careers of San Diego musicians. Artists from all musical styles can come and learn from industry professionals about a wide variety of music business topics. Rockpress has invited music industry insiders from L.A., San Diego and across the country to share their knowledge and advice through panel discussions, demo tape critique sessions and intensive workshops. Don't miss this chance to get valuable feedback on your music and learn more about the record industry.

Independent and major label A&R staff will discuss what they're looking for and accept demo tapes. In addition to the two days of panels, the IMS features a trade show / exhibit area and there will be bands playing live at the Marriott. At night, over 100 bands and artists of all styles will perform showcase concerts at 12 venues all over San Diego, Friday, Saturday and Sunday nights.

Registration includes: Unlimited access to all panels, workshops and presentations at the IMS, access to the IMS Trade Show, an IMS Freebie Bag full of promotional goodies, and free entrance to over 25 showcase concerts. Register early and save $$$.

FOR MORE INFO. CALL 274-7685.

SPONSORED BY

ROCKPRESS   OFF THE RECORD   CARGO RECORDS   BOOKSHELF *INFORMATION RESOURCES FOR MUSIC PROFESSIONALS*   BMI

Over 20 panels and demo critique sessions. Panel topics include:

• Releasing An Independent Record
• Touring
• Low Budget / High Quality Recording
• Press Kit Workshop
• Music Video Production
• The A&R Panel
• The State of San Diego's Live Music Scene
• Getting Radio Airplay
• The San Diego Press Panel
• The Zen of Hype
• A Manager's Role in Artist Development
• Making Money In The Music Business
• The Musician's Role Socially & Environmentally
• Music Law
• & More Panels TBA.

ATTENTION MUSIC-RELATED BUSINESSES: There are a very limited number of exhibit spaces left for the IMS Trade Show. Please call 274-7685 for a reservation ASAP.

REGISTRATION IS $20 BEFORE OCTOBER 1, $30 AFTER AND $40 WALK UP. ATTENDANCE IS LIMITED!!! REGISTER EARLY!

IMS REGISTRATION FORM

Advance Registration:
$20 per person before October 1.
$30 per person after October 1.
Showcase Only Passes: $10

Of Registrations____
Amount Enclosed____
Check☐   Money Order☐

MAKE CHECKS PAYABLE TO:
ROCKPRESS
P.O. BOX 99090 SAN DIEGO CA 92169

NAME(S)____
COMPANY OR BAND____
ADDRESS____
PHONE____
Please send me info. on advertising and promotional opportunities at the IMS. ☐

ATTENTION: Attendance for this event is on a first paid – first served basis, so register early. Advance registrations received after the event has reached capacity will be returned to sender.

Registration form for San Diego's Independent Music Seminar.

With the focus on independent, DIY methods of production, Hustwit and his codirector, Kevin Chanel, were determined to limit the influence of the major labels. They had seen how corporate conglomerates were taking over other music seminars, and so the Independent Music Seminar (IMS) refused an estimated $50,000 from major labels who wanted to sponsor the event, host music industry parties, or give away free CDs and other promotional packages. "We don't allow the major labels to advertise themselves and their bands, and every one of them has asked," Hustwit explained to the *San Diego Union-Tribune*. "The thing is that you can't compete with that kind of money. It kind of drowns out the indie labels. It prices the small labels and small bands out of the ballpark."[69] Hustwit and Chanel financed the IMS entirely through registration fees and money solicited from local businesses, and it was a tremendous success by any standard. In 1992, the seminar's first year, 1,000 people attended the concerts and panel discussions, including over 100 people participating as panelists and guest speakers. Panel topics centered on how-to discussions about recording, touring, management, and music law, as well as broader discussions like "The Musician's Role–Socially and Environmentally" and "The Zen of Hype." Hustwit recalled that many of the panels, especially those pertaining to musical production, were "standing room only." Hustwit and Chanel decided to expand in the following years, and in 1993 and 1994 the conferences drew audiences of between 1,500 and 2,000. The concerts showcased 250 bands, approximately 150 of which were from San Diego, and the organizers had to turn away another 200-plus bands who wanted to perform at the event.

Ultimately, however, the IMS came to be known for the series of major-label signings of local bands that grew out of the showcase performances, and not for the instruction in how to do it yourself. Hustwit and Chanel limited the corporate presence in sponsorship and promotion, but they actively encouraged A and R representatives (the talent scouts of the music industry) to attend the concerts. There probably would have been no interest among the major labels in previous years, but during the commercial breakthrough of Nirvana, grunge, and alternative rock, A and R scouts came from New York and Los Angeles determined to outdo one another in pursuit of new talent. Among others, Interscope, Geffen, and Atlantic Records all signed at least one San Diego band. The IMS organizers knew there might be some major-label interest, but the money and contracts changed the focus of the event in ways they hadn't intended. As Hustwit explained to me, "My original idea was that the panels were the main thing, and then the shows afterwards. Not the other way around, and that's how it ended up being. The attitude was: 'I want to get a show because I want label people to see me and I want to get signed,' and not, 'I want to go to this thing so I can learn more about the industry,' like what does a music attorney do, what does a producer do, how do I get an agent.'"[70] Hustwit grew frustrated because he felt that local musicians had missed his point: even if one aspires to a major-label deal, musicians are better off if they learn how to produce their own music and a build a reputation through touring, rather than waiting to be magically discovered by a record company.

The major-label contracts were followed by media speculation that the San Diego scene could be a potential successor to Seattle grunge. *Entertainment Weekly*, *Billboard*, *Spin*, *Details*, and the *New Yorker* all included blurbs that proclaimed that the San Diego scene was "hot." A journalist for the *Los Angeles Times Magazine* quipped, "They're young, disaffected, and suddenly they have record contracts. Can a few post-punk bands turn

San Diego into the next capital of alternative rock?"[71] *Rolling Stone* profiled Rocket From the Crypt and Drive Like Jehu, two of the local bands who signed with Interscope Records, and dubbed the Casbah "a den of slack." *Rolling Stone* and the cable television station E! also combined to produce a *History of Style*, hosted by aging teen idol Luke Perry, which announced that the San Diego scene was "the next big thing" in alternative rock. The ensuing report featured interviews with musicians and footage of local bands performing, but it made it seem as if the music was closely linked with the region's surfing and beach culture, when in fact many of the musicians had consciously identified themselves against these activities. For example, one musician is asked about local style and responds, "San Diego fashion can be summed in two words: No Fear." His remark was meant to be sarcastic, for it is a disparaging swipe at a line of T-shirts bearing macho slogans about sports and competition that were popular with the jocks, frat boys, and military recruits who dominate the region's style. But the sarcasm was lost within the context, as the program cut from the band to more footage of surfers, rollerbladers, and bikini-clad female bodies, as if his words had been a sincere endorsement.

As alternative rock reached its commercial zenith in 1993, a band called the Stone Temple Pilots appeared with an MTV video and an album on Atlantic Records that climbed into *Billboard*'s top ten. On their debut record, the band sounded so similar to the megapopular Seattle grunge band Pearl Jam that many music reviews and rock critics commented on the obvious derivation. The band was selling a lot of records, but their lack of originality and credibility made them an object of ridicule in alternative rock circles. Sensing the need to respond to this crisis of authenticity, the band's management and their record company claimed that the Stone Temple Pilots were a product of San Diego's thriving alternative music scene. In fact, although some of the members had once lived in San Diego, the band was never part of the local music scene. Many people in the San Diego scene were infuriated because they did not want to be associated with a band that was considered to be impostors by so many. When the Stone Temple Pilots were nominated for the San Diego Music Awards, a petition was circulated and T-shirts were created bearing the message "STP ain't from SD." As one participant explained to me, "There was a lot of animosity because there were bands that have been busting their ass around here for a real long time. . . . They were an LA-based band and they had no business claiming they were from here. . . . They became so huge, and it was like, 'This is what's going to represent us?'"[72]

An investment in subcultural capital was being threatened, as this became an issue of identity and the representation of one's community. The sense that the subculture felt itself to be under attack from the forces of misrepresentation was vividly apparent in a disgusting story that assumed legendary status within the scene. When the Stone Temple Pilots played in San Diego amid this controversy, a musician from the group Rocket From the Crypt purportedly substituted a bottle of urine for a beer that was onstage, unbeknownst to the band's guitar player, who took a long drink and then immediately spit up the urine (henceforth known as "Rocket fuel") into the crowd. This story was narrated to me on several different occasions during the course of my research, testifying to its symbolic value as a kind of cultural mythology. Whether the story is true is less important than the function served by retelling it over and over again, for it enabled insiders to solidify symbolic boundaries between themselves and fake poseurs, embodied in the defilement of "sellout" imposters by an "authentic" local band, so as to preserve subcultural capital.

In San Diego the attention from media and major labels had a noticeable impact on the sense of community that had developed within the local scene. The audience for live music expanded considerably, to the benefit of many of the bands as well as Tim Mays and the Casbah. The attention certainly conferred some sense of validation for those who felt like they were part of the scene, even though many did their best to appear aloof to the sudden fascination emanating from the organs of mainstream culture. On the other hand, musicians and fans discovered that they were now sharing their space with people whom they believed to be less knowledgeable or committed to the subculture. These newcomers seemed to embody more conventional sensibilities and behaviors, which the insiders had consciously identified themselves against since they were teenagers. Subcultural capital was being liquidated, and the insiders responded by reaffirming the boundaries between themselves and those they derided as imitators. In the San Diego scene, subcultural capital was threatened by the expansion of the Casbah into a larger club that could accommodate more customers as interest in the local music scene increased. John, a musician in the local scene, described an encounter that for him symbolized the negative consequences of the Casbah's expansion:

> The new Casbah opens, and I go there for the first time and realize it's a bigger club now, it feels kind of strange. I'm turning the corner and there's this guy who I've never seen in my entire life—kind of a big guy—and he

bumps into me and I look at him and say, "Hey, excuse me," and he's staring me down like he wants to kick my ass. The only thing that was going through my head was, "Go back to Pacific Beach, you motherfucker. Go back and fight, whatever. This used to be a fun place before your kind came here."[73]

Thus for John the problem was that the media hype was attracting the wrong kind of people to the Casbah, "just so they could say they saw the latest thing." The new crowd seemed to embody the kind of machismo and propensity for violence that many alternative rockers opposed. To John, that kind of behavior belonged on the beach, the site of San Diego's more mainstream nightlife.

The hype about the "next Seattle" never translated into any real commercial breakthroughs. Within a few years all of the San Diego bands who had signed with major labels were dropped from their contracts. Two of those bands endured lengthy legal disputes with their record companies, who owned the music they had recorded but refused to release it on the grounds that it had limited commercial appeal, prompting the bands to try to get out of their contracts so they could at least release their music on an independent label. In both cases the disputes and delays were ultimately detrimental for the musicians, eventually causing their groups to disband. A musician from the band Three Mile Pilot told me that as a result of their conflicts with the David Geffen Company, "We lost two and a half years of out music, and it really put a wrench in our progress. . . . It took this long period and it really wore us down."[74]

During their hunt for the next Seattle, the record companies came to the IMS with the imperative that, as Gary Hustwit put it, "they needed to sign a San Diego band—any San Diego band." All the bands who signed were beginning to receive critical acclaim and develop a following, but for the most part even the musicians themselves knew they had little chance for commercial success because their music was too abrasive or complex for radio. Once the initial period of excitement had worn off, many musicians became frustrated by the pressures to write some "radio-friendly" singles, tone down the experimental noise, make the vocals more understandable, and agree to a particular type of packaging, artwork, or song sequencing. Moreover, the opportunity to "sell out" to the major labels actually resulted in major financial debts in addition to a loss of artistic control. The "advance" a label gives to a band, after all, is actually a loan on the costs of producing an album in the studio, buying new instruments, and going on tour, and it must be repaid through royalties on retail sales.[75] One local band, Inch, understood this and tried to protect themselves by negotiating with Atlantic Records for a small advance and recording with a lower budget. What they did not understand is that when a label has little invested and the band is not a priority, the band loses most of the advantages of working with a corporation: financial support, advertising and promotion, even the commitment to release music that has already been recorded. Inch learned a hard lesson that, despite the risk of debt, "it's still in the band's interest to sign for the most money they can."[76]

The presence of major labels had important and mostly negative consequences for the San Diego scene, but not for the reasons assumed in the typical narrative about a "feeding frenzy" or corporate "invasion" that ends in the co-optation of an otherwise-pristine underground community. In the first place, the floodgates to local talent were opened from the inside, by Gary Hustwit and the Independent Music Seminar. The major-label presence certainly redirected the emphasis of the IMS away from its stated mission to educate musicians about how to do it themselves, but this competition to sign local bands seemed to have been anticipated by IMS organizers in assessing the extent of talent and the major labels' newfound interest in alternative rock. Once the bands were signed, their major-label contracts turned out to be more damaging than profitable, but this had less to do with the demand for artistic compromises than the way that corporations passed the financial risks of investing in unknown talent onto the musicians themselves. Bands who were accused of "selling out" were in fact more likely to end up in debt and without any musical product to sell. For those who felt this was "their" scene, the problem with the hype about San Diego being the next Seattle was that it threatened their subcultural capital, meaning that it brought all the wrong kinds of people to the Casbah and compelled insiders to distinguish themselves from those hopping on the proverbial bandwagon. But when corporate interests tried to use the subcultural capital conferred by the apparent authenticity of an underground scene—most infamously when Atlantic Records claimed that the Stone Temple Pilots were a San Diego band in an attempt to give them the credibility they lacked—their machinations were transparent and met with outraged resistance.

The Battle of Seattle

The 1990s are likely to be remembered as the decade when neoliberalism finally took hold over the entire world after the collapse of the Soviet

Union and the concoction of an ideological consensus about free markets. In popular music, the ascendance of grunge from Seattle and riot grrrl from Olympia symbolized a cultural change away from the hedonism and greed that defined the 1980s. The movement of grunge, riot grrrl, and alternative rock into the mainstream of popular culture was linked to the evolution of a new form of capitalism, one that profits from cultural expressions of difference, authenticity, and rebellion. This development has been heralded as either a fusion of bourgeois and bohemian traditions or the advancement of a new class of creative workers, and it has been condemned as a process of co-optation that puts the cool and the hip in the service of consumer capitalism. Grunge and riot grrrl took shape along with other postpunk subcultures in opposition to corporate forms of capitalism embodied in the culture industry of global media conglomerates. But precisely because those subcultures seemed to personify smallness and sincerity, they could be integrated into the emerging form of creative capitalism and used in marketing to young people who had grown suspicious of the deceitful and grandiose claims of conventional advertising.

From a functionalist perspective, the commercialization of anticorporate subcultures might be seen as exemplary of the recuperative powers of capitalism to co-opt dissent. But if from this viewpoint the breakthrough of Nirvana and their peers appears to be the metaphorical starting point for 1990s capitalism, its endpoint can also be traced to events emanating from Seattle, namely the protests that shut down the meetings of the World Trade Organization in the final weeks of 1999. The extent and ferocity of the anti-WTO protests clearly came as a shock to the agents of global capitalism and the mainstream media, but they were the cumulative effect of "a movement of movements" that had been mobilizing and networking with one another during the 1990s, uniting in their common opposition to the lack of democratic accountability among corporations and global financial institutions.[77] During the protests, an impromptu band calling itself the NO WTO Combo performed with Jello Biafra of the Dead Kennedys on vocals, Soundgarden's Kim Thayil on guitar, and Krist Novoselic of Nirvana on bass. From the functionalist perspective that sees reconciliation between capital and cultural rebellion, this anti-WTO protest among prominent punk and grunge musicians was not supposed to happen. Richard Florida, for instance, recalled that his epiphany about "the big morph" between business and bohemia came when watching a rock band in Austin, Texas, and then later realizing that all the musicians were high-tech CEOs and venture capitalists.[78] Thomas Frank spent the better part of the 1990s mocking countercultural figures from Henry Rollins to William S. Burroughs to Grateful Dead lyricist John Perry Barlow for presenting pseudorebellious ideas that in Frank's view were no different from those found in management texts. If Florida or Frank had been right, we would have expected to find Biafra, Thayil, and Novoselic in a cozy little niche of the New Economy and nowhere near the WTO protests.

It wasn't just the NO WTO Combo, either. About one month before what would come to be known as the "Battle of Seattle," Rage Against the Machine released *The Battle of Los Angeles*, an album that was a sort of *London Calling* for the neoliberal globalization era. *The Battle of Los Angeles* debuted at number one upon its release on November 2, 1999, selling 450,000 copies in its first week and eventually going double platinum. As *London Calling* represented the Clash's triumphant synthesis of punk and reggae at the dawn of the rightward turn in the United Kingdom and the United States, the music of Rage Against the Machine brought the metal, punk, and hip hop styles that had developed since the 1970s into dialogue with radical anticapitalist politics. Singer Zack de la Rocha had performed in a hardcore band based in Orange County called Inside Out, but in Rage Against the Machine his ferocious vocal style began to include more rapping and rhyming. His father had been part of the art collective Los Four that grew out of the Chicano movement in Los Angeles, and in appearance de la Rocha himself looked something like a simulacrum of Bob Marley or Che Guevara. Guitarist Tom Morello also had roots in the social movements of the previous generation, as his mother had been involved in the civil rights movement and the Chicago Urban League and his father was a Mau Mau guerilla and the first Kenyan ambassador to the United Nations. As a guitar player Morello was initially influenced by heavy metal, but in Rage Against the Machine he also developed a unique style that impersonates the sound of hip hop's turntable scratching by rubbing his hands over the strings on the guitar's pickups.

The Battle of Los Angeles situates the global within the local, and vice versa, in the same spirit that brought protestors against the WTO to Seattle. Its opening track features de la Rocha recruiting us all to join the worldwide struggle whose signs are visible wherever we happen to be: "Testify!" he exhorts to the listener, "It's right outside your door!" By the end of this song he has moved from matters of space to those of time and history (the central theme of chapter 5): "Who controls the past now controls the future / Who controls the past now?" There is enough swagger in de la Rocha's rhymes to make their political radicalism and literary allusions fit credibly within the style of rap music, while at the same time the horror of global injustice is assimilated into the violent morbidity of heavy metal and punk. The mixture of a rapper's bravado and a punk's outrage is evident when de la Rocha introduces himself on "Calm Like a Bomb": "I be walking God like a dog / My narrative fearless / My word war returns home to burn / Like Baldwin home from Paris / Steel from a furnace / I was born landless / It's tha native son / Born of Zapata's guns / Stroll through the shanties / And tha cities remain / Same bodies buried hungry / But with different last names." At other moments the images of injustice are fired in a Surrealist style of juxtaposition, as in the same song when de la Rocha spits out: "Pick a point on the globe / Yes tha picture's tha same / There's a bank a church a myth and a hearse / A mall and a loan a child dead at birth." As social critics complained that rebellion had been co-opted, many rock fans were also accusing Rage Against the Machine of hypocrisy because their attacks on global capitalism were launched with a recording contract with Sony Entertainment. But the band's success also suggested the possibility of infiltrating and subverting the system from within by exploiting the contradiction that capitalists will sell anything that turns a profit: "A fire in the master's house is set," de la Rocha repeatedly cries out to punctuate "New Millennium Homes."

Whether it is couched in celebratory or critical terms, the analysis of capital's capacity to absorb cultural creativity or dissent leaves no room for the possibility that capitalism continues to be ripe with contradictions—that the bourgeoisie creates its own grave diggers, as Marx famously put it.[79] It is unquestionable that capital seeks to appropriate and profit from the authenticity and rebellion embodied in youth culture—and that it does this faster and more thoroughly than ever—but does that mean it can easily restore hegemony in the process? In this chapter we have seen how the attempts to use alternative culture to market to Generation X during the early 1990s were absurdly transparent and met with a fierce backlash. At the WTO protests, two of the main targets of protestors' rage were Nike and Starbucks, both of which wound up with rocks thrown through the windows of their stores in Seattle. Nike has been at the forefront of commercializing youthful expressions of cool ever since it used the Beatles' "Revolution" in a television commercial in 1987. Starbucks has gone to great lengths to cultivate an image for itself as a purveyor of culture and community, not simply coffee. And yet these corporations did not fool anyone who showed up in Seattle as the 1990s came to an end, and they still inspire resistance all over the world as the march of globalization continues.

5

Retro Punks and Pin-Up Girls

Your inspiration is a memory that you know you never had.
> —Rocket From the Crypt, "Born in '69"

One day you will be nostalgic for now.
> —Slogan of Suicide Girls' first U.S. tour

San Diego, 1995: In the beginning stages of my ethnographic research, I arrange to meet Matt Reese for an interview in a bar called the Live Wire. Matt had been a singer in various punk rock bands in San Diego for almost 10 years at that point, most recently in a band called Jalopy that centered on the band members' shared enthusiasm for old cars. When I started interviewing people around the local scene and discussed plans to do further research, I was told on more than one occasion, "You gotta talk to Matt Reese," because he was known and respected by so many. He showed up for our interview looking like a 1950s greaser, with an upper torso full of tattoos, slicked-back hair, and a cigarette perched on his ear. Matt was a burly and affable guy, a supreme storyteller who always seemed to have a crowd around him. As far I could see, the retro/tattoo/punk aesthetic permeated every aspect of life, as I later learned that he painted tattoo-style designs on plywood and built a large tiki bar in his backyard.

When I started asking about his background, Matt described himself as "blue-collar." His father worked as an electrician, and Matt worked in building maintenance. After I got to know him better, I asked Matt if he thought his retro style was connected to his social class identification and the "blue-collar" masculinity of his father: "What's tougher and cooler than a guy who busts his ass his whole life? Nothing," he put it to me emphatically. "My dad's an old fuckin' greaser guy and I'm a real American traditionalist." "It all comes back to *Rebel Without a Cause*," he continued, trying to find the links between his father's generation and his. "You think you got [something original], and then you come to find out you're the same as your father was. I am my old man, I am."[1] Matt and I would have many conversations like these again, ones in which he moaned about getting old, being stuck in his job, and steadily accumulating adult responsibilities while the next generation of kids went out and tried to recreate punk rock without realizing that it had all been done before. In time I would begin to notice an undercurrent of wishful thinking beneath Matt's hard-boiled exterior. He sounded like he was complaining about "turning into his old man" and becoming "Middle America," but I think this was also secretly what he wanted and hoped for, so that he could reproduce his social class status as solidly "blue-collar" and lay claim to the masculinity personified by his father.

He may not have understood how it happened, but Matt was acutely aware of the fact that there had been a breakdown in the social process of reproducing masculinity and social class from generation to generation. Growing up in the 1980s and 1990s, Matt was surrounded by right-wing ideological discourses that insisted that "blue-collar" people had been thrown out of the center of American society not as a result of economic processes but by social and government programs designed to advance the interests of minorities. These ideological discourses also typically expressed analogous complaints about the emasculation of American men. When I asked Matt about politics, he told me that he was "raised Republican, kind of conservative," but was not registered with either of the two main political parties. Like so many other Americans, Matt said he votes for "the lesser of two evils" and that politics is "all bullshit, realistically." His image of the ideal president was "the foreman from the construction site that actually works. A working foreman, not some guy going, 'Lift this, do this, do that.'" As he was getting older, Matt found himself starting to sympathize with "liberal politics, starting to believe more and more like, 'Hey, we gotta help these people out, we gotta do this, we gotta do that.'" And yet at other times Matt was still in agreement with conservative views on social programs and the backlash against "bleeding heart" liberals: "My upbringing is so cynical, like, 'You fucking hippies, get your ass a job.'"[2]

This guy whom everyone in the San Diego punk scene directed me to turned out to be as much Ralph Kramden or Archie Bunker as he was

Matt Reese singing for Jalopy sometime in the mid-1990s. Ryan Moore.

Matt and a friend in the punk rock days of the 1980s. Ryan Moore.

Henry Rollins. This surprised me. As a teenager, Matt had been the lead singer for a band called Funeral March, who called themselves punk band but also had heavy metal and comic book influences in their fascination with death, violence, and vampires. When I listened to Matt, then in his late twenties, I heard someone complaining about getting old and settling down but also secretly aspiring to reproduce the "blue-collar" existence established by his father. And when I looked at Matt, I looked into the past, and I saw both what had Matt had been—the ghoulish punk rock kid who traded in his makeup for tattoos—and what he had become—a retro 1950s image of rebel masculinity derived from the white American working class' highest point of power and stability. When he described himself as "a real American traditionalist," Matt was trying to anchor his identity in things that appear solid, like the nation, tradition, and authenticity. Meanwhile, in the way he dressed and presented himself, Matt was trying to superimpose the old masculine image of an "American traditionalist" onto that of a punk with his slicked hair, vintage shirts, and mesmerizing array of tattoos.

On the night of my first interview with Matt at the Live Wire in 1995, MTV was scheduled to air the new video for "Born in '69" by Rocket From the Crypt, the most popular band in the local scene. The bar had suddenly gotten very crowded, and Matt and I went to jockey for position with the other patrons so we could see the television. There was a sense of anticipation building from what felt to me like the collective energy when someone from the neighborhood or hometown is making it in sports and some other form of entertainment. I looked at this community of spectators and saw people who would have looked like they were at a costume party ten years ago, guys with chain wallets and gas station jackets and gals with multiple tattoos and dark hair and short bangs in the style of 1950s pin-up model Bettie Page. They were a stylistic hodge-podge that took a little from the flappers, a little from the greasers, and a little from the original punks, and the only consistency I could discern in these styles was their common status as old and past. Inside the bar, the jukebox had been turned off and the crowd fell silent when "Born in '69" came on the TV. The video was also a pastiche of retro imagery, as it incongruously combined Fifties B movies from the genres of science fiction, juvenile delinquency, and horror. The video begins with the band's front man John Reis ("Speedo") on a motorcycle in an image reminiscent of Marlon Brando in *The Wild One*, when suddenly he is shot down by a UFO (using some crude and thus campy special effects), and then the rest of the band removes his brain and turns him into a vampire or some sort of monster.

After the video Matt muttered something to me with a joking tone about John Reis having "stolen that whole Misfits thing" (i.e., horror punk) from him, and then he began to tell me about Rocket From the Crypt's last video. Matt explained to me that he and John Reis had known each other and been friends since their teen years, when they both grew up in the neighborhoods around San Diego's Pacific Beach and often hung out together at punk shows. He told me that Rocket From the Crypt's previous video, for "Sturdy Wrists," had been shot at a party in the backyard of John Reis and his fiancée, who invited their friends in the scene to appear in the video and asked them to dress in Mexican or Hawaiian garb. As Matt named all the locals who can be spotted in the video, it was becoming clear to me that part of this band's appeal was its ability to inspire feelings of community, loyalty, and belonging.

Some years earlier, when Rocket From the Crypt was touring relentlessly after signing their contract with Interscope Records, they announced that anyone who had a tattoo of their band's logo could get into any of their shows for free. The Rocket logo is a pretty simple design of a basic rocket shape enclosed within a circle. It was part of a merchandising strategy to promote the band while selling symbolic forms of membership to a community of fans, and indeed there was a brief vogue for Rocket tattoos after Kennedy, the VJ for MTV's *Alternative Nation*, got one. Now, in light of my continuing conversation with Matt and observation of San Diego's retro scene, the symbolic significance of Rocket From the Crypt and the Rocket tattoo was becoming clear. The city of San Diego had been built on military spending, especially aerospace. For the entire duration of the cold war, the manufacture of rockets had allowed working-class people to realize the Southern California version of the American Dream long after the auto factories and steel mills began laying people off in other parts of the country. Of course, rockets are also notoriously phallic symbols, and in this sense it is also true that the military-industrial complex had supported a particular image of masculinity and the breadwinner ethic behind the nuclear family.

None of this was consciously intended by John Reis or anyone else in Rocket From the Crypt, who named themselves after a 1970s Cleveland-based noise band called Rocket From the Tombs. But that made this form of class (sub)consciousness and masculinity all the more interesting to me. I imagined how their parents had come to San Diego riding the long wave

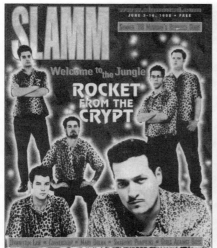 

Rocket From the Crypt in a leopard-skin motif in 1998 (*left*).
Rocket From the Crypt named San Diego's number one artist of all time in 2002
(*right*). From the cover of *Slamm: San Diego's Music Magazine*. Issue #175, January 16–29, 2002.

of military Keynesianism, gobbling up some prime real estate if they were
lucky but otherwise settling into one of Southern California's endlessly
sprawling suburbs. The rocket was a symbol of that way of life made possible by the likes of General Dynamics and McDonnell Douglas, and now
it was rapidly becoming a symbol of the past. With the end of the cold
war, the unemployment rate in San Diego County increased dramatically
from 3.9 percent in 1989 to 9.2 percent in mid-1993.[3] The most dramatic
round of layoffs hit during the summer of 1994, when Martin Marietta
announced that it was moving 1,800 jobs to Denver and, two weeks later,
General Dynamics closed its jet fuselage operations, eliminating an additional 2,000 jobs.[4] In the social scene that had gathered around guys like
Matt Reese and the members of Rocket From the Crypt, I was looking at a
generational cohort that wasn't young anymore and was facing the reality
of getting older in an economy that doesn't have much use for tough guys;
over the next 10 years or so, some of them would be altogether priced out
of the skyrocketing real estate market and forced to leave San Diego. They
had been living as if there were no future since their teen years, and now
they were looking to the past, to these retro combinations of rebellion and
masculinity that they imagined their fathers had once embodied.

Marie, Suicide Girl (*above*). From *Suicide Girls*. Missy Suicide. Los Angeles: Feral House.

A gaggle of Suicide Girls on tour in 2004 (*left*). From *The Encyclopedia of Punk*. Brian Cogan. New York: Sterling, 2008.

The Past in the Present

The epigraphs quoted at the beginning of this chapter are derived from an aspect of contemporary popular culture that has literally lost track of time. Rocket From the Crypt was a band who combined punk rock noise with 1960s garage rock and soul as well as a touch of 1950s rockabilly, employing a horn section, call-and-response vocals, and an ethic of old-time showmanship and performance. In "Born in '69," they are talking about being inspired by and "stealing" from sounds and styles that originated before they were born. Suicide Girls are young women who pose in various states of undress for a Web site that mixes World War II–era "pin-up" photography with punk and goth styles of female sexuality, and their touring performances are modeled after old-style burlesque shows. Like Rocket From the Crypt, Suicide Girls have been inspired by memories its creators never had, and moreover their tour slogan suggests that perhaps the culture of the present will one day be looked back on fondly in the same way that people like them look to yesterday's styles.

In this chapter I discuss various retro styles in music and subculture that have animated the likes of Rocket From the Crypt and Suicide Girls as well as people like Matt Reese. Retro styles have been gaining momentum in popular culture since at least the 1970s. One could glimpse various instances of a retro style emerging prior to this, perhaps none more humorous than Sha Na Na's performance at Woodstock, but it was during the 1970s that a revival of Fifties culture took firm root, not only with the popularity of *American Graffiti*, *Happy Days*, and *Grease*, but also in sock hops and "greaser days" on college campuses, the revisiting of "golden oldies" on FM radio, and even a resurrection of the juvenile delinquent look within punk subculture.[5] The Fifties took on a different glow when viewed through the rubble of the Sixties, as many people expressed nostalgia for this time of supposed simplicity and social order, while the rock 'n' roll music and youth culture that had once been denounced as deviant came to be seen as relatively innocent and naïve. The Sixties appeared to return with full force during the 1980s, as many popular films (e.g., *Born on the Fourth of July*, *1969*, *Flashback*) and a few television shows (e.g., *The Wonder Years*) revisited the Vietnam War and generational conflicts of the time, complete with psychedelic rock soundtracks. This too had political import, for the legacy of the Sixties was at the center of the U.S. culture wars, and it was also connected to marketing strategies that sought to profit from the nostalgia of baby boomers.

During the 1990s, the retro turn expanded into new dimensions of hip culture with young people rummaging through thrift stores in search of vintage clothing, furnishings, and frivolous commodities. Especially once grunge had been played out and "alternative" was codified as a commercial genre, many musicians who had grown up with punk and hardcore began to incorporate swing, country, the blues, lounge, rockabilly, or soul into their newest musical projects, and they redesigned their style of dress and performance to go with it. Just as people looked back to the Fifties in the 1970s and the Sixties in the 1980s, many within "Generation X" turned their gaze to the pop culture of the Seventies, embracing all the schlock embodied in bell-bottoms, *The Brady Bunch*, and the Bee Gees. Others revisited the posthippie culture depicted in Richard Linklater's film *Dazed and Confused* and the TV series *That '70s Show*. A parallel trend occurred in hip hop during the 1990s, when "G-funk" emerged using beats and riffs sampled from 1970s funk music, particularly George Clinton's groups Parliament and Funkadelic, and an accompanying change of style included a resurgence of Afros and "throwback" sports jerseys. But the reach of 1990s retro culture also extended back to the mid-twentieth century and beyond, times that twenty-somethings hadn't experienced in childhood, and thus created a sensibility that cannot be explained in terms of nostalgia or collective memory. As demonstrated by Matt Reese, Rocket From the Crypt, and the San Diego scene, I argue that retro styles have much to tell us about both the uses of the past in a postmodern society and the anxieties of the present that derive from the shifting hierarchies of class, race, and gender.

Retro and Postmodern Culture

As Elizabeth Guffey puts it in her excellent overview of the topic, "Retro quotes styles from the past, but applies them in anomalous settings; it regards the past from a bemused distance, its dark humour re-mixing popular mid-century drinks and serving them up as 'atomic cocktails.'"[6] The retro aesthetic therefore shares affinities with nostalgia and revivalism on the one hand, and camp and kitsch on the other, but it must be analytically distinguished as something different from all of these. For instance, both nostalgia and retro express an indirect critique of modernity and our faith in progress, suggesting that the new and improved doesn't deserve the hype, that things are actually getting worse, and that the best is to be found in the forgotten ways of yesteryear. But whereas nostalgia flourished in the age of industrialization and urbanization as people came to romanticize the traditional ways of life associated with the preindustrial, rural past, retro is a development of postmodern society in which it is commodities, styles, and outdated technologies from a more recent past that are revisited, not necessarily ways of life and traditions.[7] Insofar as nostalgia idealizes historical experiences, it is "a complex emotion, often representing the past with a sadness that is blended with a small measure of pleasure," Guffey writes, and therefore is "emphatically earnest" and "always characterized by a certain seriousness."[8] By contrast, because retro involves commodities, styles, and technologies it is not simply more superficial than nostalgia but also less serious or sentimental, as there is always some degree of irony and detachment entailed in a retro aesthetic. This also makes retro distinct from the type of revivalism that thrived in the nineteenth century and continues to be evident today, in which there is a premium placed on reconstructing historical facts and events with complete accuracy. The retro sensibility does not fetishize historical accuracy, and it has no qualms about taking objects or images out of their original context and reusing them inconsistently in the present.

Because it always contains some amount of irony and even "dark humor," retro also overlaps with what is called camp or kitsch.[9] As Susan Sontag elucidated in her landmark essay on the subject, camp is a mode of performance that appropriates bad taste and melodrama in an exaggerated manner, a style that initially developed in gay subcultures and especially among drag queens.[10] Retro styles also frequently include objects and images with kitschy qualities, particularly those from the Fifties or Seventies, and they tend to do so with a self-conscious, tongue-in-cheek sensibility, but there are significant differences between retro and camp. Although Sontag celebrated camp as a key example of the fusion between high and low culture in the postmodern culture of the 1960s, its humor still depends on a modernist divide between aesthetes and the schlock they appropriate, a divide that is more blurred within retro. To put it differently, retro styles may also revive goods that are widely considered "corny" or "cheesy," but they do so with less of the spirit of condescension that characterizes camp. Performers like Rocket From the Crypt and the Suicide Girls are more selective and sincere in choosing which styles to emulate and which ones to avoid, even if they do so with a knowing smirk that indicates they are fully aware of the fabricated nature of their image.

We therefore locate retro as somewhere between the poles of nostalgia and camp on a spectrum of aesthetic and affective approaches to the past. A consideration of retro music and style also gives us the opportunity to address theoretical questions about simulacra and pastiche on the one hand and collective memory and dialogics on the other. Indeed, Jean Baudrillard was the first major social theorist to address the emergence of retro as part of his renowned *Simulacra and Simulation*.[11] For Baudrillard, "the great trauma" of what would be called postmodern society "is this decline of referentials, these death pangs of the real and of the rational that open onto an age of simulation."[12] The retro sensibility, which Baudrillard discussed via 1970s films like *Chinatown* and *The Last Picture Show*, is symptomatic of this "decline of referentials," a simulacrum of history. While there had been an upsurge of films set in the past, Baudrillard concluded that "today one has the impression that history has retreated, leaving behind it an indifferent nebula, traversed by currents, but emptied of references."[13] In short, he saw retro as a poor substitute for the loss of history and emblematic of a larger implosion of meaning in a society saturated with media simulations.

Though writing from a Marxist perspective that Baudrillard had deserted, Fredric Jameson reached similarly glum conclusions in his essay "Nostalgia for the Present" about the "loss of historicity" and its relation to pastiche in postmodern culture.[14] In analyzing the Fifties recreations of *American Graffiti* and the science fiction of Philip K. Dick, and comparing them with the historical novel, Jameson observed a waning of historical consciousness occurring alongside a resurgence of interest in seemingly more superficial styles from the past. After pronouncing "an ultimate historicist breakdown," Jameson observed a countervailing trend: "Everything in our culture suggests that we have not, for all that, ceased to be preoccupied by history; indeed, at the very moment we complain, as here, of the eclipse of historicity, we also universally diagnose contemporary culture as irredeemably historicist, in the bad sense of an omnipresent and indiscriminate appetite for dead styles and fashions; indeed, for all the styles and fashions of a dead past."[15] Cultural producers imitate these "dead styles" as a form of what Jameson called pastiche, which is like parody in the sense of intending to provoke humor through mockery yet seems to lack a political bite, for it is "without any of parody's ulterior motives, amputated of the satiric impulse."[16] Jameson thus provides an important theoretical framework for understanding retro as a mixture of irony, nostalgia, and a pseudohistorical imitation of fashions and commodities from a "dead past" that come to substitute for what used to be meant by history.[17]

While surveying retro youth culture and music in this chapter, we will periodically return to Baudrillard's and Jameson's conceptions of retro as simulacra of images of the past, commodities whose links to their historical context of social relations have been abstracted, and a sentimental yet cynical form of blank parody. Retro certainly should not be confused with what sociologists and historians have referred to as collective or social memory, which focuses on how societies commemorate national events and political crises through ceremonies and monuments.[18] The subject matter of retro is more trivial by comparison, and its arbitrary reconstruction of the past is actively acknowledged. Nonetheless, after closely investigating retro forms of youth culture and music we will find considerable hyperbole in Baudrillard's and Jameson's claims about the death of historicity and the meaninglessness of commodities and simulacra. I therefore situate their notions at one end of a spectrum of possibilities for retro culture, an extreme state of simulated emptiness that is only rarely realized. In many other instances, we find that retro pop culture does maintain some sort of symbolic dialogue with its original historical conditions, and even that the past can be resurrected to subvert the present.

An alternative conception of the ways the past can be used in the present, and in turn how the present creates the need for history, is proposed in Mikhail Bakhtin's "dialogic" theory of literature and language.[19] In his essay "Epic and Novel," Bakhtin contrasted these two genres of literature in terms of their approaches to the past. Whereas the epic sought to preserve history such that "it is impossible to change it: the tradition of the past is sacred," the novel incorporates the past into a more active and critical dialogue with a multitude of languages, genres, and artifacts.[20] The epic is an expression of the feudal era, dominated by tradition, patriarchy, and mythic narratives of history. By contrast, the novel is a product of modernization, in which revered traditions are overwhelmed by a volatile present and an uncertain future, and cultures become increasingly diverse as a consequence of urbanization and mass migration. In the novel, history is not revisited to be conserved in a sacred or heroic manner, but rather to speak to the conditions of the present. The novel is composed of a multitude of voices representing what Bakhtin called "chronotopes" of time and place, each of which sheds new light on the other in facilitating a dialogue between different worldviews and ways of life.[21] Every cultural producer thus enters a dialogue that began long ago, and every cultural product contains traces of history that shape its meaning, even in ways that are beyond its author's intentions.

George Lipsitz has examined rock 'n' roll as an especially dialogic medium of popular culture that exemplifies Bakhtin's idea that "culture is cumulative."[22] Although many musicians and fans have made a fetish of originality, rock music's capacity to combine styles and traditions in seemingly infinite permutations is, in Bakhtin's words, the product of "a world where there is no first word (no ideal word), and the final word has not yet been spoken."[23] As Lipsitz illustrates, rock 'n' roll originated as a hybrid of the blues and country music that rural black and white Americans brought to the cities in the mass migrations during and after World War II, and those forms of music were blended further with emergent genres like rhythm and blues, swing, and jump blues in the creation of rock 'n' roll in the 1950s. Country and the blues were both forms of music that recalled preindustrial ways of life, and so as it took shape in a new urban context, rock 'n' roll offered an oblique critique of postwar society in championing leisure and community against work and rationalization. In the decades since the 1950s, Lipsitz argues that contemporary rock music has "never been totally severed from the energy and imagination of the postwar American industrial communities in which it originated."[24] In some cases this dialogic aspect has been explicit, like with the first generation of punk musicians (e.g., the Ramones, the Clash, X), who sought to recapture the original spirit of rock 'n' roll that they felt had been betrayed. But even when the cultural debts remain unacknowledged, the various offshoots of rock 'n' roll continue to be engaged in dialogue with the social conditions that originally spawned it, particularly resistance against authority, conformity, work, and discipline. If rock music seems to have lost some of its bite over the years, perhaps it has something to do with the consumer culture's increasing capacity to absorb these demands for leisure and freedom into socially reproductive forms of individualism and instant gratification.

Using Bakhtin's methodology, Lipsitz develops a notion of history and collective memory as not only elements of cultural dialogue but also objects of social struggle. Cultural producers and social movements battle with hegemonic powers over representations of history and employ the collective memories fossilized in popular culture to critique the present. This understanding of music and popular culture as an ongoing dialogue and enduring struggle that recalls the past with meaning and purpose will thus serve as the alternate possibility in our investigation of retro. While the retro aesthetic is distinguished by an ironic dimension, it also looks back to old styles and sounds as gold mines of cultural expression that were too quickly forgotten but are preferable to the newest and allegedly best that today's culture industry offers. The question will be to what extent retro's commodity form erases the historical context, which both enables cultural dialogue to continue and debases it into a simulacrum of the past.

Gender, Class, and "Whiteness" in the 1990s

To comprehend the potential meanings of retro culture, we must therefore investigate the purposes the past may serve within the social conditions of the present. As previous chapters have suggested, the emergence of post-Fordist capitalism and postmodern culture have had profound implications for gender roles and identities. If examined seriously, retro styles do indeed expose a crisis of masculinity that young men have been trying to resolve in looking to the past. Different retro scenes and subcultures have adopted sounds and styles from many time periods, but the most frequently revisited have come from the mid-twentieth century, especially with the revival of swing, rockabilly, and images of pin-ups and juvenile delinquent "greasers." If viewed through the prism of a crisis of masculinity, the selective adoption of styles and sounds from this era seems like less than a coincidence. After all, the period between World War II and the mid-1960s is widely remembered as a time when white American men seemed to be in control and working-class men in particular enjoyed their greatest moments of affluence and stability. In drawing from early rock 'n' roll or the juvenile delinquent image, male retro styles harked back to a time when rebellion was firmly connected with the masculine performance of defiant independence, as opposed to the softer and gentler sensibility embodied by the hippies who followed them. Reared in insecure times, the young males who adopted retro styles reached for a time when the codes of masculinity at least appeared to have been solid.

The central cultural artifact for articulating this retro form of masculinity in the 1990s was the film *Swingers* (1996). The protagonist, played by the film's writer Jon Favreau, is portrayed as a sensitive guy of the times moaning over an ex-girlfriend who left him for another man. Meanwhile, his circle of friends, the central character of which is played by Vince Vaughn, represent an "old school" style of masculinity characterized by unflinching confidence in dealings with women and an overall sense that everything is cool and under control. The characters were in fact modeled after the "Rat Pack," which included Frank Sinatra, Dean Martin, and Sammy Davis Jr.; it is as if the ghosts of masculinities past have been summoned to help Favreau's character get over his broken heart and in-securities about women, similar to the way Humphrey Bogart haunted an anxious Woody Allen in *Play It Again, Sam* (1972). The movie is set against the swing revival that was thriving in the hip Los Angeles neighborhood of Los Feliz during the mid-1990s, and it is peppered with music, clothes, slang, and cocktails recycled from the swing era. All the characters are depicted as struggling to break into some form of show business, which creates some moments of emasculation (like when one character considers taking a job as Goofy at Disneyland), but in the nightclubs they are able to channel styles and sensibilities from the past to become masters of their environment. Toward the end of the movie, we know that Favreau's character has overcome his timidity when we see him in the company of a young woman perfecting old dance moves to the tune of swing music.

Women have also recreated styles from a similar period of time in their appropriations of the pin-up look. As Maria Elena Buszek has illuminated in her history of the genre, the pin-up is as old as photography itself, but the style that contemporary women continually revisit is personified by the World War II–era "Varga Girls" and the more underground photos of Bettie Page from the 1950s.[25] Painted by Alberto Vargas for *Esquire* magazine, the Varga Girls represented a new kind of pin-up who exuded confidence, independence, and assertive sexuality, in distinction from the cute and somewhat comical portrayals of sexualized women who had previously filled the pages of men's magazines. Their appearance overlapped with the massive entry of women into the workforce as part of the war effort and a recruitment campaign that showed females as strong, capable, and self-assured. As these images dovetailed with one another, Buszek writes, the wartime pin-up was fashioned as "a new kind of sexual ideal in which the independent, self-esteem, and ambition that the nation sought to groom in female workers spilled over into their sexual identities as well."[26] With the end of the war, mass firings of women workers, and reestablishment of the domestic ideal, mainstream representations of female sexuality reverted to the familiar virgin/whore dichotomy. But the more empowered and aggressive types of pin-ups continued to circulate through the 1950s, albeit with a more deviant twist, in the modeling of Bettie Page and specialty magazines that catered to sadomasochistic tastes. Even by current standards, photographs of Page are striking in the way they radiate with playfulness, a lack of shame, and even self-conscious awareness of the performative nature of her poses and role-playing. As she represented an alternative to the prevailing forms of sexuality and a tongue-in-cheek style that anticipated postmodern expressions of irony and camp, Page is arguably more famous and influential as an icon for contemporary femininity than she was in the 1950s.

Like retro masculinity, the pin-up revival embodies many of the contradictions faced by young women today. The pin-up, by definition, is a sex object primarily intended for male consumption, and yet the genre has been appropriated by women, including many self-professed feminists, because she also represents the promise of sexual subjectivity. The revival is therefore linked to a broader transformation of the women's movement in which feminist performers have sought new ways to play with the forms of sexual objectification and pornography that earlier generations of feminists could only see as instruments of subservience. As the Varga Girls expressed the newfound independence and confidence that accompanied women's growing labor power, and Bettie Page continued and escalated this tradition in the face of 1950s repression, it is little wonder that their images hold such appeal for young women who have gained unprecedented freedoms in matters of sex and work. And yet because the pin-up is inextricably linked to the forms of sexual objectification and commodity fetishism that have long imprisoned women, there are no guarantees that she will serve as a medium of liberation in any given context. After all, the pin-up form is also part of retro masculinity's imagery of sex and commodities. Paula Kamen has succinctly summarized this contradictory state of affairs: "Sexualized pictures are everywhere, used to sell every product possible, but in a market still dominated by male tastes and defining female sexuality as what is attractive to men. On the other hand, women now have more control over their sex lives because of their access to sex education, erotica, and information about their bodies."[27]

For many decades, rock 'n' roll music and hip youthfulness have been constituted through a complex and curious interplay between white people and black culture. The dynamic at work in the creation of this style of "whiteness" was inherited from the dialectic of "love and theft" that Eric Lott uncovered in antebellum U.S. minstrel shows, which expressed a "mixed erotic economy of celebration and exploitation."[28] This interplay between the desire for black male bodies and the mimicry and commercial exploitation of black music and style is ongoing in American popular culture, but it was particularly strong in the early days of rock 'n' roll and white appropriations of the blues.[29] Likewise, the "white negroes" who defined hipster style in the mid-twentieth century borrowed from a romanticized image of black rebellion and marginality.[30] Thus, when retro subcultures revisit these past forms of music and style, they are inevitably in dialogue with the social conditions in which whites have idealized and then expropriated black culture. They do so from a postmodern position, however, where the use of self-conscious irony seems to afford them the distance to resume these stylistic appropriations without having to take responsibility for them, even after their exploitative relations have been widely exposed.

As with gender, socioeconomic changes and social movement organization have also reshaped the meanings of race and whiteness in American society. A shift of racial identities among white people has occurred as deindustrialization and downsizing threaten economic privilege and security on the one hand, while multiculturalism and antiracist social movements have issued devastating challenges to the normative foundations of whiteness on the other. Historically, in the words of George Lipsitz, whiteness has been "the unmarked category against which difference is constructed," so that it "never has to speak its name, never has to acknowledge its role as an organizing principle in social and cultural relations."[31] Whiteness became more visible in popular culture during the 1990s, however, especially in stereotypes about "white trash" and other cultural forms in which the peculiarities of white culture were exposed rather than idealized. In stereotypes about white trash, racial discourses are substituted for an awareness of social class: "Because the U.S. has extremely impoverished political language of class, certain racial representations are used as allegories for it."[32] The white trash stereotype became increasingly prominent as the American class structure became more polarized as a consequence of deindustrialization and the evisceration of public education and the welfare state.[33] In popular culture this caricature of the poor and ignorant white person is typically personified with a high degree of irony, which is where its affinities with retro style can be seen.

All Yesterday's Parties

To consider the possibilities for retro music and culture ranging from pastiche and camp at one end to dialogic collective memory at the other, we now turn to four bands from the 1990s: Uncle Tupelo, Rocket From the Crypt, the Jon Spencer Blues Explosion, and the Supersuckers. Each of these groups got their start in various regional punk and alternative music scenes, but in time they began to incorporate different genres of traditional music, such as country, rockabilly, and the blues. None of them achieved anything more than modest commercial success, but because their popularity was concentrated among other musicians, critics, and hip insiders, their cultural impact exceeded their limited market niche. As we examine each group's music and performance style, the analysis will more or less proceed from dialogic uses of the past (beginning with Uncle Tupelo, the forefathers of "alternative country") to the forms of blank parody associated with postmodern pastiche (ending with the hyperironic Supersuckers). It is important to note, however, that these performers typically exhibit a mixture of dialogic and ironic uses of history and should not be categorized absolutely; the point is to reveal the multiple possibilities and contradictory impulses of retro culture. In the course of the analysis, we will also consider how the different retro styles and uses of history intersect with the bands' performances of whiteness and masculinity (they are all men and predominantly white), which are again infused with postmodern irony.

Uncle Tupelo

Uncle Tupelo formed in 1987 in Belleville, Illinois, a city of about 40,000 in the Greater St. Louis metropolitan area, and disbanded in 1994 after releasing just four albums. Though the band's career was relatively brief, they are frequently credited with launching the "alternative country" or "alt.country" movement by integrating country and folk music with punk rock. Uncle Tupelo exemplified the dialogic approach to putting the past in the service of the present and mixing genres to reveal the affinities between seemingly disparate cultural forms. Uncle Tupelo was not, however, the first group to smuggle country into punk, as the Meat Puppets and the Replacements had done so some years earlier, as had the Mekons in Britain. To stretch things a little further, alt.country is in some ways a continuation of the earlier crossover between country and the hippie counterculture that gave birth to the "cosmic cowboy" scene in Austin, Texas, and country rock performers like Neil Young and Gram Parsons.[34] Country music does not easily lend itself to these forms of hybridization, as it is a conservative genre whose standards of authenticity were affixed during the first half of the twentieth century and continues to call on its performers to recreate an imaginary past rooted in preindustrial society.[35] But the cultural dialogues with rock and punk have accentuated country's more populist tendencies and outlaw spirit as an alternative to patriarchy and patriotism, while musically they have utilized rougher sounds against the slick production associated with the Nashville country scene.

Uncle Tupelo put punk and country into dialogue with each other from the beginning with their first record, *No Depression* (1990). The opening track, "Graveyard Shift," is the first of their many laments and protests against working-class life. In his distinctively deep and solemn voice, Jay Farrar begins by singing over a jangling guitar, "Hometown, same town blues / Same old walls closing in / What an awful mess life can be / Well I'm sitting here thinking of you once again / Won't you give thought to me?" The music then erupts with the guitars and drums congealing into a fast but choppy tempo, a sound composed of dramatic starts and stops, which was predominant throughout Uncle Tupelo's first two albums and had been mainly inspired by the Minutemen (to whom they later wrote a tribute, "D. Boon"). "Graveyard Shift" continues to build to its hard-boiled conclusions about the division between haves and have-nots in the United States: "Some say land of paradise / Some say land of pain / Well which side are you looking from? / Some people have it all / And some have it all to gain."

No Depression's title track was arranged in 1936 by A.P. Carter of the Carter Family, one of country music's first and most significant recording groups, in all likelihood based on different versions Carter had heard during "song-catching" trips around Virginia, Tennessee, and Kentucky.[36] It is in "No Depression" that we find Uncle Tupelo's most dialogic use of the past to critique the present. The song paints a harrowing portrait of the Great Depression in the rural United States and prays for salvation in the afterlife:

> Fear the hearts of men are failing
> For these our latter days we know
> The Great Depression now is spreading
> God's word declared it would be so
>
> I'm going where there's no Depression
> To a better land that's free from care
> I'll leave this world of toil and trouble
> My home's in heaven
> I'm going there
>
> In this dark hour, midnight nearing
> The tribulation time will come
> The storms will hurl the midnight fear
> And sweep lost millions to their doom

This is a simple song, which Farrar sings accompanied only by an acoustic guitar, but its evocations of fear and impending doom make it well suited for punk rock appropriation. What makes Uncle Tupelo's use of "No Depression" dialogic is that it is not merely reproduced as an artifact of history but rather inserted into a totality of songs that portray capitalist exploitation of working-class and rural peoples as an ongoing crisis of the present. Their drummer, Mike Heidorn, later recalled that Uncle Tupelo adopted the song in part because it seemed relevant to the socioeconomic conditions they were witnessing in Belleville: "I think it was the timelessness of that song because, at the time, we could see in my hometown things, economically, weren't always that great. There's depression everywhere, I guess."[37] The past comes alive with the power to speak to the songs on *No Depression* that delve into the intersection between the political forces of greed and deception and the personal experiences of broken spirits and alcoholic escapism ("depression" seemed to have a double meaning in this regard). Singing as if perched on a barstool on "Whiskey Bottle," Farrar sneers at "One too many faces / With dollar sign smiles," while "Factory Belt" ends with a flurry of thrashing and guitar noise that sounds like a dust storm or an industrial accident. Collectively, these songs revealed that neither the Great Depression of the past nor the deindustrialization of the present were isolated moments but were in fact part of the same cycle of crisis endemic to capitalism.

Uncle Tupelo would incorporate even more traditional folk and country songs in their later recordings, especially an album they recorded with R.E.M. guitarist Peter Buck plainly titled *March 16–20, 1992*. This record included the song "Coalminers," which pleads, "Dear miners, they will slave you / Until you can't work no more / And what will get for your labor / But a dollar at the company store," and ends by exhorting, "Let's sink this capitalist system / To the darkest pits of hell." It also featured a version of the old gospel "Satan, Your Kingdom Must Come Down" and the foreboding antiwar song "Atomic Power." But the thrust of these recordings was less dialogic than purely revivalist, as by this point Uncle Tupelo had moved away from punk rock and gone almost exclusively acoustic to the point of including banjos, mandolins, and fiddles in their music. The songs on both this recording and their finale, *Anodyne*, were certainly more exquisite and touching than the rougher *No Depression* and its follow-up, *Still Feel Gone*, but they cut off dialogue with the present at the risk of anachronism in both sound and subject matter—while the suffering of coal miners and dangers of atomic power are still with us, they make for antiquated battle cries. It is here that we find the boundary analogous to Bakhtin's distinction between the dialogic novel and the epic, the latter of which preserves the past for its own sake. Perhaps it is not coincidental that the original songs on these later albums were also more personal than political in their lyrical content.

After the breakup of Uncle Tupelo, the band's founding members, Jay Farrar and Jeff Tweedy, went on to found the groups Son Volt and Wilco, respectively. Son Volt and Farrar's solo recordings have maintained a more revivalist approach to traditional American music, while Tweedy and Wilco have increasingly distanced themselves from country music in the process of becoming one of the most renowned (and experimental) groups in contemporary rock music. In the aftermath of Uncle Tupelo, a new zine by the name of *No Depression* was founded in 1995 and was immediately crucial for giving a name and a focal point to an emerging alt.country genre that included performers like Whiskeytown, the Old 97's, Freakwater, and the Bottle Rockets.[38] In its most dialogic moments, alt.country recovered the rebellious strains submerged within the history of country music, and indeed it persisted as an alternative to mainstream country at a time when Nashville was being articulated with the fabricated populism of conservative hegemony. But those dialogic elements can easily slide into purist concerns for preservation, particularly because country music is so firmly linked to nostalgia and is frequented dismissed as inauthentic when mixed with other genres. Likewise, country music is strongly connected with symbolic constructions of whiteness and patriarchal notions of gender, and alt.country does not typically challenge these associations even as it resurrects a resistant spirit rooted in class consciousness. In sum, the uses of history by Uncle Tupelo, and alt.country more broadly, were greatly concerned with tradition and authenticity, straddling the line between dialogic incorporations of the past into the present and a preservationist impulse to remain faithful to established standards.

Rocket From the Crypt

Rocket From the Crypt emerged as the preeminent band of a San Diego music scene that evolved from hardcore punk and alternative rock in becoming the subject of music industry hype during the search for the next Seattle in the early 1990s. While amassing a devoted following, the band helped set the standard for a retro style of vintage clothing and tattooing in San Diego and beyond. Rocket From the Crypt took their name from Rocket From the Tombs, a 1970s protopunk band from Cleveland with an ambitious but raw sound, and it also alludes to *Tales from the Crypt*, the horror comic book series published during the 1950s that has since been periodically revisited in film and television. For several reasons, this choice of names perfectly encapsulates the aesthetic of Rocket From the Crypt, who combined punk rock noise with the more polished sound and performing style inherited from rock 'n' roll, concocted their musical and visual style from a wide assortment of cultural debris, and made no pretense about the fact that most of their shtick was stolen and contradictory. This puts them firmly in line with Jameson's notion of pastiche, and yet Rocket From the Crypt also positioned themselves within an enduring lineage of rock 'n' roll, especially through a working-class sensibility that shaped their approach to music and performance.

Rocket From the Crypt began by playing house parties in the San Diego area. Their founder and front man, John Reis, had another band called Drive Like Jehu, which was a more serious venture in musical complexity and noisy experimentation. Rocket From the Crypt was conceived as a more fun band that intended to engage and entertain its audience with Reis, now using the moniker "Speedo," adopting a swaggering personality as the group's lead singer. In the beginning, Rocket From the Crypt's sound was indistinctive and certainly inferior to that of Drive Like Jehu, but they began to develop a uniquely compelling aesthetic after Reis added a saxophonist, Apollo 9. The use of saxophone augmented the group's boisterous sound and live performances, but it was used somewhat differently than in the ska bands that had become popular with a good number of California punks. Whereas ska bands' use of horns gives the music a peppy, upbeat feeling, in Rocket From the Crypt the saxophone and the trumpet (which they added in 1994) were lower and therefore sounded more sinister and ominous. Rather than taking the lead ahead of the rest of the music, the horns were more often used to add additional density to the band's two guitars, "like spackle for the bricks," as Apollo 9 once put it to me.[39] The inspiration to add a horn section had come in part from the soul groups of the 1960s who recorded on the Stax label (e.g., Booker T. and the MGs, Otis Redding, Wilson Pickett); as a further homage to that genre, Reis began to incorporate more call-and-response vocals between he and his bandmates. The results were far too loud and guitar-oriented to be mistaken for soul music, but they furthered the dialogue between punk and past genres that had begun with Rocket From the Crypt's old-fashioned showmanship and retro appearance.

Rocket From the Crypt came into their own in 1992 with their second album, *Circa: Now!*, whose kitschy cover featuring a mod-era photograph of a woman with a brightly colored disco ball called attention to their emerging retro sensibility. *Circa: Now!* retained more of a punk sound than their later music, but by then they had added the saxophone to the recording process, keeping it relatively low in the mix and primarily using it to thicken the wall of noise. The album's finale, "Glazed," ends with a good five minutes of the band repeatedly chanting "Take that!" while the guitars and sax drone on behind them. The effect is like being continually jabbed in the head by a heavyweight boxer—"Take that!" "Take that!" "Take that!"—until the saxophone grows even louder and more sour in its tone, at which point the chant evolves into "Smoke pot / Smoke pot / Everybody smoke pot," an homage to the faintly recorded chant at the end of the Beatles' "I Am the Walrus." After the release of *Circa: Now!* and at the peak of the music industry's interest in the San Diego scene and alternative rock, Rocket From the Crypt found themselves in the middle of a bidding war among the major labels in 1993, with Reis finally negotiating a deal with Interscope Records that also included his other band, Drive Like Jehu. Reis put Rocket From the Crypt on hiatus and went to work with Drive Like Jehu to record *Yank Crime*, an album that continues to be hailed as a masterpiece of noise on account of its squealing guitars, thunderous rhythms, piercing screams, and arrangements so lengthy and complex that some have dubbed it "math rock."

The following year, 1995, marked the high point of Rocket From the Crypt's recording career, with the release of not only what is widely considered to be their best album, *Scream, Dracula, Scream*, but also two heralded EPs with a more hurried and unprocessed sound, *Hot Charity* and *The State of Art Is on Fire*. *Scream, Dracula, Scream* opens with the band in call-and-response mode: "Are you stuck in the middle?" Reis asks with a drumroll pacing him, and his choir of postmodern greasers confirms that, indeed, they are. "Are you stuck?" "YEAH!" "Are you broke?" "YEAH!" "Stuck?" "YEAH!" Broke?" "YEAH!" The horns come in, the guitars peel out, and the drums speed up as Rocket From the Crypt then launches into their manifesto of retro, "Born in '69." *Scream, Dracula, Scream* has more of an ironic and even campy feel to it, beginning with its title lifted from a Seventies blaxploitation film, but it still has many moments of menacing punk rock noise accentuated by Reis's snarling vocals. The album ends with a trilogy of songs: "Come See, Come Saw," where the horns come in after the sound of a car peeling out; "Salt Future," the horribly dystopian thought of the world remade in the image of Salt Lake City; and "Burnt Alive," a slow dirge in which Reis asks, "Do you remember 1968? / Too dumb to worry / Too dumb to hate," whatever that means.

Rocket From the Crypt had some minor hit songs and music videos in the United States and United Kingdom, but they never broke through to major commercial success, and Interscope eventually dropped them when the label underwent restructuring in the late 1990s. They continued recording and touring until 2005 and earned a reputation for being an especially spirited live act, as they would usually take the stage in matching costumes (e.g., in glittery Vegas-style threads or as police officers) with Reis employing an ironic swagger while referring to his group in the third person. Thus, in contrast to Uncle Tupelo and many other alt.country groups, their retro style was never intended to hold any deeper meanings or be taken totally seriously. And yet there was a sincere identification with older genres of music developed through a dialogue with punk, particularly in the populist simplicity of early rock 'n' roll. This dialogue was mediated by Rocket From the Crypt's construction of a working-class image and their simulation of the rebellious masculinity associated with the 1950s; their embodiment of this proletarian masculinity was never completely ironic. The inclusion of old-time music and hipster showmanship also revisited the history of white appropriations of black music and style, but this was never acknowledged, ironically or otherwise.

The Jon Spencer Blues Explosion

The Jon Spencer Blues Explosion has a misleading name, not necessarily because the band doesn't play the blues, but because they play the blues at four or five degrees removed, and they perform this music so strongly associated with authenticity with such irreverent sarcasm that they can really only be called postmodern (as they so often are). Jon Spencer himself cut his teeth in the late 1980s New York music scene playing a sort of antimusic with the band Pussy Galore. He founded the Blues Explosion in 1991 with the same deconstructionist impulses, but in time the group really began to draw from the blues, along with funk and a little hip hop, flinging these sounds together with some noisy guitars and drums in a chaotic but frequently groovy mix. Spencer remade himself from a slumming New York art punk into the swaggering cliché of an Elvis impersonator, singing as if his upper lip had been permanently curled and periodically interrupting his songs to tell anyone who would listen that the Blues

Explosion was the greatest band in the world. He knew better than to fall for the authenticity trap like so many of the white men who played the blues before him; yet Spencer never found a constructive outlet for his whiteness, so he simply wore it on his sleeve with a knowing smirk.

Jon Spencer's introduction to punk came by way of the Washington, D.C., scene of the mid-1980s, but it is difficult to imagine anyone more out of place with the earnest and abstemious ethic promoted by the Dischord Records crowd (indeed, Pussy Galore would eventually write a song called "Fuck Ian MacKaye").[40] Spencer and Julia Cafritz founded Pussy Galore with the intention of irritating and defiling everyone in their path, beginning with their decidedly unfeminist name taken from a James Bond character and an obnoxious approach to making sickeningly unharmonious "music." One of their earliest recordings was a deconstruction of the Rolling Stones' classic *Exile on Main Street* in which Pussy Galore redid each and every song in the most grating style possible while banging on a drum set made with scrap metal. These excursions in junk rock lasted until 1990, after which Spencer formed the Blues Explosion and a side project called Boss Hog with his wife, Cristina Martinez.

With the Blues Explosion, Spencer and his bandmates continued the process of creating music by first taking it apart, but at this stage the musical dialogue expressed more appreciation than avant-garde antagonism for its influences, even though it was still dripping with irony. Released in 1994, *Orange*, widely considered the band's best album, improbably begins with a string section taking the lead over some funky guitar and drums, and then it suddenly stops so that Spencer can take the role of postmodern emcee to announce, "Thank you very much, ladies and gentlemen. Right now I can gotta tell you 'bout the fabulous, most groovy . . . bell-bottoms! Bell-bottoms!" The band is off to the races again in a song that sounds a lot like its sartorial subject matter—a relic of Seventies soul and funkiness—and comes to an end soon after Spencer tells us, "I remember 1970!" This is a pretty superficial form of collective memory, but it is still light-years removed from Pussy Galore's nihilistic rendering of *Exile on Main Street*. Spencer spends the remainder of the album alternating between Elvis Presley and James Brown alter egos, punctuating nearly every song with tongue-in-cheek cries of "Goddamn!" and brandishing a bravado that is so over-the-top—for much of one song he simply lists all the cities where the Blues Explosion is supposedly "number one"—that it can't be taken as fully sincere. So even though Spencer's admiration for the music he quotes seems sincere—as with Rocket From the Crypt,

The Jon Spencer Blues Explosion, *left to right*: Judah Bauer, Russell Simmons, Jon Spencer. From the interior CD case.

the sounds of Stax Records were a big influence—the end result is much closer to the blank parody of pastiche and it is difficult to detect any sort of meaningful dialogue emerging from his fusion of punk and the blues.

The prevalence of postmodern irony complicates the appropriation of black music by Spencer, an upper-middle-class white person who attended Brown University and is the son of a Dartmouth chemistry professor. Although there is none of the romanticism that characterized previous treatments of the blues by the Rolling Stones, Eric Clapton, and Led Zeppelin, many have commented on the minstrel show element of Spencer's constant posturing and boasting. "If Spencer really loves black music," the rock critic Jim DeRogatis asked, "how come he can't get beyond making fun of it?"[41] In the mid-1990s, the Blues Explosion began touring and recording with R.L. Burnside, a Mississippi-born African American bluesman who was about 70 years old at the time, and they served as Burnside's backup band on his

1996 album *A Ass Pocket of Whiskey*. From a strictly musical perspective, this collaboration worked better than one might expect given the vast differences of race, class, and generation between the parties involved, but it still perpetuated the enduring caricature of the southern bluesman as drunken amoral misogynist. And yet it was as if the heavy dose of self-conscious irony gave them license to revisit the cultural minefield where intellectual white kids play the blues with black southerners, at least as long as they were the first to call attention to the game they were playing (in one snippet of mid-song banter, for example, Spencer asks to borrow some money and Burnside threatens to kick his ass). It may not be fair to say that Spencer was "making fun" of black music, but rather that he saw all the pitfalls in loving black music in a way that has historically preceded its theft.

The Supersuckers

It seems that the Supersuckers arrived in Seattle from Tucson, Arizona, just an instant too late, at the moment that the grunge scene was blowing up beyond the confines of the Pacific Northwest. They started recording on Sub Pop with producer Jack Endino in 1992, but they didn't really hit their stride until a couple of years later. As the grunge moment came and went, the Supersuckers mixed their original punk and metal sound with more traditional rock 'n' roll music and eventually began to include country in the mix. They became known as great live performers who played with all the drunken sloppiness of Mudhoney and the other Sub Pop bands, but they substituted a southwestern image of cowboy hats and trailer park lifestyles in place of the northwestern lumberjack. Most of their deliberately simple songs revolved around drugs, liquor, women and sex, and Satan, but even though these seemed to be genuine interests for the band members (with the possible exception of Satan), the Supersuckers were really exploiting these themes for their value as rock 'n' roll clichés. When they recorded an album of country music in 1997, the results were markedly different from Uncle Tupelo or most other alt.country bands, and yet there was still a dialogic element to this crossover that was superimposed over their ironic pastiche.

Like Mudhoney, the Supersuckers played up their white trash, proletarian image with such ironic flair that they risked being exposed as too self-conscious to truly be white trash proletarians. Their earliest recordings document them in a juvenile stage espousing clichés before they were aware that they were espousing clichés, with songs like "Hell City, Hell"

The Supersuckers, hamming it up for their album *The Sacrilicious Sounds of the Supersuckers*. From the interior CD case.

and "I Say Fuck" played at drag racing speeds. On subsequent records they slowed the music to a tempo that was more like an overcaffeinated AC/DC, while their tales of hedonism became more self-consciously exaggerated and overconfident. The Supersuckers also linked their cartoonish depiction of the rock 'n' roll lifestyle with an image of dysfunctional white poverty, like on "Doublewide" (referring to a large mobile home) from the 1995 album *The Sacrilicious Sounds of the Supersuckers*:

> Got a beat up car up on blocks in my yard
> Got a beat up wife that I hit too hard
> . . . .

> Brats at my feet, I'm gonna tan their hide
> Yeah, ain't life sweet? Doublewide!
> . . . .
> Could have turned into something but I'm digging a ditch
> I'm the son of a bastard and the son of a bitch
> Everything's OK, I got it under control
> Put a septic tank in the new hole

This song intends to be humorous through the use of crude stereotypes about poor whites and a casual attitude toward spousal and child abuse. As with the Jon Spencer Blues Explosion, ironic distance is used as a shield against being taken too seriously, but the Supersuckers seem to get away with employing these stereotypes because, unlike Jon Spencer, they resemble the caricatures they are parodying and vocalist Eddie Spaghetti sings in the first person. As noted above, a self-conscious form of white trash identity began to appear during the 1990s in popular culture, finding expression in music with bands like Southern Culture on the Skids, the Reverend Horton Heat, and Nashville Pussy. Although mediated by postmodern irony, in many ways this resumed a dialogue with the origins of rock 'n' roll, or at least the rockabilly and country elements of rock 'n' roll developed by the southern white working class.

After solidifying their reputation as a punk band with a retro rock 'n' roll approach, the Supersuckers moved on to record a country music album titled *Must've Been High*. The band continued to employ their raucous sense of humor with songs about hangovers and loneliness on the road, and in this sense they stood apart from the more somber and politicized alt.country bands of their time. But otherwise *Must've Been High* was surprisingly respectful of the genre and included contributions by country music luminaries Willie Nelson and Jesse Dayton. Though their dialogue between punk and country was carried forth in very different terms than in Uncle Tupelo, the Supersuckers found common ground between these ostensibly conflicting genres not only in the image of the outlaw but also in their shared sense of accessibility and honesty. The Supersuckers inscribed this message on the back side of the *Must've Been High* packaging:

> Honest. Pure. Simple. These are the qualities that attracted us to punk rock. The fact that the four of us, or any other bunch of like-minded jackasses for that matter, could get up on a stage and rock out is remarkably

appealing. And it has been our search for the best that rock-n-roll has to offer which inevitably led us down the road that old dirt road to the country. Simple, (there's that word again) three-chord songs, sung from experience, played on an old, beat up acoustic guitar—that's what we're talkin' about here. We're no virtuosos, but we had a damn good time makin' this record and we're hoping you have a damn good time listening to it. We Must've Been High . . . [42]

This idea of country music is informed by a constructed sense of authenticity—the images of dirt roads, beat-up acoustic guitars, and songs sung from experience—which allows the Supersuckers to dialogically connect it with punk rock, whose simplicity and honesty is embodied in the do-it-yourself ethic. This distinguishes their approach from that of Ween, another obnoxious, irony-filled band who recorded an album of country songs in the mid-1990s that was a pure parody of the genre and its allegedly backward worldview. The Supersuckers' identification with and defense of country music is most humorously evident in "The Captain," a song that tells the story of their encounter with an unnamed British musician during a recording session. The Supersuckers suggest that they might include a piano in the studio, but he continues using a synthesizer. As their incompatible tastes come to a head, the British musician storms out of the studio after uttering the insult "Country sucks." Eddie Spaghetti retorts: "I know you're so-and-so from some band / You might've been good, but I'll be damned / If I'm gonna sit here and take that anymore."

All Tatted Up with Nowhere to Go

Our consideration of these four musical acts has begun the process of mapping the different possibilities of retro culture. At one end of the spectrum, retro is little more than a blank parody of the past that recycles the most superficial signifiers of history with a self-reflexive sense of humor. At the other extreme, retro facilitates a meaningful dialogue in which the past is not simply preserved or recreated for its own sake but rather engaged with the social conditions and cultural practices of the present. Both of these possibilities can be described as postmodern and are achievable because of the vast wealth of images, commodities, and musical styles available for reuse by young people. Of the four bands we examined, Uncle Tupelo exhibited the most dialogic approach to the past as they exhumed subordinate traditions of country music in mixing it with punk, while Rocket From the Crypt, the Jon Spencer Blues Explosion, and the Supersuckers revisited older music with a more ironic approach but still made deliberate decisions about the forms they chose to appropriate.

Moving from musical texts to ethnographic contexts, I will now consider how a retro scene developed in Southern California leading up to the night that I met Matt Reese and the Live Wire was packed with people to watch Rocket From the Crypt's "Born in '69" video. The fusion between punk and what came to be known as "roots music" in Southern California was evident from at least the early 1980s, particularly with the rockabilly style of the band X's guitarist Billy Zoom. X often shared their bills with a group known as the Blasters who delved even further into the blues, R & B, and country. The preeminent revivalists to emerge from San Diego were the Beat Farmers, who began playing shows in the area in 1983/84 and invented a style that some called "cowpunk" with its merger of country and blues and the provocative antics of singer Country Dick Montana. They were closely linked to another performer who emerged from San Diego in the mid-1980s who called himself Mojo Nixon, a political satirist in the tradition of punk who put celebrity-bashing songs like "Debbie Gibson Is Pregnant with My Two-Headed Love Child" and "Don Henley Must Die" to the tune of rockabilly music in a manner that was aptly dubbed "psychobilly." With this revival in full swing, we can recall from the previous chapter that it was Tim Mays's intention to open the Casbah in San Diego in 1989 as a host to locally popular variations of roots rock and R & B music.

Another local performer who exemplified both the dialogic and ironic dimensions of retro performance was El Vez, the self-proclaimed "Mexican Elvis," who began playing shows in Los Angeles and San Diego in the early 1990s. El Vez certainly embodies the campy sensibilities befitting an Elvis impersonator, but at the same he seriously incorporates a radical viewpoint on issues of racism, poverty, and American imperialism from a Chicano perspective. Describing himself as "the hardest migrant working man in show business," El Vez combined kitsch with Chicano politics in the way he would talk about the rebellion in Chiapas while wearing a pair of gold lamé pants, for instance. Born Robert Lopez, his career began in the late 1970s as the rhythm guitarist for the Zeros, a late 1970s punk band based in Los Angeles that was sometimes called "the Mexican Ramones." El Vez continues to make use of the punk style of self-reflexive performance, but while doing so he brings the music of Elvis Presley and a host of other rock 'n' roll icons into a satirical dialogue with the Chicano experience in songs like "You Ain't Nothin' But a Chihuahua."

As I began my research, San Diego was emerging out of a deep recession and was in the process of economic restructuring. More so than other parts of California, San Diego's regional economy had historically been linked to military spending. During the 1980s, while other parts of the United States were reeling from the consequences of deindustrialization and capital flight, the Southern California region was among the main beneficiaries of the Reagan administration's reescalation of the cold war, as military expenditures in San Diego County increased from $2.1 billion in 1979 to almost $10 billion by 1988.[43] Local economists and business leaders bragged that San Diego was "recession-proof" as defense contracts helped sustain and create high-paying jobs with good benefits in the manufacturing of aircraft missiles and parts, electronic equipment, instruments, and industrial machinery. The big change came after the end of the cold war, when defense cuts of between 20 and 30 percent resulted in the permanent loss of approximately 28,000 jobs in San Diego County over the next five years. Those hit hardest were working-class people in jobs that were "closest to the manufacturing process (production workers and factory support personnel)."[44] A study of the regional impact of layoffs in the aerospace industry found that 55 percent either left California or were still unemployed two years later, while those that did find new jobs saw their earnings decrease by an average of 33 percent: "They ended up at low-wage firms, in the retailing sector and the service sector, where they often did not have health insurance."[45]

Those coming of age in the 1980s and 1990s grew up in a time of structural convulsion. The young people who had good educations were on their way to inheriting a New Economy, which has since proven no less volatile and unforgiving than the military-industrial economy, but one that nonetheless depends on the kind of technological savvy and creative skills they possess. But those who had failed in school, and who in the process had developed a rebellious intolerance for all forms of authority and become immersed in a culture of violence, drugs and alcohol, and various other forms of (self-)destructive behavior, would have no future in this New Economy and would not have the factory floor of the military-industrial economy to fall back on. A great number of these young people were growing up surrounded by the fallout from the economic and social crisis of their time—broken families, alcoholism and drug addiction, problems with the police and the legal system, violence, domestic abuse, poverty, homelessness, and so on. San Diego's hardcore punk scene had a reputation for being especially violent, even in comparison to the other hardcore scenes in Southern California. The zines from this era are full of stories about shows being broken up by the cops came because some punks were drunk and got in a fight, for instance. In many ways, the regional hardcore scene was a monstrous amplification of the *Top Gun* militarism and racism that fuelled both the prosperity and the misery in Southern California.

Many years before he named himself Speedo, Rocket From the Crypt's John Reis had become a punk rocker while growing up in San Diego during the 1980s; he formed his first, short-lived band, Conservative Itch, and then formed Pitchfork, a band that has been described as "post-hardcore," in 1986. In his teen years Reis also organized local hardcore shows, hosted "scene meetings," and wrote a column in the local anarchist-punk newsletter, *San Diego's Daily Impulse*. Reis often wrote reviews of the local hardcore shows, and some of these reviews describe the violence and self-destructive behavior of punks and how this was destroying the ability to maintain a local scene. In one review, he writes: "Amidst Crabgrass' lengthy barrage of sludge, massive violence broke out and blood was splattered everywhere. One guy was getting beat up by ten others. Some were kicking the shit out of him and bashing him with folding chairs. . . . The fact that paramedics had to be called caused the closing of the show."[46]

As he got older, Reis focused his musical energies on Pitchfork, and after they broke up in 1990 he and Rick Froberg moved on to form Drive Like Jehu, which featured Reis on guitar and Froberg screaming his head off. In contrast, Reis intended for Rocket From the Crypt to be more like a "party band" that would involve their audience by going for more of a good-time rock 'n' roll sound and putting Reis on vocals. In the early days, when Rocket From the Crypt was playing a party they might pass out lyric sheets or various noisemakers to involve their audience, and at one point Reis vowed that Rocket From the Crypt would never play on a stage. As their bass player, Pete Reichert (aka Petey X) once explained to me, these efforts to generate audience participation were partly a response to the violent atmosphere of the local punk scene: "Even from day one, like our very first show, right before we went on we were like, 'Let's do something like paint our faces or make it more like a show,' because when we started the band it was a time when San Diego was a really violent scene. . . . [We] did anything that made people not feel alienated from the band, be a part of the music, get involved, put on a show."[47]

Drive Like Jehu: Rick Froberg on vocals and guitar, John Reis on guitar. From *Music [619] Magazine*. Vol. 1, #4, July–August 1993.

Up and down the coastal towns of Southern California, from Santa Barbara to San Diego, the supreme band to emerge from the party circuit of this era was Sublime, the Long Beach–based ska-punk band who began playing parties in exchange for free beer in the summer of 1988, when their first gig ended in a riot on the Fourth of July. In their early days Sublime was once described as the "below average garage punk band that every kid wanted to play at his party." A collective social atmosphere always surrounded the band, and here again we could find a wide range of social strata among young people in the Southern California beach towns, from the affluent to the runaways, burnouts, and junkies. The members of Sublime—Bradley Nowell, Bud Gaugh, and Eric Wilson—met as students at Long Beach State and played many college parties in their early years. The music and larger persona of Sublime is probably best thought of as "skunk," which is the name they gave their record label to describe their musical fusion of punk and ska (while also making reference to marijuana). As they were developing as a band, Sublime's performances were often sloppy, and their lyrics and overall style were mostly juvenile, but in time they created a highly unique sound by including not only punk and ska but also a host of other musical influences, thus fashioning a hybrid aesthetic that was not necessarily retro but certainly can be considered dialogic. Because Sublime was involved with a large social environment—from the inner circle, whom the band members referred to as their "family," to the networks of partygoers, groupies, and hangers-on—their music can be heard from a sociological perspective as the register of a particular social world. Indeed, Sublime wrote many songs about the troubled young people they encountered, and they tended to present these characters as social types; the most tragic story of all, however, is personified by their front man, Bradley Nowell, who died from a heroin overdose in May 1996, two months before the release of his musical masterpiece.

Bradley Nowell appears to have grown up like one of those beach bum youths who are formulaically replicated in all the various media set in Southern California, a middle-class white kid who loved to play the guitar and surf, and who certainly looked the part with the shaggy blond hair he sported in his adolescent years. And yet he was obviously quite a troubled child, one who had an especially difficult time after his parents' divorce, was clearly intelligent but a failure in school, and was eventually diagnosed with Attention Deficit Disorder and medicated through the stimulant Ritalin. As an adolescent, he was drawn to the spastic Southern California style of punk rock and hardcore exemplified by Black Flag, the Circle Jerks, the Minutemen, the Descendents, and Bad Religion. Nowell first encountered reggae music as a youngster when he was on a trip with his father to the Virgin Islands, and in later years he always maintained that this experience was fundamental in shaping his approach to creating music. By all accounts Nowell was a gifted guitarist who had a great ear, and he developed a unique style in alternating between Caribbean rhythms and punk aggression.

As they continued playing the party scene and embarked on some regional tours, Sublime began to amass a devoted following of young people concentrated in Southern California's beach cities. In 1992 they recorded an album through their own Skunk Records called *40 Oz. to Freedom*, and they claim to have sold tens of thousands of copies primarily from the trunks of their cars. Eventually they scored with a single called "Date Rape," which became a cult hit on local radio stations and led to their signing by MCA Records. "Date Rape" is ostensibly an antirape song, but it is also a good example of how the party scene shaped Sublime's music, as it is an upbeat number that includes some sadistic humor about how the rapist is later raped when he is in prison; you can almost hear the collective voices of all the young, drunk and stoned, mostly male partygoers singing and laughing along.

Sublime had their major breakthrough in 1997 with an eponymous album released by MCA that is responsible for the vast majority of the 17 million albums the band has now sold worldwide. Its most popular single and music video, "What I Got," is a cheerful tribute to living and loving, but in other songs, behind the breezy Caribbean sound of the music, there are also some harrowing portraits of a generation of exploited and wasted youth. "The Wrong Way," for instance, is a song about incest and child prostitution with an infectious ska beat. One of the most intriguing cuts is "April 29, 1992 (Miami)," a song with a hip hop beat where Nowell describes his actions on the first night of the riots following the Rodney King verdict. This is no plea for reconciliation and peace, but instead a song where Nowell portrays himself as a looter, first hitting the liquor store and setting it on fire, then moving on to get some musical equipment and furniture. At other moments, the violently distressed aspects of Nowell's psyche are exposed, like "Santeria," which finds him looking to take revenge on another man who has stolen his woman, and especially in "Doin' Time," a reggae/hip hop rearrangement of George Gershwin's "Summertime" that ends with Nowell thinking about drowning his girlfriend. On these last few minutes of *Sublime*, the music is as gorgeous as its lyrical subject matter is gruesome, as "Doin' Time" slouches into a hypnotic beat and the smooth chanting of "Summertime / The livin's easy," but then Nowell comes back to warn us, "She's evil," and his voice was rarely as tender or soulful as when he sang, "The tension / Is getting hotter / I'd like to hold her / Head under water."

Throughout the 1990s, the beach cities of Southern California, from Los Angeles to Orange County to San Diego, were host to forms of cultural innovation that were largely energized by young castoffs from the old white working class. The culture of tattooing experienced a renaissance in this period as bands like Sublime and Rocket From the Crypt achieved regional popularity, and fashion took on more of a retro style as grunge receded into history. Those who had come of age in the punk and hardcore movements of the 1980s were turning to music and styles from other places and times, creating new cultural hybrids by putting a punk spin on them. There was a celebratory air to much of this culture that largely developed from the social atmosphere of house parties, but it was the kind of partying that also has a desperate quality to it, the sort of hopelessness that comes from thinking that nothing good can from the future and therefore one only has the present to live for.

A strong sense of community developed in the San Diego scene around Rocket From the Crypt and a group of other bands, with the Rocket tattoo becoming an emblem of membership. But the reconstructions of working-class masculinity and whiteness were also exclusionary in some of the same ways that the original Southern California suburban order had been. It was a scene primarily composed of white people and some Latinos, and its musical and stylistic norms of whiteness were only rarely in dialogue with the neighboring Mexican culture in any serious way. During my years of research in San Diego I got to know a Korean American musician named John Lee who was the singer, guitarist, and songwriter for the locally popular band aMiniature. John was one of only a handful of Asian Americans in the scene, and he spent most of his time playing and touring with almost exclusively white musicians and for a predominantly white audience. He maintained friendships with many in the San Diego scene, but he never embraced their retro style or ironic images of working-class life:

> In San Diego, all the guys I know, I mean I love them to death but it's like the whole white trash thing. . . . So what are you, are you going to live in a trailer park or no? Are you going to live in a trailer park but still get the Martha Stewart trim? Go to the Casbah any night and you know what I mean. I love all those guys anyway. . . . I talk to a lot of my friends who nothing traumatic has happened to them. There was never an issue of who they were in this society. They were white. That's it. I'm not saying that's bad. I really wanted that when I was a kid, just so I wouldn't have to explain what I had for dinner: "Yeah, I ate this really spicy stew with cabbage and squid and shit," and my friends were like, "What?"[48]

The Southern California region has large populations of Korean and Asian Americans, but John became estranged from that Asian youth culture, which he derisively described to me as "hip hop meets Euro-disco fashion." As he entered the subcultures of punk and alternative rock, John became immersed in a social network that was overwhelmingly white, and he sometimes made passing references to how his friends in the San Diego scene were "all white." And yet John had maintained a strong attachment to Korean culture, especially as it had been mediated through his family. John had taken several trips back to South Korea, where he still had lots of family, and after aMiniature signed a major-label deal with Restless Records, Korean magazines and newspapers began contacting John for interviews. In the United States, John maintained links to

Korean culture through the Chicago music scene, where the band Seam, led by Sooyoung Park, had established themselves. Park eventually organized the "Ear of the Dragon" tour across North America featuring bands fronted by Asian Americans, including Seam and aMiniature as well as the groups Versus and Cub. Around this time, some Korean American friends of John's made him a T-shirt bearing the words, "Punk Rock Asian Redneck." John felt that those words expressed the hybrid identity he had forged through punk rock and the conflicts between his background and the culture of whiteness in the music scene.

The retro greaser look accompanied by a return to various forms of roots music can be seen as symbolic work on the part of young men to anchor their identity in an image of white working-class masculinity. For women in the scene who also adopted a retro look, however, there seemed to be much less attachment to the social-historical values embodied in the styles and fashions they recycled. This was most humorously illustrated in an interview between V. Vale of V/Search Publications and two swing dance instructors named Dana and Mango during the height of the 1990s swing revival. Mango comments: "In the same respect, the way we live our lives now is a lot more glamorous than it was in the '40s. If we were girls our age then, we'd be working in steel mills waiting for our husbands to come home from the war." Dana responds: "No way would I prefer to live back then. I'd just like to go back and get the clothes and immediately return [laughs]."[49]

Certainly, these young women in the contemporary retro scene had far more agency and opportunity than their grandmothers' generation had during the World War II era. But they were also facing new challenges brought on by service work and the temporary/part-time job market, the collapse of the "family wage," and the prevalence of poverty among female-headed households. The young women who began to model their style after Bettie Page and retro pin-ups also did so because they were dissatisfied with the hegemonic standards of beauty and sexuality in the mainstream media and commercial culture. A style that employed vintage fashions and the pin-up look mixed the punk and goth subculture of tattoos and piercing became increasingly evident among youth women in various alternative music scenes during the 1990s.

This retro/pin-up and punk/goth look came together with developing "alt porn" media (made possible by the Internet) in the creation of Suicide Girls, as the Web site began posting its photos and profiles of young women in late 2001. Suicide Girls is largely the invention of a young female photographer who calls herself Missy Suicide, who started by photographing women in the various subcultures and music scenes in Portland, Oregon. Missy Suicide often makes reference to being influenced by Alberto Vargas and pin-up photographers of that era, and her style has been shaped with an eye for models like Bettie Page who can be confident yet playful and imaginative. Virtually all the Suicide Girls have some combination of tattoos and piercings, and the intent is to capture the individuality of the model and highlight her idiosyncrasies and imperfections rather than airbrushing them to conform to a homogenous standard. Those who criticize Suicide Girls, however, have often said that its models are still limited to a relatively narrow range of what can be described as young, white, and skinny, only with a more alternative look. Each Suicide Girl has her own page where all her photo shoots can be accessed, and there is a blog and a personal profile of interests in music, movies, and books; in this way Suicide Girls has tried to project more individuality than is typical in other media of female sexual objectification. As of 2007, there were more than 1,500 Suicide Girls on the Web site, and the company claimed to receive about 1,000 applications from would-be models every few days.[50]

Our Retro Future

We began this chapter by considering two theoretical prognoses of the emergence of a retro style in popular culture. Baudrillard and Jameson both saw retro as nothing less than a signal of modernity's crisis of historical consciousness under the influence of the commodity form (Jameson) or media simulacra (Baudrillard). There is an ethos of revival and a desire for authenticity embedded in the retro sensibility, but past styles are approached with the spirit of irony and camp in ways that are distinct from other forms of historical preservation. Retro thus implodes the modernist categories of temporality and aesthetics with a sensibility that is too makeshift and lighthearted to be called nostalgia while being unwilling to simply caricature past styles in the manner of kitsch.

In examining a retro scene in San Diego and Greater Southern California from an ethnographic standpoint, however, we can find can deep meanings beneath the retro music and fashion that young people selectively appropriated. We have witnessed how these young people not only endowed the past with cultural significance but also actively used it to speak to the social conditions of the present—as they mixed the greaser or pin-up look with contemporary fashions or put a punk rock spin on various forms of roots music. This would seem to further validate the dialogic theory of culture and history first proposed by Bakhtin and later extended in Lipsitz's studies of popular culture and collective memory. In focusing on the San Diego scene of the 1990s, we have seen how the past was summoned in an attempt to symbolically resolve the structural crises pertaining to masculinity and, less visibly, whiteness that have been provoked by deindustrialization and disempowerment in the era of post-Fordist capitalism. This retro subculture must be analytically situated within the social conditions of postmodernity, for it is only possible because the proliferation of media and commodification of culture have exponentially multiplied the volume of imagery and music now available for reproduction and juxtaposition. The dialogic approach differs from the more apocalyptic strains of postmodern theory by allowing for the possibility that people will look to the past with an active, creative eye, not to rediscover and preserve some notion of authentic history, but rather to shed critical light on the present in a playful spirit.

Specific trends recycled from different eras will inevitably come and go, but the retro sensibility now appears to be a permanent fixture in popular culture, and youth culture in particular. In 2001 a new crop of bands—the Strokes, the White Stripes, and the Hives—emerged to great fanfare in the American and British music media, which portrayed them as the new saviors of rock. Each of these three bands had a different look and sound, but they all had a strongly retro feel, and each of them had indeed become excellent rock bands insofar as they mastered the existing methods for recreating different variations of a compelling rock sound and the mystique of rock stars. The White Stripes have become one of the most celebrated bands in contemporary rock music with a sound that draws heavily from both the original Delta blues and the whitened blues rock of the Sixties and Seventies. The Hives sound like a Sixties garage rock band accelerated to the pace of Eighties hardcore, and although they are Swedish they look a group of American mobsters dressed in black-and-white suits. But the pièce de résistance was certainly the Strokes, who came out of New York City looking and sounding like they had been assembled in some Warholian factory of cool; they looked like movie stars dressed in the Ramones' clothing while making music that sounded like the Velvet Underground, Television, or Sonic Youth with the noise tightened up and trimmed down.

When we examine existing retro subcultures from an ethnographic standpoint we are bound to see the agency of young people actively engaged in creating culture instead of just trying to replicate the past. But from a more distanced perspective, with a longer view of trends in popular culture, the retro phenomenon does pose some significant and possibly discomforting problems. What is the significance of the fact that there has been a shift in youth culture from forward-looking moderns to retro recyclers rummaging through the past? Is it symptomatic of a greater loss of faith in progress in a postmodern society as compared to modernity? Is it symptomatic of collective feelings of exhaustion within the music world and the end of the notion of youth as a collective subject of social change? Insofar as these questions center on the purported "death of rock" and the future of youthful cultural politics, they will be addressed in the next chapter.

6

The Work of Rock in the Age of Digital Reproduction

One might generalize by saying: the technique of reproduction detaches the reproduced object from the domain of tradition. By making many reproductions it substitutes a plurality of copies for a unique existence. And in permitting the reproduction to meet the beholder or listener in his own particular situation, it reactivates the object reproduced.

—Walter Benjamin[1]

For all contemporary musical life is dominated by the commodity form; the last pre-capitalist residues have been eliminated. Music, with all the attributes of the ethereal and sublime which are generously accorded it, serves in America today as an advertisement for commodities which one must acquire in order to be able to hear music.

—Theodor W. Adorno[2]

In April 2000 Lars Ulrich, the drummer for Metallica, filed suit against Napster, the online music file sharing service that Ulrich charged with giving Metallica's music away for free through the Internet. At roughly the same time, Napster would also be sued by the Recording Industry Association of America (RIAA), a coalition of recording companies led by A&M Records, as well as the rapper and producer Dr. Dre. Their actions targeted not only Napster but also individual consumers; the RIAA began prosecuting people for downloading music while Metallica and Dr. Dre collected lists of hundreds of thousands of Napster users who were subsequently banned from the service. After being found guilty of violating copyright infringement under the Digital Millennium Copyright Act, Napster shut down operations in 2001, declared bankruptcy, and sold off its assets in 2002. Nonetheless, this certainly did not put an end to the free online exchange of music, as peer-to-peer file-sharing systems like Kazaa and LimeWire have since emerged with more cunning means of technical and legal protection. Every semester I ask the students in my Sociology of Popular Culture course how many of them download free music over the Internet. The vast majority of them raise their hands, and without much hesitation or embarrassment. The consensus is that it's pretty easy and safe to get free music—though as college students they are certainly more technologically adept than the rest of the population—and most of them don't feel guilty about doing it.

The twenty-first century has been a tough time for the music industry, or at least for the aspect of the music industry that depends on selling recorded music. Overall music sales (in units) steadily declined from 788.6 million in 2000 to 348.7 million in 2008.[3] The best-selling compact disc in 2004 was the blank and recordable kind, with an estimated 1.8 billion sold annually.[4] In 2006 the Tower Records chain and the Musicland entertainment company (including the Sam Goody and Media Play retail stores) declared bankruptcy. Observers of the music business continue to debate how much of this financial distress can be attributed to file sharing.[5] In the past, the industry has been able to withstand the introduction of new technologies that allow people to reproduce music and share it with others. In the early 1980s, for example, the record companies were so anxious about music being copied and circulated on blank cassettes that they launched a campaign featuring the slogan "Home taping is killing music." But tape trading turned out to be an essential part of building the underground subcultures of hardcore punk and thrash metal. To offer a personal anecdote that might have assuaged Lars Ulrich's worst fears about Napster, the first time I heard Metallica was on a mixtape that a friend made for me in 1985, and I cannot recount all the money I spent on Metallica records, tapes, CDs, concerts, T-shirts, posters, and videocassettes and DVDs in the ensuing years. It remains to be seen how the recording industry will assimilate the latest technological developments, but the initial response has simply been resistant and antagonistic.

At the same time that new digital technologies of reproduction have been introduced, the music industry, along with the rest of the corporate media, has undergone processes of concentration, conglomeration, and hypercommercialism.[6] As a result of concentration, the number of companies who dominate the American and world market has now shrunk considerably, with this "big four" (Universal Music Group, Sony BMG Music Entertainment, Warner Music Group, and EMI Group) accounting for over 80 percent of the U.S. market and over 70 percent of the world market for recorded music.[7] On the retail side, during the 1990s the major labels began to focus more on distribution through the "big box" chains like Wal-Mart, Best Buy, and Target, all of whom sell CDs at discounted prices, which is certainly an important factor in explaining why so many record stores have gone out of business in recent years. In radio, the passage of the Telecommunications Act of 1996 deregulated media ownership and thus allowed Clear Channel Communications to purchase multiple radio stations in every market and establish a dominant position in broadcasting with over 1,200 stations nationwide. They have since become the subject of controversy after banning airplay of over 100 songs (including the entire Rage Against the Machine catalog) after the attacks of September 11, 2001, and in subsequent years Clear Channel, a major contributor to the Republican Party, censored critics of president George W. Bush and the Iraq war.[8]

While concentration refers to the domination of a market by a decreasing number of companies within a particular industry, conglomeration is the process whereby firms have expanded their holdings across multiple industries and media. Each of the big four is now a subsidiary of a horizontally integrated conglomerate with assets in media such as television, film, telecommunications, video games, publishing, and the Internet. As the major labels have become subsidiaries of larger conglomerates, they are now more oriented toward immediate profits and are impatient when it comes to developing new artists. As Ben Shapiro, former copresident of Atlantic Records, explained: "Corporations want irrational growth, but the music business has historically worked on long-term artist development. Now there is an incredible lack of patience for developing artists. Where you program for your parent company's immediate gratification, you sign stuff that's easy to digest, not what you consider brilliant."[9] Because the major labels are subsidiaries of conglomerates, music has also increasingly been subjected to a process of hypercommercialism in which artists or songs are cross-promoted with other forms of media owned by the same parent company. More than ever, popular music is not simply a commodity in its own right but also a central medium for greasing all the various wheels of the consumer culture as the boundary between content and advertising is obliterated. The opportunities for cross-promotion or "synergy" within conglomerates has put a premium on developing pop stars who can transcend the music world and become celebrities in multiple forms of media; the corollary, of course, is that it devalues those whose talent is restricted to music alone.[10]

In sum, popular music and popular culture more generally are caught in a conflict between the democratizing possibilities opened by digital technologies and the monopolistic tendencies of global media conglomerates. More people have greater access to the tools of media production and communication, but anything that is popular enough to be consumed by a large audience inevitably falls under the domain of corporations that maximize profit by expanding the scope of the commodity form. While this may be the most urgent cultural issue of our times, there is precedent for it in the debate between Walter Benjamin and Theodor W. Adorno during the late 1930s. Benjamin speculated about how new media technologies of reproduction could empower audiences and allow consumers to become cultural producers in his essay "The Work of Art in the Age of Mechanical Reproduction." Adorno condemned and lampooned what he called "the culture industry," as he believed it to be producing a series of standardized and mindless commodities that effectively pacified their consuming audience. I will therefore revisit this seminal intellectual debate between two of the twentieth century's most esteemed cultural Marxists with the idea that it continues to hold prognostic value for understanding our own times of technological change and capitalist control.

While Benjamin and Adorno direct us to different aspects of technology and capitalism, they quickly advance us from these structural issues to questions of aesthetics and cultural meaning. These two thinkers will be our guides from a consideration of digital reproduction and global conglomeration to the debate that has been raging for some time about the "death" of rock music. Benjamin and Adorno each expose a different side of the crisis of authenticity that has led many musicians, critics, and fans to argue that rock music and the culture surrounding it is no longer significant. Adorno's perspective leads us to the dispiriting conclusion that rock will only survive if it can somehow heroically avoid the lethal process of incorporation by the culture industry. Benjamin, however, offers us some more ambiguous possibilities. Benjamin also leads us to the conclusion that the aura that illuminates rock cannot survive the mediated reproduction of the digital age. And yet this may ultimately be a liberating development, for Benjamin's ideas suggest the possibility of an oppositional culture forged through new technologies, though this can only be achieved once rock's ideal of authenticity has been demolished.

Benjamin Versus Adorno

Writing in 1936, Walter Benjamin sought to anticipate the effects that new media technologies would have on art and culture. In more traditional societies, what Benjamin called "the ritual function" of art and culture had been dependent on a sense of authenticity and the "aura" conferred by sacred objects and rituals. This authenticity was derived from the singularity of the sacred in space and time, but the new media technologies of the early twentieth century, especially photography and film, were based on reproduction, and these acts of reproduction undermined the pseudoreligious aura surrounding artworks. Though Benjamin expressed some ambivalence about these developments in other writings, in "The Work of Art in the Age of Mechanical Reproduction" he welcomed them as nothing less than revolutionary contradictions of capitalism.[11] Media technologies of reproduction made art more accessible to mass audiences and closed what Benjamin referred to as the "distance" from which art casts a mystifying and pacifying spell over its beholders. The democratizing effects of media technologies enabled audiences to act more like critics, Benjamin believed, and the reproducibility of these media permitted people to take on a participatory role as cultural producers. Benjamin was an enthusiast of montage as a form of artistic technique and political statement, and he saw that media reproduction allowed images to be recombined in ways that exposed new meanings, associations, and contradictions. In one of his most oft-quoted passages, he imagined that a new revolutionary culture would supplant the vanishing traditions of authenticity, ritual, and aura: "The instant the criterion of authenticity ceases to be applicable to artistic production, the total function of art is reversed. Instead of being based on ritual, it begins to be based on another practice—politics."[12]

Of course, the revolution Benjamin envisioned in this essay never came to fruition. But in many other respects his ideas are remarkably prescient as we consider the changes in not only art but also music and popular culture in the decades since his essay was written. For instance, the history of DIY punk and independent rock we have traced was facilitated by the development of media technologies that made it both easier and cheaper for people to produce and distribute their music, writing, or artwork. In matters of style and performance, punk and many of the subcultural permutations that followed have made use of montage by reproducing and juxtaposing media images from the present and past, typically with a sense of self-conscious irony if not politicized parody. The technologies of reproducibility that Benjamin identified are even more favorable to hip hop music and subculture, especially in the technique of sampling, where music is produced by those master consumers who possess an encyclopedic knowledge of records and the skills to recycle and remix those sounds into new musical creations.[13] Now, in the age of digital media, the outlets for the production and distribution of music are multiplying, along with many other forms of cultural production, and are thus becoming more accessible to anyone with the time and money to create or circulate them via their computer. There are infinitely more opportunities to create networks of people linked through channels of communication and creativity, and so the technological possibilities for a revolutionary culture have redoubled, regardless of whether there is the popular will or collective imagination to make it happen.

In presenting a hopeful forecast of the cultural contradictions of capitalism, Benjamin badly underestimated capital's ability to recreate the aura's allure in the form of commodities and celebrities. He dismissed this problem in his "Work of Art" essay when he wrote that "the cult of the movie star" exudes nothing more than "the phony spell of the commodity."[14] Benjamin failed to anticipate the mystifying spell of commodities not just in the movies but also among celebrities in music and sports. The aura certainly has not evaporated as quickly as Benjamin thought it would as commercial media, now on a global scale, has increasingly dominated popular culture. In the church of rock 'n' roll, for instance, the aura takes the form of legends about its rebellious origins in the repressive Fifties, the sacred/profane duality of Woodstock and Altamont to symbolize the rise-and-fall narrative of the Sixties, and so many martyrs who have accumulated mythic status for their ability to live and die the rock 'n' roll lifestyle. Punk took great joy in defaming these idols and myths, but punk has also subsequently amassed its own alternative collection of sacred times, places, and people; and as we have seen on multiple occasions in previous chapters, punk is motivated by nothing if not its "criterion of authenticity."

Benjamin's friend and intellectual rival Theodor W. Adorno developed his infamous critique of the culture industry in no small part as a response to the "Work of Art" essay. Adorno had already penned some notorious denunciations of jazz, and in light of Benjamin's essay and his own exile from Nazi Germany to the United States in 1938, he began a series of far-reaching broadsides against popular music and commercial entertainment.[15] Adorno mourned the development of a music industry that he saw as an assembly line designed to crank out an endless parade of formulaic, predictable hit songs and star performers whose differences from one another were merely cosmetic in nature. In the process, he believed, the audience for popular music forfeited its capacity to listen actively or critically and was reduced to the passive consumption of diversionary forms of entertainment. Distinguishing himself from more conservative intellectual critics who feared that "mass culture" would lead to cultural and political anarchy, the Marxist Adorno perceived that the commodification of culture and music would serve to reproduce capitalism by pacifying its proletarian victims. At the same time, Adorno defended the modernist conception of art and the avant-garde whose declining aura had been trumpeted by Benjamin, for he felt that the consciousness of the working class was too mystified and reified under capitalist conditions; in the meantime it fell on the avant-garde to express a radical negation of the existing society. For Adorno, great art, like the music of Schoenberg or the novels of Kafka, should be imbued with dissonance in a way that is artistically innovative while exposing social contradictions, in contrast to the "affirmative" culture assembled in the commodity form, which represents a false ideal of harmony.[16]

In much of the contemporary scholarship on media and popular culture, Adorno is held up as a caricature of either a conspiratorial Marxist or an elitist snob who believes that passive audiences fully absorb ideological messages in automatic fashion.[17] But from the perspective of political economy, the critique of popular music in its commodity form continues to be relevant, though perhaps not wholly persuasive, due to the expansion in the era of global capitalism of what Adorno and Max Horkheimer would call "the culture industry." While there has been a proliferation of media accessible to people at the grassroots level, the vast majority of all music sold is owned by a shrinking number of what are now global conglomerates with interconnected holdings in film, publishing, and television.[18] These criticisms of the contemporary political economy of music and popular culture can be affirmed even if one strongly rejects Adorno's assumption that audiences uncritically absorb the culture industry's ideological messages. What has changed in the decades since Adorno first formulated his critique, however, is that the culture industry has also found new ways to profit not just from standardization and conformity but also from expressions of resistance and authenticity on the part of those who experience alienation from mass culture.

Needless to say, Adorno's elitist and Eurocentric assumptions about the inherent superiority of what he called "serious music," along with his stereotyped view of the hypnotic banality of popular music, are highly problematic. But as music is increasingly integrated into the consumer culture and functions as a vital element in the globalization of culture and entertainment, it has become impossible (or at least foolish) to develop a sociological analysis of contemporary music without engaging the culture industry critique in some fashion. Following Adorno, we should consider the role of popular music in reproducing social relations of capitalism, the co-opting consequences of the commodity form, and the obstacles to creating music that expresses a radical negation of society. Moreover, even if Adorno's ideas are revealed to be extremely flawed in the end, he still must be reckoned with because so many people inside the different subcultures of contemporary music continue to think along the same lines that he did: they make relatively firm distinctions between serious music and pop music (and their respective audiences), and they fear that music risks losing its innovative edge or political bite if it becomes too commercialized. The Adornoesque critique of the culture industry is thus important in its own right for the questions of political economy it forces us to confront, but it also allows us to interrogate the central ideology that circulates within punk, indie rock, and many other subcultures.[19]

On "The Death of Rock"

The death of rock 'n' roll, as Kevin Dettmar has noted with a paradoxical tone, is one of the most enduring mythologies of the genre's half-century history. Rumors of the death of rock began spreading at the end of the 1960s and had reached commonsensical status by the 1970s. As Dettmar has chronicled, academics and journalists have spilled much ink on the subject in recent years, so much so that rock's "death" or "rise and fall" could be classified as its own subfield of popular music studies and rock criticism.[20] And yet writers and intellectuals are not the only ones to have eulogized rock, as Dettmar has collected and classified some 200 songs that proclaim the death of rock or use the death of a rock star as an allegory for the whole genre's demise. And rock is apparently not the only musical corpse roaming the earth, for people started talking about the death of punk almost immediately after it was born, and everything from jazz to rhythm and blues to hip hop (e.g., in the title of an album by the rapper Nas) has been declared "dead."[21]

It is tempting to dismiss all this, as Dettmar does, as the narcissistic discourse of baby boomers who have stopped listening to music and thus pronounce rock dead when in reality they just don't get it anymore. But the issue seems more serious than this. It is not a question of whether it is still possible to make great rock music, but instead whether rock can ever reestablish the cultural and political significance it once occupied. In this spirit, the absence of musicians with the currency to be recognized not only as great artists but also as leaders of social transformation has caused David Shumway to ask, "Where have all the rock stars gone?"[22] The answer to Shumway's question seems to have less to do with the music itself than the sociopolitical conditions surrounding it. As Lawrence Grossberg, the most prominent scholar of the death of rock and one of Dettmar's principle targets, has put it, "Rock's conditions of possibility have been transformed so radically as to suggest that rock's operating logic might no longer be either effective or possible."[23] In short, rock 'n' roll originated from a social context, spanning from World War II to the early 1970s, that we have identified with high Fordism—a period of economic affluence in which a large demographic of young people constituted a mass market and were poised to take over the world. Now that these social conditions have been undone as capital has extended its global reach and broken its social compact with labor and the nation-state, what are "the conditions of possibility" for rock in the age of digital media and transnational conglomerates?

The most common explanation for the death of rock is a close cousin of the culture industry thesis, even when Adorno or other members of the Frankfurt School are not mentioned by name. In simple terms, it maintains that if rock is dead, it was killed by profiteering record companies and concert promoters, rich rock stars with inflated egos, and advertisers capitalizing on the coolness of youth culture. This sort of lament can be found in Fred Goodman's attack on "the head-on collision of rock and commerce" personified by Dylan, Springsteen, and Neil Young on one side and David Geffen on the other, or in James Miller's caustic complaint that "a music that once provoked the wrath of the censors has become the Muzak of the Millennium."[24] Thomas Frank included an addendum to this thesis when he announced in his title that "Hip Is Dead" in a cover story for *The Nation* in 1996.[25] For Frank, the death of hip is a result of contemporary capitalism's confluence between bohemian sensibilities and the consumerist assertions of individualism and difference.

While this may be the most common explanation for the purported death of rock, it is also the one most often and easily refuted. It is unquestionable that rock is firmly in the grips of the culture industry; it is a routine aspect of the consumer culture pumped into sporting events, movie soundtracks, and TV shows (and, yes, turned into Muzak for shoppers). But it is quite another thing to say that this commodification has killed rock, for this depends on a host of assumptions about the incompatibility of art and commerce and imagines some golden age when rock supposedly was not a commodity. Frank's argument is somewhat more nuanced because he posits that hip has always been tied to the consumer culture, and so a more accurate but infinitely less catchy title for his essay would have been "Hip Was Never Alive." Nonetheless, Frank shares with the death-of-rock crowd a tendency to assume that capitalism has an unlimited capacity to murder every piece of culture it discovers and transform consumers into its willing accomplices, all without leaving any evidence of struggle at the scene of the crime.

A second and more plausible explanation for the death of rock has emerged from the perspective of political economy, though it is not one that could have been foreseen by Adorno in the 1940s. This argument maintains that rock is dead because the music and its audiences have splintered into so many different subgenres and niche markets that there is nothing to unify people into something like a Woodstock Nation. This is supplemented by the assertion that the means of musical consumption have become increasingly privatized (e.g., the iPod, Internet radio, etc.), while public media like radio no longer enjoy the common currency they once did. Shumway presents these changes as his explanation for the declining significance of rock stars: "In popular music, the decline of a genuine mass audience has meant that it is harder and harder for a performer to attain recognition beyond his or her niche. . . . Now, each listener creates his or her own playlist, taking individual songs and, typically, ignoring their presentation within an album."[26] These changes can be further contextualized as the consequences of a post-Fordist economy that targets more specialized niche markets, in distinction from the mass culture that characterized the middle decades of the twentieth century. Adorno, who primarily feared standardization and did not expect that a mass audience would translate into a mass movement during the 1960s, could not have anticipated such fragmentation and individualization resulting from the restructuring of the culture industry.

Specialized markets and privatized technologies have undoubtedly contributed to a splintering of the rock audience, but by themselves they are not sufficient explanations for why rock music and rock stars seem to have lost so much of their cultural power. In the first place, one suspects that those who use the Sixties as their point of comparison are overestimating and idealizing the extent to which rock music was the central element in unifying an entire generation of youth. But the bigger problem is that these arguments use quantitative measures—the size of the audience and the lack of a critical mass—to assess the death of rock, when in fact the situation seems to have more to do with qualitative factors like the capacity to empower an audience or the degree of resonance across popular culture. The case of punk, for instance, is proof that music does not need to reach a mass audience to achieve cultural significance as an expression and catalyst of social change.

To return to Benjamin's ideas, we might say that the death of rock is a result of the erosion of its aura. Rock's aura is attached to values and rituals that are nonreproducible by definition, particularly youthfulness, the singular time and space of live performance, and the demand for artistic originality. The culture of rock music creates an aura for particular events, like Woodstock or the birth of punk, or moments when legendary performers like the Rolling Stones or the Sex Pistols were at the acme of their powers. But this is also what can make it sad and embarrassing to be a rock fan when corporate interests align to hold another Woodstock concert that is exponentially more expensive and commercialized than the original, or to sponsor the latest tours of the Rolling Stones, the Sex Pistols, or any number of other bands who are long past their creative peak and heading toward middle age (or well beyond).[27] As Benjamin would have seen it, the halo surrounding these moments and idols is profaned with each successive act of reproduction and simulation. This is a process driven by the culture industry, but its profaning consequences cannot simply be attributed to commercialization, for the original moments and idols were always commodities to begin with. In short, the rock ideals of youthfulness and originality are inevitably thwarted by conglomerates that have the technological and promotional means to maximize profits through reproduction. This might explain why the most mythologized rock stars are often the ones who died young, because even if the culture industry is always finding new ways to release music and paraphernalia with their name attached to it, their image and voice are frozen in a specific moment and cannot be coaxed out of retirement for one more farewell tour.

Rock's criteria of authenticity most recently and scathingly came under attack in a 2004 *New York Times* editorial by Kelefa Sanneh titled "The

Rap Against Rockism." According to Sanneh, most rock critics cling to unspoken assumptions about authenticity that include "idolizing the authentic old legend (or underground hero) while mocking the latest pop star; lionizing punk while barely tolerating disco; loving the live show and hating the music video; extolling the growling performer while hating the lip-syncher."[28] As it disparages pop music, disco, R & B, and most forms of hip hop, Sanneh also charges rockism with upholding the aesthetic norms of the straight white men who dominate contemporary rock music and rock criticism. Although the critique of rockism is not entirely new, Sanneh's article touched off a firestorm of debate on the Internet and at popular music conferences among music critics.[29] Sanneh and others have thus identified rockism as a source of privilege, but the fact that they are able to stand outside its taken-for-granted assumptions and challenge its aesthetic claims may in itself be proof that rockism's hegemony is in decline. In Sanneh's portrait, "rockists" are holdovers from the Sixties and Seventies whose standards are increasingly out-of-touch with the new realities of the music (and, by extension, social) world. Rockism thus amounts to a form of nostalgia in the context of hypercommercialism, digital reproduction, and multiculturalism.

The sense that the struggle to preserve rock's aura and criteria of authenticity are inherently losing battles is evident in the fact that authenticity is so often defined negatively, as a lack of originality or sincerity on the part of sellouts, rip-offs, lip-synchers, and all-around poseurs. The continuing development of technologies of reproducibility and the expansion of commercial culture make it extremely unlikely that any form of rock music will ever again fulfill the criteria of authenticity established by Sixties rock or Seventies punk. If the newest incarnations of rock music continue to be held to these standards, it will become increasingly easy to dismiss them as "a routinized package of theatrical gestures, generally expressed in a blaze of musical clichés," as James Miller grumbles.[30] Miller compares rock's fate to that of jazz and other musical genres in that it "has many of the features of a fixed cultural form—a more or less fixed repertoire of sounds and styles and patterns of behavior."[31] If true, this means that rock has nowhere to go but back to its past, a development we began following in the previous chapter among retro bands who have made some great music but nonetheless embody the sense that it's all been said and done. Rock has become or will become a "fixed cultural form" like jazz or the blues in the sense that it is impossible to perform without the traditions of all dead generations weighing like a nightmare on the brains of the living, to paraphrase Marx.[32] In the future, rock will continue to make money in a host of different media, perhaps more money than ever, but as a cultural and artistic practice it will merely be a ghost of its former self.

And yet this sort of pessimistic view about the death of rock can really only be espoused by those who are far removed from their teen years and the experience of youth, who might still be avid listeners and fans but cannot possibly invest the music with the same meaning or emotion and have since moved on to different sources of identity in their adult years. If rock has a saving grace, it is its connection with young people, who are simply too ignorant of history to know it's been said and done before and might not care anyway, who experience it all as new and exciting because they need music to help get them through the emotional trauma of their youth. This was articulated to me during an interview with Rocket From the Crypt's saxophonist, Paul aka Apollo 9, when we were talking about how he would like his band to be remembered and the conversation drifted into why and how rock matters when you are young. "I heard [Paul] Westerberg talk about 'Sixteen Blue' and 'Unsatisfied,'" he said in reference to two ballads of youthful alienation penned by the front man for the Replacements for their celebrated 1984 album *Let It Be*, "and he admits it sounds totally cheesy, but it's like someone else understands. He has people come up and say, 'Hey, you changed my life in high school.' It sounds totally cheesy, but to be honest with you I would have freaked out if I didn't have the Clash and the Jam and the Replacements when I needed them. I would have lost my shit." He believed that this powerful identification on the part of young people guaranteed that rock will never die: "[Rock] definitely changes lives. The minute you want to give up on rock, somebody turns you on to a band or a song and it's like 'Exactly! I wrote that song when I was fourteen, I just never put it on paper and put it to music!'" "You're just about to start listening to jazz," the punk rock saxophonist said with a laugh, "and then someone turns you on to a great rock record. Yes! It's back!"[33]

As an example of rock's resiliency, in just the past 10 years or so it has made significant inroads—to many people's surprise—in the world of evangelical Christianity. In the summer of 2005 there were an estimated 35 Christian music festivals attended by more than 5,000 youths, a veritable explosion considering that there were only five such festivals as recently as the summer of 2000.[34] The largest of these, the Cornerstone Festival, which is held annually in Illinois with additional concerts in other parts of the country, features Christian variations of every conceivable subgenre of rock including hardcore punk, heavy metal, and rap. In the past decade, Christian bands such as Creed, P.O.D., Jars of Clay, MxPx, and As I Lay Dying have crossed over to achieve success in the larger markets for rock, alternative, and metal music. Evangelical Christianity has also made its presence felt in youthful forms of rebellion like skateboarding, tattooing, and body piercing. Such recent cultural trends have baffled many observers, but the point of intersection among religion, rock, and rebellion is the quest for authenticity. As the journalist Lauren Sandler wrote of her encounters with this new youth culture, "This was a Christianity I had never seen before, faith rebranded as a subculture for a country of angst-laden kids craving meaning and authenticity, a paradigm shift in the lives of disaffected American youth as formidable as the advent of the skateboard."[35] Not unlike their secular peers, these youths had come to the Church in retreat from the banality, superficiality, and excess of consumer capitalism: "With its hunger for an experience that feels gritty and true, this generation is sick of being treated like mindless consumers. Its broken record plays the same refrain from coast-to-coast: *it wants authenticity*. And often, authenticity takes the form of reckoning."[36]

A lot of academics, journalists, musicians, and fans have been talking about the death of rock for a long time now, but it periodically seems to recover or at least shake with a "death rattle," as the Lester Bangs character called it in the movie *Almost Famous*. Contrary to detractors like James Miller, who dismisses everything that followed the death of Elvis Presley and the birth of punk in 1977, we have examined the various histories of hardcore, metal, alternative, riot grrrl, and garage rock under the assumption that they have both artistic merit and sociopolitical meaning. But there can be no doubt that none of these have approximated the significance that was achieved during the Sixties, and so although it is an exaggeration to speak of rock's sudden death, it seems accurate to say it has undergone a long, drawn-out decline periodically interrupted by momentary gasps of revival. Perhaps the most rejuvenating trend in recent years has been the increasing presence of women in rock, in part because there has been so little precedent for women to reproduce and so they have been able to reinvent the genre in relatively fresh fashion. But even if rock is already dead or will soon die, there are contradictions in the socioeconomic system of contemporary capitalism that have the potential to spur new forms of youthful revolt and cultural innovation, and it is to these contradictions and possibilities that we will now turn.

The Shape of Punk to Come

Benjamin's diagnosis of the decline of the aura may have been premature, yet he did have the foresight to see that the aura and the criteria of authenticity are under constant siege from commodification and media technologies of reproduction and simulation, despite capital's best efforts to fabricate or preserve them. Benjamin thus anticipated one of the central conflicts and contradictions of our day, when the commodity form and media simulation are constantly undermining authenticity, originality, and our notions of the sacred at the very moment that capital is trying to package and sell them to consumers. We witnessed this dynamic at work in chapter 4, as advertisers tried to capitalize on the authenticity and subcultural capital of alternative culture but wound up liquidating their hip qualities in the process of bringing them to market. Consumers crave authenticity and anything sacred, and capital tries to invent and design something like an aura for its commodities; but processes of commodification and reproduction are inherently profane, and so consumers are destined to live in a state of perpetual disappointment. Of course, such disappointment is somewhat functional for the consumer culture, as capital continues to package its newest products or experiences as remedies for the boredom and alienation that capital itself has wrought. But it also guarantees that capitalism must exist in a constant crisis of legitimacy, for it destroys aura and authenticity at the same time that it tries to create them, and so its idolized stars and hallowed myths are continually threatened by the specter of instant obsolescence.

It is with these contradictions in mind that we must recall the revolutionary optimism that stirred Benjamin in writing that the function of art becomes based on political practice once criteria of authenticity are no longer applicable. Punk, after all, was born in celebration of the withering of rock's aura during the 1970s. Punk mocked the artistic pretensions epitomized by progressive rock, and it demystified the process of musical production in demonstrating that anyone could do it once they had seized the technological media. From the shocking juxtapositions in its sartorial style to the ransom note lettering in its flyers and fanzines to the "piss-take" deconstructions of its music, the original punk scene utilized montage for purposes of symbolic defilement in ways that likely would have received Benjamin's endorsement. What Benjamin could not have anticipated was how a new kind of halo would later be thrown around punk in the form of legends about its outrageous acts and larger-than-life

Walter Benjamin in 1927 (*left*). From *Walter Benjamin: An Aesthetic of Redemption*. Richard Wolin. New York: Columbia University Press, 1982.
Theodor W. Adorno at the piano in 1967 (*right*). From *Theodore W. Adorno: One Last Genius*. Detlev Claussen, translated by Rodney Livingstone. Cambridge: Belknap, 2008.

personalities, which are now glorified in an assortment of documentaries, photographs, oral histories, and repackaged musical collections designed to capitalize on people's hunger for the authenticity of the original. Ironically but perhaps predictably, the punk movement, whose stated intent was to kill idols and rock stars, has been absorbed into the very rock establishment that it opposed.

The aesthetic of appropriation, fragmentation, and juxtaposition that Benjamin championed can still be heard in a number of albums composed during the punk era and beyond, such as Wire's *Pink Flag* or the Minutemen's *Double Nickels on the Dime* or the Jon Spencer Blues Explosion's *Orange*. But in the present this style is more easily and more often realized in forms of sample-based hip hop that utilize digital media of reproduction. The cultural practice of disassembly and reassembly that Benjamin championed is alive today in the form of auteur DJs all over the world. The interlinking of sampling and new digital media will continue to reshape the music world and provoke crises in the music industry, and these changes seem to favor the various permutations of hip hop music. It will certainly still be possible to create and more easily distribute rock music through this media, but it remains to be seen how and to what extent rock can "matter" in this context without its sense of authenticity. Sample-based hip hop will have several technological and economic advances over rock music performed with instruments. The practice of sampling is also better equipped to absorb the beat and sounds of the global city and mix them into creative hybrids, much in the same way that Benjamin juxtaposed quotations and snippets of life he glimpsed in Paris for his unfinished *Arcades Project.*

It is easy to imagine Benjamin reincarnated as a kind of DJ or hip hop engineer, given not only his style of montage and urban sensibility but also his penchant for hashish and study of Jewish mysticism. I imagine him as someone like DJ Shadow, Danger Mouse, or a fourth Beastie Boy. Adorno, on the other hand, probably finds his counterpart in today's jaded hipsters and noise rock bands whose sonic forms of destruction are obliquely linked to sociopolitical dissent. Many of these noise groups are the cultural children and grandchildren of Sonic Youth, who started playing their experimental guitar noise alongside avant-garde composer Glenn Branca in 1981. As Adorno discovered brilliant innovation in Arnold Schoenberg's atonality, we might guess that his present-day counterpart would have a taste for noise that expresses chaos and confusion, and he would find more political substance in the way that bands destroy musical structure than in anything they might say in their lyrics. As Adorno indiscriminately despised the music churned out by the culture industry, so too our indie rock hipster is predisposed to reject almost everything you might hear on the radio and is immediately suspicious when any performer achieves commercial success.

In examining the Adorno-Benjamin debate with an eye to the future of music, we are returned to the dialectic between rhythm and noise introduced in the first chapter. The Adorno side of music and politics represents extraordinary innovations in noisemaking and an almost complete absence of rhythm. In terms of cultural politics, the implication is that noise is especially potent in destroying, defiling, and mocking all manifestations of structure, but it is missing the aspects of rhythm that prefigure alternate possibilities of time and space as well as relations between the individual and community. Rhythm is indispensable for imagining and creating new paces of time, new uses of space, new ways of experiencing the body through dance, and new methods of integrating producers and consumers. It is not a matter of choosing between rhythm and noise but rather of dialectically overcoming the opposition between them, for rhythm also needs noise to ensure that it cannot be smoothly absorbed into the formulaic and manipulative harmonies of the culture industry. Without a sense of rhythm, noise just creates more indie rockers who don't dance, just as Adorno believed that music should be an object of contemplation engaged with at a mental rather than physical level. Adorno looked at dancing in the modern age in the same way he looked at laughter and applause in commercial entertainment, as illusions of agency on the part of programmed audiences who exemplify the rote conformity of advanced industrial capitalism. Benjamin, in contrast, had written in favor of a "distracted" mode of perception among mass audiences, and he believed that the function of art should be a matter of "tactile appropriation," which he likened to architecture.[37]

One of the most innovative compositions of noise in recent years is the Refused's *The Shape of Punk to Come* (1998). The record title is named for Ornette Coleman's seminal avant-garde jazz album from 1959, *The Shape of Jazz to Come*, and the Refused do in fact meld jazz and many other musical genres into a sound that violently vacillates from soft and quiet to loud and screaming in the best traditions of hardcore punk. In fact, their signature song is called "New Noise," which begins musically by building anticipation until the singer suddenly shrieks, "Can I scream?" and then continues yelling: "We lack the motion / To move to the new beat." This is a song of noise that is bemoaning our collective lack of rhythm, our inability to move and to find a new beat. Midway through "New Noise," the Refused's singer is screaming, "We dance to all the wrong songs / We enjoy all the wrong moves," and then chanting "We're not . . . leading!" Indeed, the Refused, who formed in Sweden, took many ideas from the Situationist International and the May 1968 revolt in France. In the first song on the album, the Refused's front man Dennis Lyxzén protests, "Human life is not commodity, fake statistics, or make-believe!" But *The Shape of Punk to Come* is not simply an intellectual exercise in Marxist theory stamped on a hardcore soundtrack; it is a document of ferocious noisemaking that convincingly inserts its revolutionary ideas into the chaos and passion of the music. By the end of "New Noise," Lyxzén is screaming his head off in search of a revolution he can dance to: "THE NEW BEAT! THE NEW BEAT! THE NEW BEAT!"

The Shape of Punk to Come has the sound of punk being stretched to its limits of noise while revolutionary ideologies confront the limits of protest and refusal in lieu of a rhythm to accompany them. Lyxzén's vocals are strained to the point where the listener can hardly decipher the slogans he's shouting. So perhaps it was inevitable that the Refused should break up after releasing their masterwork, with Lyxzén moving on to form a new band, the (International) Noise Conspiracy, which was groovier and less noisy, drawing on rhythm and blues and 1960s garage bands as its influences. The (I)NC strikes a better balance between rhythm and noise and joy and dissent, most notably on their single "Capitalism Stole My Virginity," a more danceable and good-humored song that features the refrain, "We're all sluts / Cheap products / In someone else's notebook." While adopting a more retro sound and performing style, Lyxzén and the (I)NC also employ self-conscious irony about their own commodification and simulation of revolutionary rock 'n' roll, though without totally succumbing to cynicism or fatalism. In one song about all the broken promises of the twentieth century, including the commercialization of rock 'n' roll, Lyxzén sings, "But what did come of us? / A borrowed intellect and a stolen pose / Dismantling the power with the rules it sets / We're as real as it's gonna get." In short, it has become impossible to realize authenticity in the society of the spectacle, but we must still look for the contradictions in capitalism and exploit them rather than resign ourselves to ironic cynicism or the imagined purity of commercial independence.

The Future Is Unwritten

Following the debate and correspondence between Benjamin and Adorno in the 1930s and Adorno's condemnation of the culture industry in the 1940s, it seemed that Adorno's analysis had been realized in the popular culture of corporate entertainment, mass markets, and widespread conformity that endured through the 1950s and most of the 1960s. Indeed, I maintain that Adorno's analysis of the culture industry continues to be relevant for understanding global media conglomerates as they secure a tenuous kind of cultural hegemony over images of the United States that are broadcast through commercial entertainment all over the world. But in light of the social changes that began taking place since the late 1960s, I think it is Benjamin's analysis that now demands closer scrutiny as a guide to the possibilities for building a revolutionary culture. The counterculture that formed in the interplay between bohemian hippie culture and New Left politics was extinguished in the matter of a few years, but it opened new opportunities for linking music, popular culture, and social movements. This countercultural uprising invalidated the notion that

popular music and the culture industry simply serve as means of conformity and social reproduction, and it revealed the possibilities for people
to create an alternative culture by seizing the means of cultural (re)pro-
duction in the media of music, film, and art.

New criteria of authenticity were established for rock music after it became linked to the cultural discourses and standards of folk culture on the
one hand and the artistic vanguard on the other. An aura continues to hang
around this moment of the Sixties when rock was intertwined with social
and personal processes of transformation and innovation. The counteraesthetic of punk was articulated over the course of the 1970s as a repudiation
of the aura that rock continued trying to build after the Sixties had passed.
Punk effectively demystified rock by asserting that anyone could do it.
And yet punk did not sever the links with folk and art, but instead intensified them. Musicians and intermediaries who brought an avant-garde approach to punk imposed a new form of distinction between art and pop,
one that has situated the punk, postpunk, and indie rock of the past three
decades on the art side of the spectrum in opposition to "mainstream" or
"commercial" rock music. Whereas the pop art and art rock movements
of the 1960s sought to transcend this boundary, with art rock moving to
the center of popular music in the form of the Beatles, Bob Dylan, and
the psychedelic groups, punk and its various subcultural offspring have
sought refuge from popular music and embraced their marginal role relative to the mainstream. Punk, postpunk, and indie rock, picking up from
folk culture, have envisaged the notion of community among artists and
audiences in terms of "the scene," a localized and downscaled successor
to the vanquished ideal of Woodstock Nation. Folk notions of community
have reinforced the discourses of art and distinction with their distrust of
commerce and celebrity, but they have also constricted cultural innovation
when insisting on a uniformity of sound and style, which has frequently
alienated some of the more artistically inclined performers.

Benjamin believed that a revolutionary culture would emerge as the
aura of art and the criterion of authenticity dissipated with the development of technologies of reproduction. Historical events certainly did not
progress in the way Benjamin thought they might, but the possibilities
have indeed multiplied with the evolution of digital technology. Two writers associated with the Berklee College of Music have concluded that in
the future, "music will be like water: ubiquitous and free flowing."[38] As a
result, there will need to be a paradigm shift within the music industry
from the idea of "music as product to music as entertainment service."[39]

This change has been necessitated by the shift from analog to digital technologies that began with the introduction of compact discs in the early 1980s, as digital technologies allow for an infinite number of perfect reproductions that can be compressed into data files. The recording industry has engaged in a protracted legal battle against the consequences of these developments, but nevertheless a major change seems inevitable.

As of this writing, the future of the music industry is still being played out in social conflicts involving a wide assortment of interested parties, including global conglomerates, musicians, and consumers. It is clear, however, that digital technologies will continue to make it easier to produce, reproduce, and circulate music along with other forms of media in the making of subcultures that allow people to participate, create, and communicate. These developments provide many more opportunities to realize the culture that Benjamin envisioned in 1936 when he wrote that mechanical reproduction "permits the audience to take the position of the critic" and allows "readers to become writers," such that "the distinction between author and public is about to lose its basic character."[40] Digital technologies can significantly augment the localized production of music and media that constituted the punk, hardcore, thrash metal, and alternative and indie rock subcultures we have examined in the preceding chapters. Of course, this will depend on the exercise of human agency and imagination, as technology cannot create culture on its own.[41] Until the advent of digital technologies, musicians needed record labels to finance the costs of recording their music, to promote their music through contacts in radio, and to distribute their music into chain record stores and big box retailers. In recent years, however, software programs like Pro Tools and GarageBand have eliminated the need for a studio and significantly reduced the costs of recording, social networking Web sites like MySpace and Facebook have largely supplanted radio as media of promotion and exposure, and intermediate distribution channels are unnecessary when music files can be shared or bought over the Internet.[42]

While history has witnessed some significant alliances between musicians and social movements, from labor to civil rights to peace movements, the role of music in social change is limited in some respects. In the first place, music primarily expresses the language of affect and emotion; while these have been shown to play a crucial if mostly unappreciated role in social movements, the efforts to make music communicate literal political messages often end up awkward and contrived, and subordination to politics can stifle the creativity that makes music relevant.[43]

On a social and organizational level, the youthful and bohemian sensibilities that circulate within the music world are notoriously resistant to the discipline, commitment, and consensus required by social movements. Nonetheless, there are forces of social energy that are unique to music and youth culture that no one hoping to change their society can afford to ignore. The nucleus of these social energies is the ability to imagine a different mode of "everyday life" that demands a radical reorganization of society and yet transcends political issues in a more sweeping utopian vision.[44] The counterculture of the 1960s dramatized these possibilities even if it failed to explicitly articulate them. Punk, as we have seen, arose with the collapse of this Sixties vision, and yet there is also a utopian dream embedded in the do-it-yourself ethic that has yet to be realized.

Independent media produced and circulated through the new digital technologies can certainly play a pivotal role in forming an alternative forum that both facilitates communication about social issues neglected by mainstream media and allows social movements to organize. In a world where media employ the democratic rhetoric of "choice" but are in fact owned by only a handful of multinational conglomerates, the most subversive thing about punk may be that its methods of production give mavericks and heretics a chance to scream from the margins of popular culture. But its significance is also greater than that, for independent media can also serve as a kind of prefigurative politics, the model for a democratic culture based on creative work and cooperative participation. Prefigurative politics are embedded in the social practices we have identified in rhythm, where new ways of being can be imagined and momentarily enacted in the libidinal ties forged among participants in a festive environment.

As Benjamin would have foreseen, a revolutionary culture can come into being only after the criterion of authenticity has been discarded. The Adornoesque desire to remain pure of the corrupting influence of commerce and the culture industry is increasingly impossible to achieve, as we witnessed in chapter 4. In the place of authenticity, political criteria would identify the revolutionary function of art in the processes that enable cultural producers to create, participate, and communicate, regardless of the commodity form that culture inevitably takes. A new kind of folk culture can emerge in the digital age, but it will have to be one that allows for considerable experimentation and innovation within a democratic context, thus abandoning the traditional notion that locates the authenticity of folk in obedience to a singular sound and style. With the death of the aura that once surrounded art and was later attached to rock, we may find a new culture being born.

Notes

CHAPTER 1

1. Naomi Klein, *The Shock Doctrine: The Rise of Disaster Capitalism* (New York: Metropolitan Books, 2007), p. 7.

2. Legs McNeil and Gillian McCain, *Please Kill Me: The Uncensored Oral History of Punk* (New York: Penguin Books, 1996), p. 204.

3. Hell has repeatedly insisted that "Blank Generation" was not a nihilistic song. Instead, he intended the "blank" to refer to the sense of possibility arising from a lack of definition. In the social context of the 1970s, however, the "blank" was more commonly interpreted as an anthemic reference to the vacancy and inanity of posthippie youth. Following that understanding, the Sex Pistols' "Pretty Vacant" was meant to be an English equivalent of "Blank Generation."

4. McNeil and McCain, *Please Kill Me*; Jon Savage, *England's Dreaming: Anarchy, Sex Pistols, Punk Rock, and Beyond* (New York: St. Martin's Griffin, 1993); Clinton Heylin, *Babylon's Burning: From Punk to Grunge* (New York: Canongate, 2007).

5. William Tabb, *The Long Default: New York City and the Urban Fiscal Crisis* (New York: Monthly Review Press, 1982); Joshua B. Freeman, *Working-Class New York: Life and Labor Since World War II* (New York: New Press, 2000), ch. 15.

6. Klein, *The Shock Doctrine*.

7. Quoted in Tabb, *The Long Default*, p. 28. Simon later served as president of the John M. Olin Foundation, a conservative think tank that would play a key role in shifting American political discourse to the right, particularly on economic issues. In one of his books, Simon wrote, "The capitalist miracle occurred in the United States, the politically freest nation in the world, precisely because this explosion of wealth is uniquely a result of *individual liberty*. That is the true defense of capitalism. That is what most people do not understand—and that is what deserves to be shouted from the rooftops" (William Simon, *A Time for Truth* [New York: Reader's Digest Press, 1978], p. 25, italics in original).

8. Freeman, *Working-Class New York*, p. 256.

9. Jeff Chang, *Can't Stop, Won't Stop: A History of the Hip-Hop Generation* (New York: St. Martin's Press, 2005), pp. 10–17; Tricia Rose, *Black Noise: Rap*

Music and Black Culture in Contemporary America (Hanover, NH: Wesleyan University Press, 1994), pp. 27–34.

10. Chang, *Can't Stop, Won't Stop*, ch. 4; Rose, *Black Noise*, ch. 2; Murray Forman and Mark Anthony Neal, eds., *That's the Joint! The Hip-Hop Studies Reader* (New York: Routledge, 2004), pt. 1; Nelson George, *Hip Hop America* (New York: Penguin Books, 1999), ch. 1 and 2.

11. David Harvey, *A Brief History of Neoliberalism* (New York: Oxford University Press, 2005); Klein, *The Shock Doctrine*; Thomas Frank, *One Market Under God: Extreme Capitalism, Market Populism, and the End of Economic Democracy* (New York: Doubleday, 2000).

12. Harvey, *A Brief History of Neoliberalism*, p. 48.

13. Zygmunt Bauman, *Liquid Modernity* (Malden, MA: Blackwell, 2000); Zygmunt Bauman, *Liquid Life* (Malden, MA: Polity Press, 2005); Richard Sennett, *The Corrosion of Character: The Personal Consequences of Work in the New Capitalism* (New York: Norton, 1998); Richard Sennett, *The Culture of the New Capitalism* (New Haven, CT: Yale University Press, 2006).

14. Theodor Roszak, *The Making of a Counterculture* (New York: Anchor Books, 1969).

15. Those interested in these subcultures should consult: Sarah Thornton, *Club Cultures: Music, Media, and Subcultural Capital* (Hanover, NH: Wesleyan University Press, 1996); Steve Redhead, Derek Wynne, and Justin O'Connor, eds., *The Clubcultures Reader: Readings in Popular Cultural Studies* (Malden, MA: Blackwell, 1997); Simon Reynolds, *Generation Ecstasy: Into the World of Techno and Rave Culture* (New York: Routledge, 1999); Rebecca G. Adams and Robert Sardiello, eds., *Deadhead Social Science: You Ain't Gonna Learn What You Don't Want to Know* (Walnut Creek, CA: AltaMira Press, 2000); Paul Hodkinson, *Goth: Identity, Style, and Subculture* (New York: Berg, 2002); David Muggleton, *Inside Subculture: The Postmodern Meaning of Style* (New York: Berg, 2002); Andy Greenwald, *Nothing Feels Good: Punk Rock, Teenagers, and Emo* (New York: St. Martin's Griffin, 2003); David Muggleton and Rupert Weinzierl, eds., *The Postsubcultures Reader* (New York: Berg, 2004); Andy Bennett and Keith Kahn-Harris, eds., *After Subculture: Critical Studies in Contemporary Youth Culture* (New York: Palgrave Macmillan, 2004); Simon Reynolds, *Rip It Up and Start Again: Postpunk, 1978–84* (New York: Penguin Books, 2006); Lauren M.E. Goodlad and Michael Bibby, eds., *Goth: Undead Subculture* (Durham, NC: Duke University Press, 2007).

16. Rose, *Black Noise*; George, *Hip Hop America*; Tony Mitchell, ed., *Global Noise: Rap and Hip-Hop Outside the USA* (Hanover, NH: Wesleyan University Press, 2001); Murray Forman, *The 'Hood Comes First: Race, Space, and Place in Rap and Hip-Hop* (Hanover, NH: Wesleyan University Press, 2002); Bakari Kitwana, *The Hip Hop Generation: Young Blacks and the Crisis in African American Culture* (New York: Basic Civitas Books, 2003); Forman and Neal, *That's The Joint!*; Imani Perry, *Prophets of the Hood: Politics and Poetics in Hip Hop* (Durham,

NC: Duke University Press, 2004); Gwendolyn Pough, *Check It While I Wreck It: Black Womanhood, Hip-Hop Culture, and the Public Sphere* (Boston: Northeastern University Press, 2004); Todd Boyd, *The New H.N.I.C: The Death of Civil Rights and the Reign of Hip Hop* (New York: New York University Press, 2004); Eithne Quinn, *Nuthin' But a "G" Thang: The Culture and Commerce of Gangsta Rap* (New York: Columbia University Press, 2005); Chang, *Can't Stop, Won't Stop*; S. Craig Watkins, *Hip Hop Matters: Politics, Pop Culture, and the Struggle for the Soul of a Movement* (Boston: Beacon Press, 2006); William Jelani Cobb, *To the Break of Dawn: A Freestyle on the Hip Hop Aesthetic* (New York: New York University Press, 2007); T. Denean Sharpley-Whiting, *Pimps Up, Ho's Down: Hip Hop's Hold on Young Black Women* (New York: New York University Press, 2007).

17. Martin Jay, *Marxism and Totality: The Adventures of a Concept from Lukács to Habermas* (Berkeley and Los Angeles: University of California Press, 1984); Perry Anderson, *Considerations on Western Marxism* (London: NLB, 1976).

18. Raymond Williams, "Base and Superstructure in Marxist Cultural Theory," in *The Raymond Williams Reader*, ed. John Higgins (Malden, MA: Blackwell, 2001), p. 165.

19. David Harvey, *The Condition of Postmodernity: An Enquiry into the Origins of Cultural Change* (Cambridge, MA: Blackwell, 1989); Fredric Jameson, *Postmodernism, or, The Cultural Logic of Late Capitalism* (Durham, NC: Duke University Press, 1991). Also see Scott Lash, *Sociology of Postmodernism* (New York: Routledge, 1990); David Ashley, *History Without a Subject: The Postmodern Condition* (Boulder, CO: Westview Press, 1997); Robert Dunn, *Identity Crises: A Social Critique of Postmodernity* (Minneapolis: University of Minnesota Press, 1998); Perry Anderson, *The Origins of Postmodernity* (New York: Verso, 1998).

20. Jameson, *Postmodernism*, pp. 136–61.

21. Todd Gitlin, "'We Build Excitement,'" in *Watching Television* (New York: Pantheon, 1986); Lawrence Grossberg, "The Indifference of Television, or, Mapping TV's Popular (Affective) Economy," in *Dancing in Spite of Myself* (Durham, NC: Duke University Press, 1999), pp. 125–44.

22. The Reagan films were *Murder in the Air, Secret Service of the Air, Smashing the Money Ring*, and *Code of the Secret Service*. Michael Rogin, *Ronald Reagan, the Movie, and Other Episodes in Political Demonology* (Berkeley and Los Angeles: University of California Press, 1988); Haynes Johnson, *Sleepwalking Through History: America in the Reagan Years* (New York: Norton, 1991).

23. Sharon Zukin, *Loft Living: Culture and Capital in Urban Change* (Baltimore: Johns Hopkins Press, 1992); Elizabeth Currid, *The Warhol Economy: How Fashion, Art, and Music Drive New York City* (Princeton, NJ: Princeton University Press, 2007).

24. Richard Gendron, *Between Montmartre and the Mudd Club: Popular Music and the Avant-Garde* (Chicago: University of Chicago Press, 2002), ch. 11–13.

25. Jameson, *Postmodernism*, p. 15.

26. Todd Gitlin, "Postmodernism: Roots and Politics," *Dissent*, vol. 36, Winter 1989, p. 106. Also see Todd Gitlin, *Media Unlimited: How the Torrent of Images and Sounds Overwhelms Our Lives* (New York: Metropolitan Books, 2001), pp. 150–53.

27. Lawrence Grossberg, *We Gotta Get Out of This Place: Popular Conservatism and Postmodern Culture* (New York: Routledge, 1992), p. 222.

28. Thomas Frank and Matt Weiland, eds., *Commodify Your Dissent: Salvos from the Baffler* (New York: Norton, 1997); Thomas Frank, *The Conquest of Cool: Business Culture, Counterculture, and the Rise of Hip Consumerism* (Chicago: University of Chicago Press, 1997).

29. Barry Bluestone and Bennett Harrison, *The Deindustrialization of America: Plant Closings, Community Abandonment, and the Dismantling of Basic Industry* (New York: Basic Books, 1982), p. 26.

30. Robert H. Frank, *Falling Behind: How Rising Inequality Harms the Middle Class* (Berkeley and Los Angeles: University of California Press, 2007), pp. 6–12.

31. Juliet Schor, *The Overspent American: Upscaling, Downshifting, and the New Consumer* (New York: Basic Books, 1998), p. 15.

32. Frank, *Falling Behind*.

33. Jean Twenge, *Generation Me: Why Today's Young Americans Are More Confident, Assertive, Entitled—and More Miserable Than Ever Before* (New York: Free Press, 2006).

34. On the "all-or-nothing" society, see David Callahan, *The Cheating Culture: Why More Americans Are Doing Wrong to Get Ahead* (Orlando: Harcourt, 2004). Also see Robert H. Frank and Phillip Cook, *The Winner-Take-All Society: Why the Few at the Top Get So Much More Than the Rest of Us* (New York: Free Press, 1995); Charles Derber, *The Wilding of America: Money, Mayhem, and the New American Dream*, 3d ed. (New York: Worth, 2004).

35. Karl Marx and Friedrich Engels, *Manifesto of the Communist Party*, in *The Marx-Engels Reader*, ed. Robert Tucker (New York: Norton, 1978), p. 475.

36. Raymond Williams, *Marxism and Literature* (Oxford: Oxford University Press, 1977), p. 132.

37. See Ron Eyerman and Andrew Jamison, *Music and Social Movements: Mobilizing Traditions in the Twentieth Century* (New York: Cambridge University Press, 1998), ch. 7.

38. Roland Barthes, "The Grain of the Voice," in *Image/Music/Text*, ed. and trans. Stephen Heath (New York: Hill and Wang, 1977), pp. 179–89. Also see Simon Frith, *Performing Rites: On the Value of Popular Music* (Cambridge, MA: Harvard University Press, 1996), ch. 9.

39. Jacques Attali, *Noise: The Political Economy of Music*, trans. Brian Massumi (Minneapolis: University of Minnesota Press, 1985); also see Theodor Gracyk, *Rhythm and Noise: An Aesthetics of Rock* (Durham, NC: Duke University Press, 1999).

40. Attali, *Noise*, p. 11.

41. Ibid.

42. Henri Lefebvre, *Critique of Everyday Life*, vol. 3, *From Modernity to Modernism: Towards a Metaphilosophy of Daily Life*, trans. Gregory Elliot (New York: Verso, 2005), p. 130. Also see Henri Lefebvre, *Rhythmanalysis: Space, Time, and Everyday Life*, trans. Stuart Elden and Gerald Moore (New York: Continuum International, 2004).

43. Lefebvre, *Critique of Everyday Life*, vol. 3, p. 135. Also see M.M. Bakhtin, *Rabelais and his World*, trans. Helene Oswolsky (Cambridge, MA: MIT Press, 1968); Peter Stallybrass and Allon White, *The Politics and Poetics of Transgression* (Ithaca, NY: Cornell University Press, 1986); Barbara Ehrenreich, *Dancing in the Streets: A History of Collective Joy* (New York: Metropolitan Books, 2007).

44. Hank Shocklee, quoted in Mark Dery, "Public Enemy Confrontation," in Forman and Neal, *That's the Joint!*, p. 418.

45. Timothy White, "A Man Out of Time Beats the Clock," *Musician Magazine*, vol. 60, October 1983, p. 52.

46. On the musicology of popular music, see Susan McClary and Robert Walser, "Start Making Sense! Musicology Wrestles with Rock," in Simon Frith and Andrew Goodwin, eds., *On Record: Rock, Pop, and the Written Word* (New York: Pantheon Books, 1990), pp. 277–92; Susan McClary, *Feminine Endings: Music, Gender, and Sexuality* (Minneapolis: University of Minnesota Press, 1991); Robert Walser, *Running with the Devil: Power, Gender, and Madness in Heavy Metal Music* (Hanover, NH: Wesleyan University Press, 1993); Harris Berger, *Metal, Rock, and Jazz: Perception and the Phenomenology of Musical Experience* (Hanover, NH: University of New England Press, 1999); Gracyk, *Rhythm and Noise*; Susan Fast, *In the Houses of the Holy: Led Zeppelin and the Power of Rock Music* (New York: Oxford University Press, 2001); Richard Middleton, *Voicing the Popular: On the Subjects of Popular Music* (New York: Routledge, 2006); Glenn Pilsbury, *Damage Incorporated: Metallica and the Production of Musical Identity* (New York: Routledge, 2006).

47. Karl Mannheim, "The Problem of Generations," in *Essays on the Sociology of Knowledge*, ed. Paul Kecskemeti (London: Routledge and Kegan Paul, 1952), pp. 351–95. Mannheim's notion of generations is also usefully employed in Rebecca Klatch, *A Generation Divided: The New Left, the New Right, and the 1960s* (Berkeley and Los Angeles: University of California Press, 1999).

48. Erik Erickson, *Identity, Youth, and Crisis* (New York: Norton, 1968); Kenneth Keniston, *Youth and Dissent* (New York: Harcourt Brace Janovich, 1971).

49. Neil Howe and William Strauss, *13th Gen: Abort, Retry, Ignore, Fail?* (New York: Vintage, 1993); Neil Howe and William Strauss, *Millennials Rising: The Next Great Generation* (New York: Vintage, 2000).

50. Fredric M. Thrasher, *The Gang* (Chicago: University of Chicago Press, 1927); Paul G. Cressey, *The Taxi-Dance Hall* (New York: Greenwood Press, 1932);

Albert K. Cohen, *Delinquent Boys: The Culture of the Gang* (New York: Free Press, 1955); Howard S. Becker, *Outsiders: Studies in the Sociology of Deviance*, rev. ed. (New York: Free Press, 1973). Also see: Michael Brake, *Comparative Youth Culture: The Sociology of Youth Culture and Youth Subcultures in America, Britain, and Canada* (New York: Routledge, 1985), ch. 2; Sarah Thornton, "Introduction to Part One," in Ken Gelder and Sarah Thornton, eds., *The Subcultures Reader* (New York: Routledge, 1997), pp. 11–15.

51. Stuart Hall and Tony Jefferson, eds., *Resistance Through Rituals: Youth Subcultures in Post-war Britain* (New York: Routledge, 1975); Paul Willis, *Profane Culture* (London: Routledge and Kegan Paul, 1978); Dick Hebdige, *Subculture: The Meaning of Style* (New York: Routledge, 1979); Phil Cohen, "Subcultural Conflict and Subcultural Community," in Gelder and Thornton, *The Subcultures Reader*, pp. 90–100; Angela McRobbie and Jenny Garber, "Girls and Subcultures," in Gelder and Thornton, *The Subcultures Reader*, pp. 112–20; Angela McRobbie, ed., *Zoot Suits and Second-Hand Dresses: An Anthology of Fashion and Music* (London: Macmillan, 1991).

52. Cohen, "Subcultural Conflict and Subcultural Community," p. 95. Also see Phil Cohen, *On the Youth Question* (Durham, NC: Duke University Press, 1999).

53. Hebdige, *Subculture*, p. 90.

54. Ted Polhemus, "In the Supermarket of Style," in Redhead, Wynne, and O'Connor, *The Clubcultures Reader*, pp. 130–33; Andy Bennett "Subcultures or Neo-tribes? Rethinking the Relationship Between Youth, Style, and Musical Taste," *Sociology*, vol. 33., no. 3, 1999, pp. 599–617; Muggleton, *Inside Subculture*; Muggleton and Weinzierl, *The Post-subcultures Reader*; Bennett and Kahn-Harris, *After Subculture*; for a more ambivalent response, see Hodkinson, *Goth*.

55. Among the social theories used in support in these claims are Michel Maffesoli, *The Time of the Tribes* (London: Sage Publications, 1996); and Bauman, *Liquid Modernity*.

56. I borrow the terms local, translocal, and virtual from Andy Bennett and Richard Peterson, eds., *Music Scenes: Local, Translocal, Virtual* (Nashville, TN: Vanderbilt University Press, 2005). The editors of this volume use "scene" as a replacement for the concept of subculture; my use of scene is restricted to localized forms, whereas I discuss the translocal and virtual forms as subcultures.

57. On scenes, see Will Straw, "Systems of Articulation, Logics of Change: Communities and Scenes in Popular Music," *Cultural Studies*, vol. 5, no. 3, 1991, pp. 368–88; Barry Shank, *Dissonant Identities: The Rock 'n' Roll Scene in Austin, Texas* (Hanover, NH: Wesleyan University Press, 1994); Sara Cohen, *Rock Culture in Liverpool: Popular Music in the Making* (New York: Oxford University Press, 1991); Ruth Finnegan, *The Hidden Musicians: Music-Making in an English Town* (Hanover, NH: Wesleyan University Press, 2007); Bennett and Peterson, *Music Scenes*; Holly Kruse, *Site and Sound: Understanding Independent Music Scenes*

(New York: P. Lang, 2003); Wendy Fonarow, *Empire of Dirt: The Aesthetics and Rituals of British Indie Music* (Hanover, NH: Wesleyan University Press, 2006).

58. Howard S. Becker, *Art Worlds* (Berkeley and Los Angeles: University of California Press, 1982).

59. David Riesman, "Listening to Popular Music," in Frith and Goodwin, *On Record*, p. 8.

60. Ibid., p. 9.

61. Pierre Bourdieu, *Distinction: A Social Critique of the Judgment of Taste*, trans. Richard Nice (Cambridge, MA: Harvard University Press, 1984); Pierre Bourdieu, *The Field of Cultural Production: Essays on Art and Literature* (New York: Columbia University Press, 1993); Thornton, *Club Cultures*.

62. With regard to music, this anti–mass culture argument has been challenged by Simon Frith, *Sound Effects: Youth, Leisure, and the Politics of Rock 'n' Roll* (New York: Pantheon Books, 1981). Also see: Angela McRobbie, "Second-Hand Dresses and the Role of the Ragmarket," in *Postmodernism and Popular Culture* (New York: Routledge, 1994), pp. 135–54; Sarah Thornton, "Moral Panic, the Media, and British Rave Culture," in Andrew Ross and Tricia Rose, eds., *Microphone Fiends: Youth Culture and Youth Music* (New York: Routledge, 1994), pp. 176–92.

63. Riesman, "Listening to Popular Music," p. 10

64. Eric Lott, *Love and Theft: Blackface Minstrelsy and the American Working Class* (New York: Oxford University Press, 1993); John Leland, *Hip: The History* (New York: Ecco, 2004).

65. McRobbie and Garber, "Girls and Subcultures"; Angela McRobbie, *Feminism and Youth Culture: From Jackie to Just Seventeen* (London: Macmillan, 1991).

66. Tania Modleski, "Femininity as Mas(s)querade: A Feminist Approach to Mass Culture," in Colin McCabe, ed., *High Theory/Low Culture: Analyzing Popular Television* (Manchester, U.K.: Manchester University Press, 1986); Sarah Thornton, "Understanding Hipness: 'Subcultural Capital' as Feminist Tool," in Andy Bennett, Barry Shank, and Jayson Toynbee, eds., *The Popular Music Studies Reader* (New York: Routledge, 2006), pp. 99–105.

67. The exceptions that do theorize the masculinity of rock music and subcultures are: Simon Frith and Angela McRobbie, "Rock and Sexuality," in Frith and Goodwin, *On Record*, pp. 371–89; Walser, *Running with the Devil*; Simon Reynolds and Joy Press, *The Sex Revolts: Gender, Rebellion, and Rock 'n' Roll* (Cambridge, MA: Harvard University Press, 1995); Mimi Schippers, *Rockin' Out of the Box: Gender Maneuvering in Alternative Hard Rock* (New Brunswick, NJ: Rutgers University Press, 2002); Matthew Bannister, *White Boys, White Noise: Masculinities and 1980s Indie Guitar Rock* (Burlington, VT: Ashgate, 2006).

68. One of the strongest criticisms of the lack of ethnographic research in the Birmingham School, especially in Hebdige's work, comes from Muggleton,

Inside Subculture (in fact, Muggleton himself has conducted some important research on a variety of subcultures). Other key ethnographies of subcultures include: Shank, *Dissonant Identities*; Lorraine Leblanc, *Pretty in Punk: Girls' Resistance in a Boys' Subculture* (New Brunswick, NJ: Rutgers University Press, 1999); Hodkinson, *Goth*; Ross Haenfler, *Straight Edge: Clean-Living Youth, Hardcore Punk, and Social Change* (New Brunswick, NJ: Rutgers University Press, 2006); Fonarow, *Empire of Dirt*; Robert Wood, *Straightedge Youth: Complexity and Contradictions of a Subculture* (Syracuse, NY: Syracuse University Press, 2006).

69. See Ryan Moore, "Friends Don't Let Friends Listen to Corporate Rock: Punk as Field of Cultural Production," *Journal of Contemporary Ethnography*, vol. 36, no. 4, August 2007, pp. 438–74.

70. McNeil and McCain, *Please Kill Me*; Savage, *England's Dreaming*; Marc Spitz and Brendan Mullen, *We Got the Neutron Bomb: The Untold Story of L.A. Punk* (New York: Three Rivers Press, 2001); Steven Blush, *American Hardcore: A Tribal History* (Los Angeles: Feral House, 2001); Mark Andersen and Mark Jenkins, *Dance of Days: Two Decades of Punk in the Nation's Capital* (New York: Akashic Books, 2003); David Konow, *Bang Your Head: The Rise and Fall of Heavy Metal* (New York: Three Rivers Press, 2002); Ian Christie, *Sound of the Beast: The Complete Headbanging History of Heavy Metal* (New York: HarperCollins, 2003); Gina Arnold, *Route 666: On the Road to Nirvana* (New York: St. Martin's Press, 1993); Michael Azerrad, *Come as You Are: The Story of Nirvana* (New York: Doubleday, 1994); Michael Azerrad, *Our Band Could Be Your Life: Scenes from the American Indie Underground, 1981–1991* (New York: Little, Brown, 2001).

CHAPTER 2

1. Greil Marcus, *Ranters and Crowd Pleasers: Punk in Pop Music, 1977–92* (New York: Anchor Books, 1993), p. 132.

2. Lisa McGirr, *Suburban Warriors: The Origins of the New American Right* (Princeton, NJ: Princeton University Press, 2001).

3. Greil Marcus, *Lipstick Traces: A Secret History of the Twentieth Century* (Cambridge, MA: Harvard University Press, 1989), p. 6.

4. Savage, *England's Dreaming*, p. 541.

5. Hebdige, *Subculture*, p. 108.

6. Lester Bangs, *Psychotic Reactions and Carburetor Dung: Literature as Rock 'n' Roll, Rock 'n' Roll as Literature*, ed. Greil Marcus (New York: Anchor Books, 1988), p. 275

7. Susan Douglas, *Where the Girls Are: Growing Up Female with the Mass Media* (New York: Times Books, 1995); Peter Braunstein, "Forever Young: Insurgent Youth and the Sixties Culture of Rejuvenation," in Peter Braunstein and Michael W. Doyle, eds., *Imagine Nation: The American Counterculture of the 1960s and '70s* (New York: Routledge, 2002), pp. 243–74.

8. Roszak, *The Making of a Counterculture*, p. xix.

9. Students for a Democratic Society, "The Port Huron Statement," in Alexander Bloom and Wini Breines, eds., *"Takin' It to the Streets": A Sixties Reader* (New York, Oxford University Press, 1995), p. 65.

10. Ibid, p. 61.

11. Kenneth Keniston, *Young Radicals: Notes on Committed Youth* (New York: Harcourt, Brace, and World, 1968), p. 283.

12. Timothy Miller, *The Hippies and American Values* (Knoxville: University of Tennessee Press, 1991); David Farber, "Intoxicated State/Illegal Nation: Drugs in the Sixties Counterculture," in Braunstein and Boyle, *Imagine Nation*, pp. 17–40.

13. Marshall Berman, "Sympathy for the Devil," *American Review*, vol. 19, August 1974, p. 68.

14. On cultural intermediaries, see Mike Featherstone, *Consumer Culture and Postmodernism* (Thousand Oaks, CA: Sage Publications, 1992), pp. 43–48; Bourdieu, *Distinction*.

15. Steve Waksman, *Instruments of Desire: The Electric Guitar and the Shaping of Musical Experience* (Cambridge, MA: Harvard University Press, 1999).

16. Featherstone, *Consumer Culture and Postmodernism*, p. 44.

17. Todd Gitlin, *The Whole World Is Watching: Mass Media in the Making and Unmaking of the New Left* (Berkeley and Los Angeles: University of California Press, 1980); Todd Gitlin, *The Sixties: Years of Hope, Days of Rage* (New York: Bantam Books, 1987); Terry H. Anderson, *The Movement and the Sixties* (New York: Oxford University Press, 1995).

18. Marcus, *Ranters and Crowd Pleasers*, p. 9.

19. Ibid.

20. Ibid, p. 10.

21. Bangs, *Psychotic Reactions and Carburetor Dung*, p. 36.

22. Ibid, p. 34.

23. Ibid, p. 32.

24. Gendron, *Between Montmartre and the Mudd Club*.

25. Quoted in ibid., p. 232.

26. Gendron, *Between Monmartre and the Mudd Club*, pp. 233–36; also see Jim DeRogatis, *Let It Blurt: The Life and Times of Lester Bangs, America's Greatest Rock Critic* (New York: Broadway Books, 2000).

27. Bangs, *Psychotic Reactions and Carburetor Dung*, p. 44.

28. Ibid.

29. Ellen Willis, *Beginning to See the Light: Pieces of a Decade* (New York: Knopf, 1981), p. 115.

30. Heylin, *Babylon's Burning*.

31. Savage, *England's Dreaming*, pp. 87–88.

32. Quoted in Savage, *England's Dreaming*, pp. 165–66.

33. Simon Frith and Howard Horne, *Art Into Pop* (London: Metheun, 1988).

34. Simon Frith, "Formalism, Realism, and Leisure: The Case of Punk," in Gelder and Thornton, *The Subcultures Reader*, p. 163.

35. David Widgery, *Beating Time: Riot 'n' Race 'n' Rock 'n' Roll* (London: Chatto and Windus, 1986); Paul Gilroy, *"There Ain't No Black in the Union Jack": The Cultural Politics of Race and Nation* (Chicago: University of Chicago Press, 1991), pp. 120–35; Simon Frith and John Street, "Rock Against Racism and Red Wedge," in Reebee Garofalo, ed., *Rockin' the Boat: Mass Music and Mass Movements* (Boston: South End Press, 1992), pp. 55–66; Ashley Dawson, "Love Music, Hate Racism: The Cultural Politics of the Rock Against Racism Campaigns, 1976–1981," *Postmodern Culture*, vol. 16, no. 1, September 2005, n.p.

36. Frith, "Formalism, Realism, and Leisure," p. 164.

37. Reynolds, *Rip It Up and Start Again*.

38. Quoted in Savage, *England's Dreaming*, p. 329.

39. Claude Lévi-Strauss, *The Savage Mind*, trans. John Weightman and Doreen Weightman (Chicago: University of Chicago Press, 1966), pp. 16–36; also see Hebdige, *Subculture*.

40. Reynolds, *Rip It Up and Start Again*, ch. 2; David Hesmondhalgh, "Post-punk's Attempts to Democratise the Music Industry: The Success and Failure of Rough Trade," *Popular Music*, vol. 16, no. 3, 1988, pp. 255–74.

41. On Los Angeles and the postmodern condition, see: Edward W. Soja, *Postmodern Geographies: The Reassertion of Space in Critical Social Theory* (New York: Verso, 1989); Rob Kling, Spencer Olin, and Mark Poster, eds., *Postsuburban California: The Transformation of Orange County Since World War II* (Berkeley and Los Angeles: University of California Press, 1991); Mike Davis, *City of Quartz: Excavating the Future in Los Angeles* (New York: Vintage Books, 1992).

42. Spitz and Mullen, *We Got the Neutron Bomb*; Barney Hoskyns, *Waiting for the Sun: Strange Days, Weird Scenes, and the Sound of Los Angeles* (New York: St. Martin's Press, 1996), ch. 8; Peter Belsito and Bob Davis, *Hardcore California: A History of Punk and New Wave* (Berkeley, CA: Last Gasp of San Francisco, 1983).

43. Quoted in Savage, *England's Dreaming*, p. 437.

44. James Stark, *Punk '77: An Inside Look at the San Francisco Rock 'n' Roll Scene* (San Francisco: RE/Search, 2006); Belsito and Davis, *Hardcore California*.

45. Quoted in Spitz and Mullen, *We Got the Neutron Bomb*, p. 199.

46. Bakhtin, *Rabelais and His World*; Stallybrass and White, *The Politics and Poetics of Transgression*.

47. See Steven Best and Douglas Kellner, "Beavis and Butt-Head: No Future for Postmodern Youth," in Jonathon S. Epstein, ed., *Youth Culture: Identity in a Postmodern World* (Malden, MA: Blackwell), pp. 74–99; Chris Turner, *Planet Simpson: How a Cartoon Masterpiece Defined a Generation* (Cambridge, MA: Da Capo Press, 2004); Judith Kegan Gardiner, "*South Park*, Blue Men, Anality, and

Market Masculinity," in Mark Hussey, ed., *Masculinities: Interdisciplinary Readings* (Upper Saddle River, NJ: Prentice Hall, 2003), pp. 100–115.

48. Gardiner, "*South Park*," p. 101.

49. Ibid, p. 106.

50. Davis, *City of Quartz*, p. 156.

51. *Flipside: The Ten-Year Anniversary Issue* (Whittier, CA: Flipside, 1987), p. 125.

52. Interview with the author, January 16, 1998.

53. Blush, *American Hardcore*.

54. Benedict Anderson, *Imagined Communities: Reflections on the Origin and Spread of Nationalism* (New York: Verso, 1991).

55. Ross Haenfler, "Manhood in Contradiction: The Two Faces of Straight Edge," *Men and Masculinities*, vol. 7, no. 1, July 2004, pp. 77–99.

56. Noah Levine, *Dharma Punx: A Memoir* (New York: HarperSanFrancisco, 2003), p. 71.

57. See Benjamin Barber, *Jihad vs. McWorld* (New York: Times Books, 1995).

58. Haenfler, "Manhood in Contradiction." On the history of this construction of masculinity, see Michael S. Kimmel, *Manhood in America: A Cultural History* (New York: Free Press, 1996); Klaus Theweleit, *Male Fantasies*, vol. 1, *Women, Floods, Bodies, History*, trans. Steven Conway (Minneapolis: University of Minnesota Press, 1987).

59. Kathryn Joan Fox, "Real Punks and Pretenders: The Social Organization of a Counterculture," *Journal of Contemporary Ethnography*, vol. 16, October 1987, pp. 344–70.

60. Thornton, *Club Cultures*.

61. The classic text of the mass culture critique is Bernard Rosenberg and David Manning White, eds., *Mass Culture: The Popular Arts in America* (Glencoe, IL: Free Press, 1957). Also see Herbert Gans, *Popular Culture and High Culture: An Analysis and Evaluation of Taste* (New York: Basic Books, 1974); Andrew Ross, *No Respect: Intellectuals and Popular Culture* (New York: Routledge, 1989).

62. Bourdieu, *The Field of Cultural Production*.

63. Belsito and Davis, *Hardcore California*.

64. Brian Edge, ed., *924 Gilman: The Story So Far* (San Francisco: Maximumrocknroll, 2004).

65. Barbara Epstein, *Political Protest and Cultural Revolution: Nonviolent Direct Action in the 1970s and 1980s* (Berkeley and Los Angeles: University of California Press, 1991).

66. Jeff Goldthorpe, "Intoxicated Culture: Punk Symbolism and Punk Protest," *Socialist Review*, vol. 22, no. 2, 1992, pp. 50–52.

67. Epstein, for instance, reports: "Many LAG people were critical of the cat-and-mouse games some of the punks played with the police." Epstein, *Political Protest and Cultural Revolution*, p. 153.

68. Andersen and Jenkins, *Dance of Days*.

69. Ibid.; Johnny Temple, "Noise from Underground: Punk Rock's Anarchic Rhythms Spur a New Generation to Political Activism," *The Nation*, October 17, 1999, pp. 17–20; Positive Force, D.C., "Projects," http://www.positiveforcedc.org/projects.html.

70. Interview with the author, June 29, 1998.

71. Ibid.

72. Ibid.

73. "He Didn't Kiss Babies, and He Didn't Kiss Asses," *Maximumrocknroll*, November 1991.

74. Ibid.

75. Enrique Larana, Hank Johnston, and Joseph R. Gusfield, eds., *New Social Movements: From Ideology to Identity* (Philadelphia: Temple University Press, 1994); Alberto Melucci, *Challenging Codes: Collective Action in the Information Age* (New York: Cambridge University Press, 1996); on the connection between music and social movements, see Eyerman and Jamison, *Music and Social Movements*.

76. John D. McCarthy and Mayer N. Zald, "Resource Mobilization and Social Movements: A Partial Theory," *American Journal of Sociology*, vol. 82, no. 6, May 1977, pp. 1212–41; Doug McAdam, John D. McCarthy, and Mayer Zald, eds., *Comparative Perspectives on Social Movements: Political Opportunities, Mobilizing Structures, and Cultural Framings* (New York: Cambridge University Press, 1996); Bob Edwards and John D. McCarthy, "Resources and Social Movement Mobilization," in David A. Snow, Sarah A. Soule, and Hanspeter Kriesi, eds., *The Blackwell Companion to Social Movements* (Malden, MA: Blackwell, 2004), pp. 116–52.

77. See Michael Azerrad's outstanding chapter about the Minutemen in *Our Band Could Be Your Life* (ch. 2), and the documentary *We Jam Econo: The Story of the Minutemen* (Plexifilm, 2005).

78. Interview with the author, July 15, 2001.

79. Ibid.

80. Quoted in Arnold, *Route 666*, p. 40.

81. Quoted in Azerrad, *Our Band Could Be Your Life*, p. 76, italics in original.

CHAPTER 3

1. James Baldwin, *The Devil Finds Work* (New York: Dial Press, 1976), p. 126.

2. Frank, *The Conquest of Cool*; David Brooks, *Bobos in Paradise: The New Upper Class and How They Got There* (New York: Simon and Schuster, 2000); Richard Florida, *The Rise of the Creative Class* (New York: Basic Books, 2002); Joseph Heath and Andrew Potter, *A Nation of Rebels: Why Counterculture Became Consumer Culture* (New York: HarperCollins, 2005).

3. For an excellent ethnography of the changes in youth culture during the 1970s and the impact of the counterculture in "Middle America," see Gary Schwartz, *Beyond Conformity or Rebellion: Youth and Authority in America* (Chicago: University of Chicago Press, 1987).

4. David Roediger, The *Wages of Whiteness: Race and the Making of the American Working Class*, rev. ed. (New York: Verso, 1999); Lillian B. Rubin, *Families on the Fault Line: America's Working Class Speaks About the Family, the Economy, Race, and Ethnicity* (New York: HarperCollins, 1995); George Lipsitz, *The Possessive Investment in Whiteness: How White People Profit from Identity Politics* (Philadelphia: Temple University Press, 1998); Thomas Frank, *What's the Matter with Kansas? How Conservatives Won the Heart of America* (New York: Metropolitan Books, 2004). On the English working class, see Paul Willis, *Learning to Labor: How Working-Class Kids Get Working-Class Jobs* (New York: Columbia University Press, 1977).

5. Michael Ryan and Douglas Kellner, *Camera Politica: The Politics and Ideology of Contemporary Hollywood Film* (Bloomington: Indiana University Press, 1988); Barbara Ehrenreich, *Fear of Falling: The Inner Life of the Middle Class* (New York: Harper Perennial, 1989), esp. ch. 3; Stanley Aronowitz, *The Politics of Identity: Class, Culture, Social Movements* (New York: Routledge, 1992), ch. 5.

6. Leigh Kreske and Jim McKay, "'Hard and Heavy': Gender and Power in a Heavy Metal Subculture," *Gender, Place, and Culture: A Journal of Feminist Ethnography*, vol. 7, no. 3, 2000, pp. 287–304.

7. The question of when heavy metal originated and who its "founding fathers" were is a subject of intense debate among fans and rock journalists, as is the case in many other genres of music. Of course, there is no definitive answer, but Black Sabbath, Led Zeppelin, and Deep Purple are the three bands most often credited with establishing the sound of heavy metal. See Walser, *Running with the Devil*; Deena Weinstein, *Heavy Metal: A Cultural Sociology* (New York: Lexington Books, 1991); Konow, *Bang Your Head*; Christie, *Sound of the Beast*; Will Straw, "Characterizing Rock Music Culture: The Case of Heavy Metal," in Frith and Goodwin, *On Record*, pp. 97–110.

8. On the musical innovations of heavy metal, especially on guitar, see Walser, *Running with the Devil*; Berger, *Metal, Rock, and Jazz*; Waksman, *Instruments of Desire*.

9. Steve Chapple and Reebee Garofalo, *Rock 'n' Roll Is Here to Pay: The History and Politics of the Music Industry* (Chicago: Nelson Hall, 1977); Straw, "Characterizing Rock Music Culture"; R. Serge Denisoff, *Tarnished Gold: The Record Industry Revisited* (New Brunswick, NJ: Transaction Publishers, 1986); Fred Goodman, *The Mansion on the Hill: Dylan, Young, Geffen, Springsteen, and the Head-On Collision of Rock and Commerce* (1997; repr., New York: Vintage, 1998).

10. The most definitive ethnographic study of heavy metal and social class is Donna Gaines, *Teenage Wasteland: Suburbia's Dead-End Kids* (Chicago:

University of Chicago Press, 1990), esp. pp. 145–73; also see Weinstein, *Heavy Metal*, pp. 113–17; Berger, *Metal, Rock, and Jazz*, ch. 11.

11. On heavy metal and juvenile delinquency, see Gaines, *Teenage Wasteland*; Jeffrey Arnett, *Metalheads: Heavy Metal Music and Adolescent Alienation* (Boulder, CO: Westview Press, 1995); Wayne S. Wooden and Randy Blazak, *Renegade Kids, Suburban Outlaws*, 2d ed. (Belmont, CA: Wadsworth, 2001).

12. Bethany Bryson, "'Anything But Heavy Metal': Symbolic Exclusion and Musical Dislikes," *American Sociological Review*, vol. 45, no. 2, 1996, pp. 884–99.

13. Weinstein, *Heavy Metal*, ch. 4.

14. Barbara Ehrenreich, *The Hearts of Men: American Dreams and the Flight from Commitment* (New York: Anchor Books, 1983); Stephanie Coontz, *The Way We Never Were: American Families and the Nostalgia Trap* (New York: Basic Books, 1992); Lisa Brush, "Gender, Work, Who Cares?! Production, Reproduction, Deindustrialization, and Business as Usual," in Myra Max Ferree, Judith Lorber, and Beth B. Hess, eds., *Revisioning Gender* (Thousand Oaks, CA: Sage Publications, 1999), pp. 161–89.

15. Rubin, *Families on the Fault Line*; Katherine Newman, *Declining Fortunes: The Withering of the American Dream* (New York: Basic Books, 1993); Lois Weis, *Working Class Without Work: High School Students in a De-industrializing Economy* (New York: Routledge, 1990); Michelle Fine, Lois Weis, Judi Addelston, and Julia Maruza, "(In)secure Times: Constructing White Working-Class Masculinities in the Late 20th Century," *Gender and Society*, vol. 11, no. 1, 1997, pp. 52–68.

16. Susan Faludi, *Stiffed: The Betrayal of the American Man* (New York: William Morrow, 1999); Frank Mort, *Cultures of Consumption: Masculinities and Social Space in Late Twentieth-Century Britain* (New York: Routledge, 1996); Sean James Nixon, *Hard Looks: Masculinities, Spectatorship, and Contemporary Consumption* (New York: St. Martin's Press, 1996); Tim Edwards, *Men in the Mirror: Men's Fashion, Masculinity, and Consumer Culture* (London: Cassell, 1997). This transformation of masculinity was lightheartedly depicted in the 1997 film *The Full Monty*, in which recently unemployed Yorkshire steelworkers find new jobs as male strippers.

17. Faludi, *Stiffed*, pp. 38–39.

18. Willis, *Learning to Labor*.

19. Gaines, *Teenage Wasteland*, p. 153.

20. Ibid, p. 155.

21. Ibid, p. 119.

22. Ibid, p. 122.

23. Mike Males, *Scapegoat Generation: America's War on Adolescents* (Monroe, ME: Common Courage Press, 1996), p. 248.

24. Stanley Cohen, *Folk Devils and Moral Panics* (New York: St. Martin's Press, 1972); James T. Richardson, "Satanism in the Courts: From Heavy Metal

to Murder," in James T. Richardson, Joel Best, and David G. Bromley, eds., *The Satanism Scare* (New York: A. de Gruyter, 1991), pp. 205–17.

25. Males, *Scapegoat Generation*, pp. 243–53.

26. Interview with the author, June 23, 1998.

27. E.P. Thompson, *The Making of the English Working Class* (New York: Pantheon, 1963), p. 49.

28. Ibid, p. 801.

29. Scott Lash and John Urry, *The End of Organized Capitalism* (Madison: University of Wisconsin Press, 1987), p. 99.

30. Ibid.

31. For Ebenezer Aldred, see Thompson, *The Making of the English Working Class*, p. 382.

32. Ibid, p. 802.

33. György Lukács, *History and Class Consciousness: Studies in Marxist Dialectics*, trans. Rodney Livingstone (Cambridge, MA: MIT Press, 1971), p. 83.

34. Karl Marx, *Capital*, vol. 1, in *The Marx-Engels Reader*, p. 321.

35. Max Weber, *The Protestant Ethic and the Spirit of Capitalism*, 3d ed., trans. Stephen Kalberg (1905; repr., Los Angeles: Roxbury, 2002); Georg Simmel, *The Philosophy of Money*, 3d ed., trans. Tom Bottomore and David Frisby (1907; repr., New York: Routledge, 2004).

36. Marx and Engels, *Manifesto of the Communist Party*, p. 478.

37. Michael T. Taussig, *The Devil and Commodity Fetishism in South America* (Chapel Hill: University of North Carolina Press, 1980), p. 17.

38. Fredric Jameson, "Reification and Utopia in Mass Culture," *Social Text*, vol. 1, Winter 1979, pp. 130–48; Ryan and Kellner, *Camera Politica*; Susan Jeffords, *Hard Bodies: Hollywood Masculinity in the Reagan Era* (New Brunswick, NJ: Rutgers University Press, 1994).

39. Walser, *Running with the Devil*, p. 10.

40. See Sam Dunn's excellent documentary *Metal: A Headbanger's Journey* (Toronto International Film Festival, 2005).

41. Lipsitz, *The Possessive Investment in Whiteness*, p. 120.

42. Berman, "Sympathy for the Devil"; Marshall Berman, *All That Is Solid Melts Into Air: The Experience of Modernity* (New York: Penguin Books, 1982).

43. Cohen, "Subcultural Conflict and Subcultural Community."

44. Quoted in Christie, *Sound of the Beast*, p. 72.

45. Walser, *Running with the Devil*, p. 154, italics in original.

46. Judy Weider, "Judas Priest's Rob Halford Is First Heavy Metal Band Member to Say He's Gay," *The Advocate*, May 12, 1998, http://www.encyclopedia.com/doc/1G1-20830600.html.

47. Walser, *Running with the Devil*, ch. 4.

48. Guy Debord, *Society of the Spectacle* (Detroit: Black and Red, 1983), p. 20.

49. Walser, *Running with the Devil*, p. 163.

50. Debord, *Society of the Spectacle*, p. 20

51. Gaines, *Teenage Wasteland*, pp. 200–201.

52. Jeffrey Arnett, "Adolescents and Heavy Metal Music: From the Mouths of Metalheads," *Youth and Society*, vol. 23, no. 1, 1991, p. 90.

53. Quoted in Gaines, *Teenage Wasteland*, p. 216.

54. Phillip Auslander, *Performing Glam Rock: Gender and Theatricality in Popular Music* (Ann Arbor: University of Michigan Press, 2006).

55. Domenic Priore, *Riot on the Sunset Strip: Rock 'n' Roll's Last Stand in Hollywood* (Berkeley, CA: Jawbone Press, 2007).

56. For other interpretations of Axl Rose and this song and video, see Fred Pfeil, *White Guys: Studies in Postmodern Domination and Difference* (New York: Verso, 1995), pp. 88–98; Walser, *Running with the Devil*, pp. 165–71.

57. Walser, *Running with the Devil*, pp. 121–23.

58. Tommy, Lee, Mick Mars, Vince Neil, and Nikki Sixx, with Neil Strauss, *The Dirt: Confessions of the World's Most Notorious Rock Band* (New York: HarperEntertainment, 2001), p. 72.

59. Faludi, *Stiffed*, pp. 498–529.

60. Lisa Sloat, "Incubus: Male Songwriters' Portrayal of Women's Sexuality in Pop Metal Music," in Epstein, *Youth Culture*, pp. 286–87.

61. Quoted in Lee et al., *The Dirt*, p. 134.

62. E. Ann Kaplan, *Rocking Around the Clock: Music Television, Postmodernism, and Consumer Culture* (New York: Routledge, 1987), p. 93, italics in original. Also see Stan Denski and David Sholle, "Metal Men and Glamour Boys: Gender and Performance in Heavy Metal," in Steve Craig, ed., *Men, Masculinity, and the Media* (Newbury Park, CA: Sage Publications, 1992), pp. 41–60.

63. Christie, *Sound of the Beast*, pp. 155–56.

64. Konow, *Bang Your Head*, p. 265.

65. Ibid., p. 266.

66. Ehrenreich, *The Hearts of Men*. Also see Reynolds and Press, *The Sex Revolts*.

67. Slash, with Anthony Bozza, *Slash* (New York: HarperEntertainment, 2007), p. 161.

68. Barbara Ehrenreich, Elizabeth Hess, and Gloria Jacobs, "Beatlemania: A Sexually Defiant Consumer Culture?" in Gelder and Thornton, *The Subcultures Reader*, pp. 523–36; Sue Wise, "Sexing Elvis," in Frith and Goodwin, *On Record*, pp. 390–98; Douglas, *Where the Girls Are*.

69. Susan Fast, "Rethinking Issues of Gender and Sexuality in Led Zeppelin: A Woman's View of Pleasure and Power in Hard Rock," in Bennett, Shank, and Toynbee, *The Popular Music Studies Reader*, pp. 362–63.

70. Ibid, p. 363; Also see Pamela Des Barres, *Let's Spend the Night Together: Backstage Secrets of Rock Muses and Supergroupies* (Chicago: Chicago Review

Press, 2007); Pamela Des Barres, *I'm With the Band: Confessions of a Groupie* (Chicago: Chicago Review Press, 2005).

71. Bennett Harrison and Barry Bluestone, *The Great U-Turn: Corporate Restructuring and the Polarizing of America* (New York: Basic Books, 1988).

72. Willis, *Learning to Labor.*

CHAPTER 4

1. Azerrad, *Come as You Are*, p. 193

2. Ibid., pp. 212–13.

3. Ibid., p. 213.

4. For instance, Gina Arnold has quoted this line as "load up on drugs." Arnold, *Route 666*, p. 142.

5. Azerrad, *Come as You Are*, p. 213.

6. Twenge, *Generation Me.*

7. Brooks, *Bobos in Paradise.*

8. Florida, *The Rise of the Creative Class*; Richard Florida, *Cities and the Creative Class* (New York: Routledge, 2005). Also see Richard Lloyd, *Neo-Bohemia: Art and Commerce in the Postindustrial City* (New York: Routledge, 2006).

9. Frank and Weiland, *Commodify Your Dissent*; Thomas Frank and Dave Mulcahey, eds., *Boob Jubilee: The Cultural Politics of the New Economy* (New York: Norton, 2003); also see Thomas Frank, *The Conquest of Cool*; Heath and Potter, *A Nation of Rebels.*

10. Daniel Bell, *The Cultural Contradictions of Capitalism* (New York: Basic Books, 1975).

11. In addition to the works previously cited, see Klein, *No Logo: Taking Aim at the Brand Bullies* (New York: Picador, 2000).

12. Daniel H. Pink, *Free Agent Nation: How America's Independent Workers Are Transforming the Way We Live* (New York: Warner Books, 2001).

13. Robert W. McChesney, *Rich Media, Poor Democracy: Communication Politics in Dubious Times* (Urbana: University of Illinois Press, 1999).

14. Luc Boltanski and Eve Chiapello, *The New Spirit of Capitalism*, trans. Gregory Elliot (New York: Verso, 2006).

15. See Andrew Ross, *No-Collar: The Humane Workplace and Its Hidden Costs* (New York: Basic Books, 2002).

16. As defined by the French Marxist Henri Lefebvre, recuperation refers to the process whereby "an idea or a project regarded as irredeemably revolutionary or subversive . . . is normalized, reintegrated into the existing order, and even revives it" (*Critique of Everyday Life*, vol. 3, p. 105). Dick Hebdige similarly diagnosed two forms of the incorporation of subcultural style, the most relevant of which for the purposes of our discussion is in the commodity form, where "as soon as the

original innovations which signify 'subculture' are translated into commodities and made generally available, they become 'frozen'" (*Subculture*, p. 96).

17. Nils Bernstein, quoted in Arnold, *Route 666*, pp. 157–58.

18. On the Seattle scene, see Azerrad, *Our Band Could Be Your Life*, ch. 12; Azerrad, *Come as You Are*; Arnold, *Route 666*; Clark Humphrey, *Loser: The Real Seattle Music Story*, updated 2d ed. (New York: Abrams, 1999).

19. On Sub Pop, see Azerrad, *Our Band Could Be Your Life*, pp. 420–53; Arnold, *Route 666*, pp. 154–63.

20. Quoted in Azerrad, *Our Band Could Be Your Life*, p. 421.

21. Charles Peterson's photos have been collected in Charles Peterson, *Screaming Life: A Chronicle of the Seattle Music Scene* (New York: HarperCollins, 1995); and Charles Peterson, *Touch Me, I'm Sick* (Brooklyn: powerHouse, 2003).

22. Quoted in Arnold, *Route 666*, p. 160.

23. Azerrad, *Our Band Could Be Your Life*, p. 441.

24. Quoted in Azerrad, *Come as You Are*, p. 71.

25. Arnold, *Route 666*, p. 106.

26. An excellent collection of interviews with various alternative rock bands published in *Option* can be found in Scott Becker, ed., *We Rock So You Don't Have To: The* Option *Reader*, vol. 1 (San Diego: Incommunicado Press, 1998).

27. Azerrad, *Our Band Could Be Your Life*, pp. 468–69.

28. Azerrad, *Come as You Are*, p. 46.

29. Quoted in Arnold, *Route 666*, p. 164.

30. Andersen and Jenkins, *Dance of Days*, pp. 307–38.

31. See the Experience Music Project's film *Riot Grrrl Retrospective*, http://www.empsfm.org/exhibitions/index.asp?articleID=666.

32. Kristen Schlit, "'I'll Resist with Every Inch and Every Breath': Girls and Zine Making as a Form of Resistance," *Youth and Society*, vol. 35, no. 1, September 2003, 71–97.

33. American Association of University Women, *Shortchanging Girls, Shortchanging America* (Washington, DC: American Association of University Women, 1991). Also see Mary Pipher, *Reviving Ophelia: Saving the Selves of Adolescent Girls* (New York: Ballantine, 1994); Peggy Orenstein, *Schoolgirls: Young Women, Self-Esteem, and the Confidence Gap* (New York: Anchor Books, 1994).

34. Pedersen quoted in Andrea Juno, "Candice Pedersen," in Juno, ed., *Angry Women in Rock* (New York: Juno Books, 1996), p. 177.

35. Marion Leonard, "Rebel Girl You Are the Queen of My World: Feminism, Subculture, and Grrrl Power," in Sheila Whiteley, ed., *Sexing the Groove: Popular Music and Gender* (New York: Routledge, 1997), pp. 230–56; Mary Celeste Kearney, "'Don't Need You': Rethinking Identity Politics and Separatism from a Grrrl Perspective," in Epstein, *Youth Culture*, pp. 148–88; Mary Celeste Kearney, *Girls Make Media* (New York: Routledge, 2006).

36. McRobbie and Garber, "Girls and Subcultures."

37. Douglas, *Where the Girls Are*; McRobbie, *Feminism and Youth Culture*; Ehrenreich, Hess, and Jacobs, "Beatlemania."

38. Reynolds and Press, *The Sex Revolts*, p. 323.

39. Interview with the author, October 4, 1995.

40. Mary Ann Clawson, "When Women Play the Bass: Instrument Specialization and Gender Interpretation in Alternative Rock Music," *Gender and Society*, vol. 13, no. 2, 1999, pp. 193–210; Mavis Bayton, "How Women Become Musicians," in Frith and Goodwin, *On Record*, pp. 238–57; Stephen B. Groce and Margaret Cooper, "Just Me and the Boys? Women in Local-Level Rock and Roll," *Gender and Society*, vol. 4, no. 2, 1990, pp. 220–29.

41. Joanne Gottlieb and Gayle Wald, "Smells Like Teen Spirit: Riot Grrrls, Revolution, and Women in Independent Rock," in Rose and Ross, *Microphone Fiends*, p. 262.

42. Karen Ritchie, "Get Ready for Generation X," *Advertising Age*, November 9, 1992, p. 21.

43. Scott Donaton, "The Media Wakes Up to Generation X," *Advertising Age*, February 1, 1993, pp. 16–17.

44. Karen Ritchie, *Marketing to Generation X* (New York: Lexington Books, 1995), p. 159, italics in original.

45. Ibid., p. 164.

46. "The Merchants of Cool," *Frontline* (first broadcast February 27, 2001, by PBS).

47. Juliet Schor, *Born to Buy: The Commercialized Child and the New Consumer Culture* (New York: Scribner, 2004).

48. David M. Gross and Sophfronia Scott, "Proceeding with Caution," *Time*, July 16, 1990, p. 57

49. Ibid.

50. Joel Achenbach, "Birth of a Protest Movement," *Washington Post*, January 17, 1991, p. C2.

51. Ibid.

52. Rick Marin, "Grunge: A Success Story," *New York Times*, November 15, 1992.

53. See Jason Cohen and Michael Krugman, *Generation Ecch! The Backlash Starts Here* (New York: Fireside, 1994).

54. Kristen Schlit, "'A Little Too Ironic': The Appropriation and Packaging of Riot Grrrl Politics by Mainstream Female Musicians," *Popular Music and Society*, vol. 26, no. 1, 2003, pp. 5–16.

55. Lorraine Ali, "The Grrrls Fight Back," *Los Angeles Times*, July 27, 1995, p. F1.

56. Thornton, *Club Cultures*; Fox, "Real Punks and Pretenders."

57. Bourdieu, *Distinction*.

58. Thornton, *Club Cultures*; Redhead, Wynne, and O'Connor, *The Clubcultures Reader*; Hodkinson, *Goth;* Muggleton, *Inside Subculture*; Muggleton and Weinzierl, *The Post-subcultures Reader*.

59. Ryan Moore, "Alternative to What? Subcultural Capital and the Commercialization of a Music Scene," *Deviant Behavior*, vol. 26, no. 3, 2005, pp. 229–52.

60. Greil Marcus, "Sleater-Kinney," *Time*, July 9, 2001, http://www.time.com/time/magazine/article/0,9171,1000294,00.html.

61. Foucault, *Discipline and Punish*.

62. Elke Zobl, "Revolution Grrrl and Lady Style, Now!" *Peace Review*, vol. 16, no. 4, 2004, pp. 445–52.

63. Interview with the author, November 8, 1995.

64. Interview with the author, January 26, 1998.

65. Ibid.

66. See Shank, *Dissonant Identities*, pp. 230–37.

67. Interview with the author, June 25, 1998.

68. Gary Hustwit, *Releasing an Independent Record*, 6th ed. (San Diego: Rockpress Publishing, 1998).

69. Karla Peterson, "Independents' Days: Concerts, Workshops Offer a Sounding Board for Struggling Musicians," *San Diego Union-Tribune*, October 4, 1994, p. E1.

70. Interview with the author, June 25, 1998.

71. Michael Walker, "San Diego, Alternatively," *Los Angeles Times Magazine*, October 18, 1993, p. 24.

72. Interview with the author, November 8, 1995.

73. Interview with the author, December 2, 1997.

74. Interview with the author, May 26, 1998

75. Steve Albini, "The Problem with Music," in Frank and Weiland, *Commodify Your Dissent*, pp. 164–76.

76. Larry Harmon, "Token Indie Band," *San Diego Weekly Reader*, April 11, 1996, p. 76.

77. Tom Mertes, ed., *A Movement of Movements: Is Another World Really Possible?* (New York: Verso, 2004); News from Nowhere, ed., *We Are Everywhere: The Irresistible Rise of Global Anticapitalism* (New York: Verso, 2004).

78. Florida, *The Rise of the Creative Class*, p. 191.

79. Marx and Engels, *Manifesto of the Communist Party*.

CHAPTER 5

1. Interview with the author, January 18, 1998.

2. Ibid.

3. Rick Shaughnessy, "County Jobless Rate: 9.2%," *San Diego Union-Tribune*, August 28, 1993, p. A1.

4. Elizabeth Douglas, "Can the Industry Be Saved? GOP Injections of Military Spending Will Help, but Don't Expect an All-Out Cure," *San Diego Union-Tribune*, November 20, 1994, p. I1.

5. Elizabeth E. Guffey, *Retro: The Culture of Revival* (London: Reaktion Books, 2006). In this chapter I spell out decades (Fifties, Sixties, etc.) when they are recycled to create the image of a time, and represent them numerically (1950s, 1960s, etc.) when referring to actual periods of time. Thus, *American Graffiti* was set in 1962, but as Guffey and others have observed, its look, sound, and feel was far more consistent with what has come to be associated with "the Fifties."

6. Guffey, *Retro*, p. 12.

7. On nostalgia, see Fred Davis, *Yearning for Yesterday: A Sociology of Nostalgia* (New York: Free Press, 1979).

8. Guffey, *Retro*, pp. 19–20.

9. Although the terms are sometimes used interchangeably, kitsch can be defined as an object or image endowed with poor taste, while camp refers to the style of performance in which kitschy objects or images are employed.

10. Susan Sontag, "Notes on 'Camp,'" in *Against Interpretation, and Other Essays* (New York: Farrar, Straus and Giroux, 1966), pp. 275–92.

11. Jean Baudrillard, *Simulacra and Simulation*, trans. Sheila Faria Glaser (Ann Arbor: University of Michigan Press, 1994).

12. Ibid., p. 43.

13. Ibid.

14. Fredric Jameson, "Nostalgia for the Present," in *Postmodernism, or, The Cultural Logic of Late Capitalism*, pp. 279–96.

15. Ibid., p. 286.

16. Fredric Jameson, "The Cultural Logic of Late Capitalism," in *Postmodernism, or, The Cultural Logic of Late Capitalism*, p. 17.

17. Another important thinker on this subject of the waning of historicity in relation to the emergence of postmodernity is Andreas Huyssen, especially in his work *Twilight Memories: Marking Time in a Culture of Amnesia* (New York: Routledge, 1995). Like Jameson and Baudrillard, Huyssen discusses both a death of historical consciousness and the resurging popularity of museums, memorials, and monuments. Huyssen was less pessimistic about these developments, however, insofar as he saw them as part of an overdue critique of teleological and totalizing philosophies of history.

18. Maurice Halbwachs, *On Collective Memory*, ed. and trans. Louis A. Coser (Chicago: University of Chicago Press, 1992); Eric Hobsbawm and Terence Ranger, eds., *The Invention of Tradition* (New York: Cambridge University Press, 1984); Robin Wagner-Pacifici and Barry Schwartz, "The Vietnam Veterans Memorial: Commemorating a Difficult Past," *American Journal of Sociology*, vol. 97, no. 2, September 1991, pp. 376–420; Lyn Spillman, *Nation and Commemoration:*

Creating National Identities in the United States and Australia (New York: Cambridge University Press, 1997); Jeffrey K. Olick and Joyce Robbins, "Social Memory Studies: From 'Collective Memory' to the Historical Sociology of Mnemonic Practices," *Annual Review of Sociology*, vol. 24, August 1998, pp. 105–40.

19. M.M. Bakhtin, *The Dialogic Imagination: Four Essays*, ed. Michael Holquist, trans. Caryl Emerson and Michael Holquist (Austin: University of Texas Press, 1981).

20. M.M. Bakhtin, "Epic and Novel," in *The Dialogic Imagination*, p. 15.

21. M.M. Bakhtin, "Forms of Time and of the Chronotope in the Novel," in *The Dialogic Imagination*, pp. 84–258.

22. George Lipsitz, *Time Passages: Collective Memory and American Popular Culture* (Minneapolis: University of Minnesota Press, 1990), p. 99.

23. Bakhtin, "Epic and Novel," p. 30.

24. Lipsitz, *Time Passages*, p. 100.

25. Maria Elena Buszek, *Pin-Up Grrrls: Feminism, Sexuality, Popular Culture* (Durham, NC: Duke University Press, 2006).

26. Ibid., p. 186.

27. Paula Kamen, *Her Way: Women Remake the Sexual Revolution* (New York: New York University Press, 2000), p. 180.

28. Lott, *Love and Theft*, p. 6.

29. Waksman, *Instruments of Desire*; David Grazian, *Blue Chicago: The Search for Authenticity in Urban Blues Clubs* (Chicago: University of Chicago Press, 2003).

30. Norman Mailer, "The White Negro" in *Advertisements for Myself* (1959; repr., Cambridge, MA: Harvard University Press, 2005), pp. 337–58; Leland, *Hip*.

31. Lipsitz, *The Possessive Investment in Whiteness*, p. 1.

32. Annalee Newitz and Matt Wray, "Introduction," in Newitz and Wray, eds., *White Trash: Race and Class in America* (New York: Routledge, 1997), p. 8.

33. John Hartigan Jr., *Racial Situations: Class Predicaments of Whiteness in Detroit* (Princeton, NJ: Princeton University Press, 1999); Doug Henwood, "Trash-O-Nomics," in Newitz and Wray, *White Trash*, pp. 177–92.

34. See Shank, *Dissonant Identities*, ch. 4.

35. Richard Peterson, *Creating Country Music: Fabricating Authenticity* (Chicago: University of Chicago Press, 1999).

36. Ibid., p. 41.

37. Quoted in S. Renee Dechert, Review of *Uncle Tupelo 89/93: Anthology*, *PopMatters*, April 22, 2002, http://www.popmatters.com/music/reviews/u/uncletupelo-8993.shtml.

38. For a collection of *No Depression*'s articles and interviews, see Grant Alden and Peter Blackstock, eds., *No Depression: An Introduction to Alternative Country Music (Whatever That Is)* (Nashville: Dowling Press, 1998).

39. Interview with the author, February 5, 1998.

40. Andersen and Jenkins, *Dance of Days*, p. 194.

41. Jim DeRogatis, "The Truth About the Jon Spencer Blues Explosion," *Penthouse*, 1997, available online at http://www.jimdero.com/OtherWritings/Spencer.htm.

42. The Supersuckers, *Must've Been High* (Sub Pop Records, 1997).

43. *The Union-Tribune's Annual Review of San Diego Business* (San Diego: Union-Tribune, 1990), p. 34.

44. San Diego Economic Adjustment Program, Defense Cutbacks Impact Assessment (March 1993), p. 12.

45. "Effects of '89 Aerospace Layoffs Found Still Painful 2 Years Later," *San Diego Union-Tribune*, June 9, 1993, p. C1.

46. John Reis, "Scene Alternatives," *San Diego's Daily Impulse*, vol. 2, no. 6, November–December 1986, p. 8

47. Interview with the author, February 2, 1998.

48. Interview with the author, December 2, 1997.

49. Quoted in V. Vale, *Swing: The New Retro Renaissance* (San Francisco, V/Search Publications, 1998), p. 172.

50. Matt Crawford, "Messy Fun with the Suicide Girls," *SF Station*, September 7, 2006, http://www.sfstation.com/messy-fun-with-the-suicide-girls-a2157.

CHAPTER 6

1. Walter Benjamin, "The Work of Art in the Age of Mechanical Reproduction," in *Illuminations*, trans. Harry Zohn (New York: Schocken, 1969), p. 221.

2. Theodor W. Adorno, "On the Fetish Character in Music and the Regression of Listening," in Andrew Arato and Eike Gebhardt, eds., *The Essential Frankfurt School Reader* (New York: Continuum, 1982), p. 278.

3. Recording Industry Association of America, "Key Statistics," http://www.riaa.com/keystatistics.php?content_selector=.

4. David Kusek and Gerd Leonhard, *The Future of Music: Manifesto for the Digital Revolution* (Boston: Berklee Press, 2005), p. 84; Sheff and Tannenbaum, "Rip. Burn. Die.," p. 338.

5. Ethan Smith, "Sales of Music, Long in Decline, Plunge Sharply," *Wall Street Journal*, March 21, 2007. Smith claims that the 20 percent drop in CD sales in the first three months of 2007 was primarily due to downloading and file sharing. The first academic study of the impact of file sharing, however, found that it had little or no effect on music sales. These findings are reported in Felix Oberholzer-Gee and Koleman Strumpf, "The Effect of File Sharing on Record Sales: An Empirical Analysis," *Journal of Political Economy*, vol. 115, no. 1, February 2007, pp. 1–42.

6. These terms are borrowed from McChesney, *Rich Media, Poor Democracy*.

7. Paul Cashmere, "Universal the Biggest Label of 2006," *Undercover*, January 5, 2007, http://www.undercover.com.au/News-Story.aspx?id=1215.

8. Eric Boehlert, "Pay for Play," *Salon*, March 14, 2001, http://archive.salon.com/ent/feature/2001/03/14/payola/index.html; Eric Boehlert, "Radio's Big Bully," *Salon*, April 30, 2001, http://archive.salon.com/ent/feature/2001/04/30/clear_channel/index.html; Oliver Burkeman, "Bush Backer Sponsoring Pro-War Rallies," *Guardian*, March 26, 2003; Kevin Brass, "GoliathSucks.net," *Austin Chronicle*, April 1, 2005.

9. Quoted in Sheff and Tannenbaum, "Rip. Burn. Die.," p. 339.

10. David J. Park, *Conglomerate Rock: The Music Industry's Quest to Divide Music and Conquer Wallets* (New York: Lexington Books, 2007).

11. Benjamin, "The Work of Art." For essays in which Benjamin expresses more ambivalent views on the decline of aura, see "On Some Motifs in Baudelaire," in *Illuminations*, pp. 155–200; and "The Storyteller," in *Illuminations*, pp. 83–109.

12. Benjamin, "The Work of Art," p. 224.

13. For views of sampling that dovetail with Benjamin's ideas, see: Rose, *Black Noise*; Joseph Schloss, *Making Beats: The Art of Sample-Based Hip Hop* (Middletown, CT: Wesleyan University Press, 2002); Andrew Goodwin, "Sample and Hold: Pop Music in the Digital Age of Reproduction," in Frith and Goodwin, *On Record*, pp. 258–73; Thomas G. Schumacher, "'This Is a Sampling Sport': Digital Sampling, Rap Music, and the Law in Cultural Production," in Forman and Neal, *That's the Joint!*, pp. 443–58.

14. Benjamin, "The Work of Art," p. 231.

15. Theodor W. Adorno, "Perennial Fashion—Jazz," in Stephen Eric Bronner and Douglas MacKay Kellner, *Critical Theory and Society: A Reader* (New York: Routledge, 1989), pp. 199–209; Adorno, "On the Fetish Character in Music"; Theodor W. Adorno, "On Popular Music," in Frith and Goodwin, *On Record*, pp. 301–14. Many of his key essays are collected in Theodor W. Adorno, *The Culture Industry*, ed. J.M. Bernstein (New York: Routledge, 2001); Theodor W. Adorno, *Essays on Music*, ed. Richard Leppert, trans. Susan H. Gillespie (Berkeley and Los Angeles: University of California Press, 2002).

16. For Adorno's views on music and the culture industry, see Robert W. Witkin, *Adorno on Music* (New York: Routledge, 1998); Robert W. Witikin, *Adorno on Popular Culture* (New York: Routledge, 2003); Tia DeNora, *After Adorno: Rethinking Music Sociology* (New York: Cambridge University Press, 2003).

17. For a debate that summarizes the long-running conflicts between political economy and cultural studies approaches, see Nicholas Garnham, "Political Economy and Cultural Studies: Reconciliation or Divorce?" in John Storey,

Cultural Theory and Popular Culture: A Reader (New York: Prentice Hall, 2006), pp. 614–25; Lawrence Grossberg, "Cultural Studies vs. Political Economy: Is Anybody Else Tired with This Debate?" in Storey, *Cultural Theory and Popular Culture*, pp. 626–36. For an excellent and more nuanced critique of Adorno's theory of popular music, see Bernard Gendron, "Theodor Adorno Meets the Cadillacs," in Tania Modleski, ed., *Studies in Entertainment* (Bloomington: University of Indiana Press, 1986), pp. 18–37.

18. Ben H. Bagdikian, *The New Media Monopoly* (Boston: Beacon Press, 2004).

19. See Thornton, *Club Cultures*; for a pioneering analysis of jazz musicians' opposition to mass culture in the person of "squares," see Howard S. Becker, "The Culture of a Deviant Group: The Dance Musician," in *Outsiders*, pp. 79–100.

20. Kevin J. H. Dettmar, *Is Rock Dead?* (New York: Routledge, 2005). Among the works Dettmar discusses are: Martha Bayles, *Hole in Our Soul: The Loss of Beauty and Meaning in American Popular Music* (Chicago: University of Chicago Press, 1994); Donald Clarke, *The Rise and Fall of American Popular Music* (New York: St. Martin's, 1995); Goodman, *Mansion on the Hill*; James Miller, *Flowers in the Dustbin: The Rise of Rock 'n' Roll, 1947–1977* (New York: Simon and Schuster, 1999); John Strausbaugh, *Rock 'Til You Drop: The Decline from Rebellion to Nostalgia* (New York: Verso, 2001); Joe Harrington, *Sonic Cool: The Life and Death of Rock 'n' Roll* (Milwaukee: Hal Leonard, 2002); Lawrence Grossberg, "Reflections of a Disappointed Popular Music Scholar," in Roger Beebe, Denise Fulbrook, and Ben Saunders, eds., *Rock Over the Edge: Transformations in Popular Music Culture* (Durham, NC: Duke University Press, 2002), pp. 25–59.

21. See Gary Giddins, "How Come Jazz Isn't Dead?" in Eric Weisbard, ed., *This Is Pop: In Search of the Elusive at the Experience Music Project* (Cambridge, MA: Harvard University Press, 2004), pp. 39–55; Nelson George, *The Death of Rhythm and Blues* (New York: Pantheon, 1988); Nas, *Hip Hop Is Dead* (Def Jam, 2006).

22. David Shumway, "Where Have All the Rock Stars Gone?" *Chronicle of Higher Education*, June 22, 2007.

23. Lawrence Grossberg, "Is Anybody Listening? Does Anybody Care? On 'The State of Rock,'" in Ross and Rose, *Microphone Fiends*, p. 52.

24. Goodman, *Mansion on the Hill*; Miller, *Flowers in the Dustbin*, p. 351.

25. Frank, "Hip Is Dead," *The Nation*, April 1, 1996, pp. 16–18.

26. Shumway, "Where Have All the Rock Stars Gone?"

27. For a humorous rant in this spirit, see Strausbaugh, *Rock 'Til You Drop*.

28. Kelefa Sanneh, "The Rap Against Rockism," in Cateforis, *The Rock History Reader*, p. 352.

29. For example, a gallery of references to "rockism" or "rockist" can be found at Scott Woods, "Gallery of Rockism Erroneous, Bizarre, and Occasionally Illuminating Usages of Today's Number-One-With-a-Bullet Buzzword,"

rockcritics.com, August 2004, http://rockcriticsarchives.com/features/rockism/gal-leryofrockism.html.

30. Miller, *Flowers in the Dustbin*, p. 17.

31. Ibid.

32. Karl Marx, *The Eighteenth Brumaire of Louis Bonaparte*, in *The Marx-Engels Reader*, p. 595.

33. Interview with the author, February 5, 1998.

34. Lauren Sandler, *Righteous: Dispatches from the Evangelical Youth Movement* (New York: Penguin Books, 2006).

35. Ibid., p. 82.

36. Ibid., pp. 114–15, italics in original.

37. Benjamin, "The Work of Art," p. 239.

38. Kusek and Leonhard, *The Future of Music*, p. 2.

39. Ibid., p. 4.

40. Benjamin, "The Work of Art," p. 228, 232.

41. For a more detailed exposition of these possibilities for popular culture in the digital age, see Henry Jenkins, *Fans, Bloggers, and Gamers: Media Consumers in a Digital Age* (New York: New York University Press, 2006); Henry Jenkins, *Convergence Culture: Where Old and New Media Collide* (New York: New York University Press, 2007).

42. Steve Knopper, *Appetite for Self-Destruction: The Spectacular Crash of the Record Industry in the Digital Age* (New York: Free Press, 2009), p. 246.

43. On the role of music in social movements, see Jeff Goodwin, James Jasper, and Donatella Della Porta, eds., *Passionate Politics: Emotions and Social Movements* (Chicago: University of Chicago Press, 2001).

44. "Everyday life" is a seemingly nebulous concept, but I introduce it here in the form it has been given in French critical theory, especially in the work of Henri Lefebvre. See Henri Lefebvre, *Everyday Life in the Modern World*, trans. Sacha Rabinovitch (New Brunswick, NJ: Transaction Publishers, 1984); Henri Lefebvre, *The Critique of Everyday Life*, 3 vols., trans. Gregory Elliot and John Moore (New York: Verso, 1991, 2002, 2005); Raoul Vaneigem, *The Revolution of Everyday Life*, trans. Donald Nicholson-Smith (Seattle: Left Bank Books, 2004); Michel de Certeau, *The Practice of Everyday Life*, trans. Steven F. Randall (Berkeley and Los Angeles: University of California Press, 1984); Michael Gardiner, *Critiques of Everyday Life* (New York: Routledge, 2000); Ben Highmore, *Everyday Life and Cultural Theory* (New York: Routledge, 2001).

Bibliography

Achenbach, Joel. 1991. "Birth of a Protest Movement." *Washington Post*, January 17.

Adams, Rebecca G. and Robert Sardiello (eds.). 2000. *Deadhead Social Science: You Ain't Gonna Learn What You Don't Want to Know*. Walnut Creek, CA: AltaMira Press.

Adorno, Theodor W. 1982. "On the Fetish Character in Music and the Regression of Listening." *The Essential Frankfurt School Reader*, eds. Andrew Arato and Eike Gebhardt. New York: Continuum.

Adorno, Theodor W. 1989. "Perennial Fashion—Jazz." *Critical Theory and Society: A Reader*, eds. Stephen Eric Bronner and Doulgas MacKay Kellner. New York: Routledge.

Adorno, Theodor W. 1990. "On Popular Music." *On Record: Rock, Pop, and the Written Word*, eds. Simon Frith and Andrew Goodwin. New York: Pantheon.

Adorno, Theodor W. 2001. *The Culture Industry*, ed. J.M. Bernstein. New York: Routledge.

Adorno, Theodor W. 2002. *Essays on Music*, ed. Richard Leppert, trans. Susan H. Gillespie. Berkeley and Los Angeles: University of California Press.

Albini, Steve. "The Problem with Music." *Commodify Your Dissent: Salvos from the* Baffler, eds. Thomas Frank and Matt Weiland. New York: Norton.

Alden, Grant and Peter Blackstock (eds.). 1998. *No Depression: An Introduction to Alternative Country Music (Whatever That Is)*. Nashville: Dowling Press.

Ali, Lorraine. 1995. "The Grrrls Fight Back." *Los Angeles Times*, July 27.

American Association of University Women. 1991. *Shortchanging Girls, Shortchanging America*. Washington, DC: American Association of University Women.

Andersen, Mark and Mark Jenkins. 2003. *Dance of Days: Two Decades of Punk in the Nation's Capital*. New York: Akashic Books.

Anderson, Benedict. 1991. *Imagined Communities: Reflections on the Origin and Spread of Nationalism*. New York: Verso.

Anderson, Perry. 1976. *Considerations on Western Marxism*. London: NLB.

Anderson, Perry. 1998. *The Origins of Postmodernity*. New York: Verso.

Anderson, Terry H. 1995. *The Movement and the Sixties*. New York: Oxford University Press.

Arnett, Jeffrey. 1991. "Adolescents and Heavy Metal Music: From the Mouths of Metalheads." *Youth and Society* 23 (1): 76–98.

Arnett, Jeffrey. 1995. *Metalheads: Heavy Metal Music and Adolescent Alienation.* Boulder, CO: Westview Press.

Arnold, Gina. 1993. *Route 666: On the Road to Nirvana.* New York: St. Martin's Press.

Aronowitz, Stanley. 1992. *The Politics of Identity: Class, Culture, Social Movements.* New York: Routledge.

Ashley, David. 1997. *History Without a Subject: The Postmodern Condition.* Boulder, CO: Westview Press.

Attali, Jacques. 1985. *Noise: The Political Economy of Music,* trans. Brian Massumi. Minneapolis: University of Minnesota Press.

Auslander, Phillip. 2006. *Performing Glam Rock: Gender and Theatricality in Popular Music.* Ann Arbor: University of Michigan Press.

Azerrad, Michael. 1994. *Come as You Are: The Story of Nirvana.* New York: Doubleday.

Azerrad, Michael. 2001. *Our Band Could Be Your Life: Scenes from the American Indie Underground, 1981–1991.* New York: Little, Brown.

Bagdikian, Ben H. 2004. *The New Media Monopoly.* Boston: Beacon Press.

Bakhtin, M.M. 1968. *Rabelais and his World,* trans. Helene Oswolsky. Cambridge, MA: MIT Press.

Bakhtin, M.M. 1981. *The Dialogic Imagination: Four Essays,* ed. Michael Holquist, trans. Caryl Emerson and Michael Holquist. Austin: University of Texas Press.

Baldwin, James. 1976. *The Devil Finds Work.* New York: Dial Press.

Bangs, Lester. 1988. *Psychotic Reactions and Carburetor Dung: Literature as Rock 'n' Roll, Rock 'n' Roll as Literature,* ed. Greil Marcus. New York: Anchor Books.

Bannister, Matthew. 2006. *White Boys, White Noise: Masculinities and 1980s Indie Guitar Rock.* Burlington, VT: Ashgate.

Barber, Benjamin. 1995. *Jihad vs. McWorld.* New York: Times Books.

Barthes, Roland. 1977. "The Grain of the Voice." *Image/Music/Text,* ed. and trans. Stephen Heath. New York: Hill and Wang.

Baudrillard, Jean. 1994. *Simulation and Simulacra,* trans. Ann Arbor: University of Michigan Press.

Bauman, Zygmunt. 2000. *Liquid Modernity.* Malden, MA: Blackwell, 2000.

Bauman, Zygmunt. 2005. *Liquid Life.* Malden, MA: Polity Press, 2005.

Bayles, Martha. 1994. *Hole in Our Soul: The Loss of Beauty and Meaning in American Popular Music.* Chicago: University of Chicago Press.

Bayton, Mavis. 1990. "How Women Become Musicians." *On Record: Rock, Pop, and the Written Word,* eds. Simon Frith and Andrew Goodwin. New York: Pantheon.

Becker, Howard S. 1973. *Outsiders: Studies in the Sociology of Deviance.* New York: Free Press.

Becker, Howard S. 1982. *Art Worlds*. Berkeley and Los Angeles: University of California Press.

Becker, Scott (ed.). 1998. *We Rock So You Don't Have To: The* Option *Reader*, vol. 1. San Diego: Incommunicado Press.

Bell, Daniel. 1975. *The Cultural Contradictions of Capitalism*. New York: Basic Books.

Belsito, Peter and Bob Davis. 1983. *Hardcore California: A History of Punk and New Wave*. San Francisco: Last Gasp.

Benjamin, Walter. 1969. *Illuminations*, trans. Harry Zohn. New York: Schocken.

Bennett, Andy. 1999. "Subcultures or Neo-Tribes? Rethinking the Relationship Between Youth, Style, and Musical Taste." *Sociology* 33 (3): 599–617.

Bennett, Andy and Keith Kahn-Harris (eds.). 2004. *After Subculture: Critical Studies in Contemporary Youth Culture*. New York: Palgrave Macmillan.

Bennett, Andy and Richard Peterson (eds.). 2005. *Music Scenes: Local, Translocal, Virtual*. Nashville: Vanderbilt University Press.

Berger, Harris. 1999. *Metal, Jazz, and Rock: Perception and the Phenomenology of Musical Experience*. Hanover, NH: University of New England Press.

Berman, Marshall. 1974. "Sympathy for the Devil: Faust, the '60s, and the Tragedy of Development." *American Review* 19 (August): 23–75.

Berman, Marshall. 1982. *All That Is Solid Melts into Air: The Experience of Modernity*. New York: Penguin Books.

Best, Steven and Douglas Kellner. 1998. "Beavis and Butt-Head: No Future for Postmodern Youth." *Youth Culture: Identity in a Postmodern World*, ed. Jonathon S. Epstein. Malden, MA: Blackwell.

Blush, Steven. 2001. *American Hardcore: A Tribal History*. Los Angeles: Feral House.

Boehlert, Eric. 2001. "Pay for Play." *Salon*, March 14, http://archive.salon.com/ent/feature/2001/03/14/payola/index.html.

Boehlert, Eric. 2001. "Radio's Big Bully." *Salon*, April 30, http://archive.salon.com/ent/feature/2001/04/30/clear_channel/index.html.

Boltanski, Luc and Eve Chiapello. 2006. *The New Spirit of Capitalism*, trans. Gregory Elliot. New York: Verso.

Bourdieu, Pierre. 1984. *Distinction: A Social Critique of the Judgment of Taste*, trans. Richard Nice. Cambridge, MA: Harvard University Press.

Bourdieu, Pierre. 1993. *The Field of Cultural Production: Essays on Art and Literature*, edited and introduced by Randal Johnson. New York: Columbia University Press.

Boyd, Todd. 2004. *The New H.N.I.C: The Death of Civil Rights and the Reign of Hip Hop*. New York: New York University Press.

Brake, Michael. 1985. *Comparative Youth Culture: The Sociology of Youth Culture and Youth Subcultures in America, Britain, and Canada*. New York: Routledge.

Brass, Kevin. 2005. "GoliathSucks.net." *Austin Chronicle*, April 1.

Braunstein, Peter. 2002. "Forever Young: Insurgent Youth and the Sixties Culture of Rejuvenation." *Imagine Nation: The American Counterculture of the 1960s and '70s*, eds. Peter Braunstein and Michael W. Boyle. New York: Routledge.

Brooks, David. 2000. *Bobos in Paradise: The New Upper Class and How They Got There*. New York: Simon and Schuster.

Brush, Lisa. 1999. "Gender, Work, Who Cares?! Production, Reproduction, Deindustrialization, and Business as Usual." *Revisioning Gender*, eds. Myra Max Ferree, Judith Lorber, and Beth B. Hess. Thousand Oaks, CA: Sage Publications.

Bryson, Bethany. 1996. "'Anything But Heavy Metal': Symbolic Exclusion and Musical Dislikes." *American Sociological Review* 45 (2): 884–99.

Burkeman, Oliver. 2003. "Bush Backer Sponsoring Pro-War Rallies." *Guardian*, March 26.

Buszek, Maria Elena. 2006. *Pin-Up Grrrls: Feminism, Sexuality, Popular Culture*. Durham, NC: Duke University Press.

Callahan, David. 2004. *The Cheating Culture: Why More Americans Are Doing Wrong to Get Ahead*. Orlando: Harcourt.

Chang, Jeff. 2005. *Can't Stop, Won't Stop: A History of the Hip-Hop Generation*. New York: St. Martin's Press.

Chapple, Steve and Reebee Garofalo. 1977. *Rock 'n' Roll Is Here to Pay: The History and Politics of the Music Industry*. Chicago: Nelson Hall.

Christie, Ian. 2003. *Sound of the Beast: The Complete Headbanging History of Heavy Metal*. New York: HarperCollins.

Clarke, Donald. 1995. *The Rise and Fall of American Popular Music*. New York: St. Martin's Press.

Clawson, Mary Ann. 1999. "When Women Play the Bass: Instrument Specialization and Gender Interpretation in Alternative Rock Music." *Gender and Society* 13 (2): 193–210.

Cobb, William Jelani. 2007. *To the Break of Dawn: A Freestyle on the Hip Hop Aesthetic*. New York: New York University Press.

Cohen, Albert K. 1955. *Delinquent Boys: The Culture of the Gang*. New York: Free Press.

Cohen, Jason and Michael Krugman. 1994. *Generation Ecch! The Backlash Starts Here*. New York: Fireside.

Cohen, Phil. 1997. "Subcultural Conflict and Subcultural Community." *The Subcultures Reader*, eds. Ken Gelder and Sarah Thornton. New York: Routledge.

Cohen, Phil. 1999. *On the Youth Question*. Durham, NC: Duke University Press.

Cohen, Sara. 1991. *Rock Culture in Liverpool: Popular Music in the Making*. New York: Oxford University Press.

Cohen, Stanley. 1972. *Folk Devils and Moral Panics: The Creation of the Mods and Rockers*. New York: St. Martin's Press.

Coontz, Stephanie. 1992. *The Way We Never Were: American Families and the Nostalgia Trap*. New York: Basic Books.

Cressey, Paul G. 1932. *The Taxi-Dance Hall*. New York: Greenwood Press.

Currid, Elizabeth. 2007. *The Warhol Economy: How Fashion, Art, and Music Drive New York City*. Princeton, NJ: Princeton University Press.

Davis, Fred. 1979. *Yearning for Yesterday: A Sociology of Nostalgia*. New York: Free Press.

Davis, Mike. 1992. *City of Quartz: Excavating the Future in Los Angeles*. New York: Vintage Books.

Dawson, Ashley. 2005. "Love Music, Hate Racism: The Cultural Politics of the Rock Against Racism Campaigns, 1976–1981." *Postmodern Culture* 16 (1): http://muse.jhu.edu/login?uri=/journals/pmc/v016/16.1dawson.html.

Debord, Guy. 1983. *Society of the Spectacle*. Detroit: Black and Red.

de Certeau, Michel. 1984. *The Practice of Everyday Life*, trans. Steven F. Randall. Berkeley and Los Angeles: University of California Press.

Denisoff, R. Serge. 1986. *Tarnished Gold: The Record Industry Revisited*. New Brunswick, NJ: Transaction Publishers.

DeNora, Tia. 2003. *After Adorno: Rethinking Music Sociology*. New York: Cambridge University Press.

Denski, Stan and David Sholle. 1992. "Metal Men and Glamour Boys: Gender and Performance in Heavy Metal." *Men, Masculinity, and the Media*, ed. Steve Craig. Newbury Park, CA: Sage Publications.

Derber, Charles. 2004. *The Wilding of America: Money, Mayhem, and the New American Dream*. New York: Worth.

DeRogatis, Jim. 2000. *Let It Blurt: The Life and Times of Lester Bangs, America's Greatest Rock Critic*. New York: Broadway Books.

Dery, Mark. 2004. "Public Enemy Confrontation." *That's the Joint! The Hip-Hop Studies Reader*, eds. Murray Forman and Mark Anthony Neal. New York: Routledge.

Des Barres, Pamela. 2005. *I'm with the Band: Confessions of a Groupie*. Chicago: Chicago Review Press.

Des Barres, Pamela. 2007. *Let's Spend the Night Together: Backstage Secrets of Rock Muses and Supergroupies*. Chicago: Chicago Review Press.

Dettmar, Kevin J. H. 2005. *Is Rock Dead?* New York: Routledge.

Donaton, Scott. 1993. "The Media Wakes Up to Generation X." *Advertising Age*, February 1.

Douglas, Elizabeth. 1994. "Can the Industry Be Saved? GOP Injections of Military Spending Will Help, But Don't Expect an All-Out Cure." *San Diego Union-Tribune*, November 20.

Douglas, Susan. 1995. *Where the Girls Are: Growing Up Female with the Mass Media*. New York: Times Books.

Dunn, Robert. 1998. *Identity Crises: A Social Critique of Postmodernity*. Minneapolis: University of Minnesota Press.

Edge, Brian (ed.). 2004. *924 Gilman: The Story So Far*. San Francisco: Maximumrocknroll.

Edwards, Bob and John D. McCarthy. 2004. "Resources and Social Movement Mobilization." *The Blackwell Companion to Social Movements*, eds. David A. Snow, Sarah A. Soule, and Hanspeter Kriesi. Malden, MA: Blackwell.

Edwards, Tim. 1997. *Men in the Mirror: Men's Fashion, Masculinity, and Consumer Culture*. London: Cassell.

Ehrenreich, Barbara. 1983. *The Hearts of Men: American Dreams and the Flight from Commitment*. New York: Anchor Books.

Ehrenreich, Barbara. 1989. *Fear of Falling: The Inner Life of the Middle Class*. New York: Harper Perennial.

Ehrenreich, Barbara. 2007. *Dancing in the Streets: A History of Collective Joy*. New York: Metropolitan Books.

Ehrenreich, Barbara, Elizabeth Hess, and Gloria Jacobs. 1997. "Beatlemania: A Sexually Defiant Consumer Culture?" *The Subcultures Reader*, eds. Ken Gelder and Sarah Thornton. New York: Routledge.

Epstein, Barbara. 1991. *Political Protest and Cultural Revolution: Nonviolent Direct Action in the 1970s and 1980s*. Berkeley and Los Angeles: University of California Press.

Erickson, Erik. 1968. *Identity, Youth, and Crisis*. New York: Norton.

Eyerman, Ron and Andrew Jamison. 1998. *Music and Social Movements: Mobilizing Traditions in the Twentieth Century*. New York: Cambridge University Press.

Faludi, Susan. 1999. *Stiffed: The Betrayal of the American Man*. New York: William Morrow.

Farber, David. 2002. "Intoxicated State/Illegal Nation: Drugs in the Sixties Counterculture." *Imagine Nation: The American Counterculture of the 1960s and '70s*, eds. Peter Braunstein and Michael W. Boyle. New York: Routledge.

Fast, Susan. 2001. *In the Houses of the Holy: Led Zeppelin and the Power of Rock Music*. New York: Oxford University Press.

Fast, Susan. 2006. "Rethinking Issues of Gender and Sexuality in Led Zeppelin: A Woman's View of Pleasure and Power in Hard Rock." *The Popular Music Studies Reader*, eds. Andy Bennett, Barry Shank, and Jason Toynbee. New York: Routledge.

Featherstone, Mike. 1992. *Consumer Culture and Postmodernism*. Thousand Oaks, CA: Sage Publications.

Fine, Michelle, Lois Weis, Judi Addelston, and Julia Maruza. 1997. "(In)Secure Times: Constructing White Working-Class Masculinities in the Late 20th Century." *Gender and Society* 11 (1): 52–68.

Finnegan, Ruth. 2007. *The Hidden Musicians: Music-Making in an English Town.* Hanover, NH: Wesleyan University Press.

Flipside. 1987. *The Ten-Year Anniversary Issue.* Whittier, CA: Flipside.

Florida, Richard. 2002. *The Rise of the Creative Class.* New York: Basic Books.

Florida, Richard. 2005. *Cities and the Creative Class.* New York: Routledge.

Fonarow, Wendy. 2006. *Empire of Dirt: The Aesthetics and Rituals of British Indie Music.* Hanover, NH: Wesleyan University Press.

Forman, Murray. 2002. *The 'Hood Comes First: Race, Space, and Place in Rap and Hip-Hop.* Hanover, NH: Wesleyan University Press.

Fox, Kathryn Joan. 1987. "Real Punks and Pretenders: The Social Organization of a Counterculture." *Journal of Contemporary Ethnography* 16 (October): 344–70.

Frank, Robert H. 2007. *Falling Behind: How Rising Inequality Harms the Middle Class.* Berkeley and Los Angeles: University of California Press.

Frank, Robert H. and Phillip Cook. 1995. *The Winner-Take-All Society: Why the Few at the Top Get So Much More Than the Rest of Us.* New York: Free Press.

Frank, Thomas. 1996. "Hip Is Dead." *The Nation,* April 1.

Frank, Thomas. 1997. *The Conquest of Cool: Business Culture, Counterculture, and the Rise of Hip Consumerism.* Chicago: University of Chicago Press.

Frank, Thomas. 2000. *One Market Under God: Extreme Capitalism, Market Populism, and the End of Economic Democracy.* New York: Doubleday.

Frank, Thomas. 2004. *What's the Matter with Kansas? How Conservatives Won the Heart of America.* New York: Metropolitan Books.

Frank, Thomas and Dave Mulcahey (eds.). 2003. *Boob Jubilee: The Cultural Politics of the New Economy.* New York: Norton.

Freeman, Joshua B. 2000. *Working-Class New York: Life and Labor Since World War II.* New York: New Press.

Frith, Simon. 1981. *Sound Effects: Youth, Leisure, and the Politics of Rock 'n' Roll.* New York: Pantheon Books.

Frith, Simon. 1996. *Performing Rites: On the Value of Popular Music.* Cambridge, MA: Harvard University Press.

Frith, Simon. 1997. "Formalism, Realism, and Leisure: The Case of Punk." *The Subcultures Reader,* eds. Ken Gelder and Sarah Thornton. New York: Routledge.

Frith, Simon and Howard Horne. 1988. *Art Into Pop.* London: Metheun.

Frith, Simon and Angela McRobbie. 1990. "Rock and Sexuality." *On Record: Rock, Pop, and the Written Word,* eds. Simon Frith and Andrew Goodwin. New York: Pantheon.

Frith, Simon and John Street. 1992. "Rock Against Racism and Red Wedge." *Rockin' the Boat: Mass Music and Mass Movements,* ed. Reebee Garofalo. Boston: South End Press.

Gaines, Donna. 1990. *Teenage Wasteland: Suburbia's Dead-End Kids*. Chicago: University of Chicago Press.

Gans, Herbert. 1974. *Popular Culture and High Culture: An Analysis and Evaluation of Taste*. New York: Basic Books.

Gardiner, Judith Kegan. 2003. "*South Park*, Blue Men, Anality, and Market Masculinity." *Masculinities: Interdisciplinary Readings*, ed. Mark Hussey. Upper Saddle River, NJ: Prentice Hall.

Gardiner, Michael. 2000. *Critiques of Everyday Life*. New York: Routledge.

Garnham, Nicholas. 2006. "Political Economy and Cultural Studies: Reconciliation or Divorce?" *Cultural Theory and Popular Culture: A Reader*, ed. John Storey. New York: Prentice Hall.

Gendron, Bernard. 1986. "Theodor Adorno Meets the Cadillacs." *Studies in Entertainment*, ed. Tania Modleski. Bloomington: University of Indiana Press.

Gendron, Bernard. 2002. *Between Montmartre and the Mudd Club: Popular Music and the Avant-Garde*. Chicago: University of Chicago Press.

George, Nelson. 1988. *The Death of Rhythm and Blues*. New York: Pantheon.

George, Nelson. 1999. *Hip Hop America*. New York: Penguin Books.

Giddins, Gary. 2004. "How Come Jazz Isn't Dead?" *This Is Pop: In Search of the Elusive at the Experience Music Project*, ed. Eric Weisbard. Cambridge, MA: Harvard University Press.

Gilroy, Paul. 1991. "*There Ain't No Black in the Union Jack*": *The Cultural Politics of Race and Nation*. Chicago: University of Chicago Press.

Gitlin, Todd. 1980. *The Whole World Is Watching: Mass Media in the Making and Unmaking of the New Left*. Berkeley and Los Angeles: University of California Press.

Gitlin, Todd. 1986. "'We Build Excitement.'" *Watching Television*, ed. Todd Gitlin. New York: Pantheon.

Gitlin, Todd. 1987. *The Sixties: Years of Hope, Days of Rage*. New York: Bantam Books.

Gitlin, Todd. 1989. "Postmodernism: Roots and Politics," *Dissent* 36 (Spring): 100–108.

Gitlin, Todd. 2001. *Media Unlimited: How the Torrent of Images and Sounds Overwhelms Our Lives*. New York: Metropolitan Books.

Goldthorpe, Jeff. 1992. "Intoxicated Culture: Punk Symbolism and Punk Protest." *Socialist Review* 22 (2): 35–64.

Goodlad, Lauren M.E. and Michael Bibby (eds.). 2007. *Goth: Undead Subculture*. Durham, NC: Duke University Press.

Goodman, Fred. 1997. *The Mansion on the Hill: Dylan, Young, Geffen, Springsteen, and the Head-On Collision of Rock and Commerce*. New York: Vintage, 1998.

Goodwin, Andrew. 1990. "Sample and Hold: Pop Music in the Digital Age of Reproduction." *On Record: Rock, Pop, and the Written Word*, eds. Simon Frith and Andrew Goodwin. New York: Pantheon.

Goodwin, Jeff, James Jasper, and Donatella Della Porta (eds.). 2001. *Passionate Politics: Emotions and Social Movements*. Chicago: University of Chicago Press.

Gottlieb, Joanne and Gayle Wald. 1994. "Smells Like Teen Spirit: Riot Grrrls, Revolution, and Women in Independent Rock." *Microphone Fiends: Youth Culture and Youth Music*, eds. Tricia Rose and Andrew Ross. New York: Routledge.

Gracyk, Theodor. 1999. *Rhythm and Noise: An Aesthetics of Rock*. Durham, NC: Duke University Press.

Grazian, David. 2003. *Blue Chicago: The Search for Authenticity in Urban Blues Clubs*. Chicago: University of Chicago Press.

Greenwald, Andy. 2003. *Nothing Feels Good: Punk Rock, Teenagers, and Emo*. New York: St. Martin's Griffin.

Groce, Stephen B. and Margaret Cooper. 1990. "Just Me and the Boys? Women in Local-Level Rock and Roll." *Gender and Society* 4 (2): 220–29.

Gross, David M. and Sophfronia Scott. 1990. "Proceeding with Caution." *Time*, July 16.

Grossberg, Lawrence. 1992. *We Gotta Get Out of This Place: Popular Conservatism and Postmodern Culture*. New York: Routledge.

Grossberg, Lawrence. 1994. "Is Anybody Listening? Does Anybody Care? On 'The State of Rock.'" *Microphone Fiends: Youth Music and Youth Culture*, eds. Andrew Ross and Tricia Rose. New York: Routledge.

Grossberg, Lawrence. 1999. "The Indifference of Television, or, Mapping TV's Popular (Affective) Economy." *Dancing in Spite of Myself*. Durham, NC: Duke University Press.

Grossberg, Lawrence. 2002. "Reflections of a Disappointed Popular Music Scholar." *Rock Over the Edge: Transformations in Popular Music Culture*, eds. Roger Beebe, Denise Fulbrook, and Ben Saunders. Durham, NC: Duke University Press.

Grossberg, Lawrence. 2006. "Cultural Studies vs. Political Economy: Is Anybody Else Tired with This Debate?" *Cultural Theory and Popular Culture: A Reader*, ed. John Storey. New York: Prentice Hall.

Guffey, Elizabeth E. 2006. *Retro: The Culture of Revival*. London: Reaktion.

Haenfler, Ross. 2004. "Manhood in Contradiction: The Two Faces of Straight Edge." *Men and Masculinities* 7 (1): 77–99.

Haenfler, Ross. 2006. *Straight Edge: Clean-Living Youth, Hardcore Punk, and Social Change*. New Brunswick, NJ: Rutgers University Press.

Halbwachs, Maurice. 1992. *On Collective Memory*, ed. and trans. Louis A. Coser. Chicago: University of Chicago Press.

Hall, Stuart and Tony Jefferson (eds.). 1975. *Resistance Through Rituals: Youth Subcultures in Post-war Britain*. New York: Routledge.

Harmon, Larry. 1996. "Token Indie Band." *San Diego Weekly Reader*, April 11.

Harrington, Joe. 2002. *Sonic Cool: The Life and Death of Rock 'n' Roll*. Milwaukee: Hal Leonard.

Harrison, Bennett and Barry Bluestone. 1988. *The Great U-Turn: Corporate Restructuring and the Polarizing of America*. New York: Basic Books.

Hartigan, John, Jr.. 1999. *Racial Situations: Class Predicaments of Whiteness in Detroit*. Princeton, NJ: Princeton University Press.

Harvey, David. 1989. *The Condition of Postmodernity: An Enquiry into the Origins of Cultural Change*. Cambridge, MA: Blackwell.

Harvey, David. 2005. *A Brief History of Neoliberalism*. New York: Oxford University Press.

Heath, Joseph and Andrew Potter. 2005. *A Nation of Rebels: Why Counterculture Became Consumer Culture*. New York: HarperCollins.

Hebdige, Dick. 1979. *Subculture: The Meaning of Style*. New York: Routledge.

Henwood, Doug. 1997. "Trash-O-Nomics." *White Trash: Race and Class in America*, eds. Annalee Newitz and Matt Wray. New York: Routledge.

Hesmondhalgh, David. 1988. "Post-punk's Attempts to Democratise the Music Industry: The Success and Failure of Rough Trade." *Popular Music* 16 (1): 255–74.

Heylin, Clinton. 2007. *Babylon's Burning: From Punk to Grunge*. New York: Canongate.

Highmore, Ben. 2001. *Everyday Life and Cultural Theory*. New York: Routledge.

Hobsbawm, Eric and Terence Ranger (eds.). 1984. *The Invention of Tradition*. New York: Cambridge University Press.

Hodkinson, Paul. 2002. *Goth: Identity, Style, and Subculture*. New York: Berg.

Hoskyns, Barney. 1996. *Waiting for the Sun: Strange Days, Weird Scenes, and the Sound of Los Angeles*. New York: St. Martin's Press.

Howe, Neil and William Strauss. 1993. *13th Gen: Abort, Retry, Ignore, Fail?* New York: Vintage.

Howe, Neil and William Strauss. 2000. *Millennials Rising: The Next Great Generation*. New York: Vintage.

Humphrey, Clark. 1999. *Loser: The Real Seattle Music Story*. 2d ed. New York: Abrams.

Hustwit, Gary. 1998. *Releasing an Independent Record*. San Diego: Rockpress Publishing.

Huyssen, Andreas. 1995. *Twilight Memories: Marking Time in a Culture of Amnesia*. New York: Routledge.

Jameson, Fredric. 1979. "Reification and Utopia in Mass Culture." *Social Text* 1 (Winter): 130–48.

Jameson, Fredric. 1991. *Postmodernism, or, The Cultural Logic of Late Capitalism*. Durham, NC: Duke University Press.

Jay, Martin. 1984. *Marxism and Totality: The Adventures of a Concept from Lukács to Habermas*. Berkeley and Los Angeles: University of California Press.

Jeffords, Susan. 1994. *Hard Bodies: Hollywood Masculinity in the Reagan Era*. New Brunswick, NJ: Rutgers University Press, 1994.

Jenkins, Henry. 2006. *Fans, Bloggers, and Gamers: Media Consumers in a Digital Age*. New York: New York University Press.

Jenkins, Henry. 2007. *Convergence Culture: Where Old and New Media Collide*. New York: New York University Press.

Johnson, Haynes. 1991. *Sleepwalking Through History: America in the Reagan Years*. New York: Norton.

Juno, Andrea (ed.). 1996. *Angry Women in Rock*. New York: Juno Books.

Kamen, Paula. 2000. *Her Way: Women Remake the Sexual Revolution*. New York: New York University Press.

Kaplan, E. Ann. 1987. *Rocking Around the Clock: Music Television, Postmodernism, and Consumer Culture*. New York: Routledge.

Kearney, Mary Celeste. 1998. "Don't Need You: Rethinking Identity Politics and Separatism from a Grrrl Perspective." *Youth Culture: Identity in a Postmodern World*, ed. Jonathan Epstein. Malden, MA: Blackwell.

Kearney, Mary Celeste. 2006. *Girls Make Media*. New York: Routledge.

Keniston, Kenneth. 1968. *Young Radicals: Notes on Committed Youth*. New York: Harcourt, Brace, and World.

Keniston, Kenneth. 1971. *Youth and Dissent*. New York: Harcourt Brace Janovich.

Kimmel, Michael S. 1996. *Manhood in America: A Cultural History*. New York: Free Press.

Kitwana, Bakari. 2003. *The Hip Hop Generation: Young Blacks and the Crisis in African American Culture*. New York: Basic Civitas Books.

Klatch, Rebecca. 1999. *A Generation Divided: The New Left, the New Right, and the 1960s*. Berkeley and Los Angeles: University of California Press.

Klein, Naomi. 2000. *No Logo: Taking Aim at the Brand Bullies*. New York: Picador.

Klein, Naomi. 2007. *The Shock Doctrine: The Rise of Disaster Capitalism*. New York: Metropolitan Books.

Kling, Rob, Spencer Olin, and Mark Poster (eds.). 1991. *Postsuburban California: The Transformation of Orange County Since World War II*. Berkeley and Los Angeles: University of California Press.

Knopper, Steve. 2009. *Appetite for Self-Destruction: The Spectacular Crash of the Record Industry in the Digital Age*. New York: Free Press.

Konow, David. 2002. *Bang Your Head: The Rise and Fall of Heavy Metal*. New York: Three Rivers Press.

Kreske, Leigh and Jim McKay. 2000. "'Hard and Heavy': Gender and Power in a Heavy Metal Subculture." *Gender, Place, and Culture: A Journal of Feminist Ethnography* 7 (3): 287–304.

Kruse, Holly. 2003. *Site and Sound: Understanding Independent Music Scenes*. New York: P. Lang.

Kusek, David and Gerd Leonhard. 2005. *The Future of Music: Manifesto for the Digital Revolution*. Boston: Berklee Press.

Larana, Enrique, Hank Johnston, and Joseph R. Gusfield (eds.). 1994. *New Social Movements: From Ideology to Identity.* Philadelphia: Temple University Press.

Lash, Scott. 1990. *Sociology of Postmodernism.* New York: Routledge.

Lash, Scott and John Urry. 1987. *The End of Organized Capitalism.* Madison: University of Wisconsin Press.

Leblanc, Lorraine. 1999. *Pretty in Punk: Girls' Resistance in a Boys' Subculture.* New Brunswick, NJ: Rutgers University Press.

Lee, Tommy, Mick Mars, Vince Neil, and Nikki Sixx, with Neil Strauss. 2001. *The Dirt: Confessions of the World's Most Notorious Rock Band.* New York: HarperEntertainment.

Lefebvre, Henri. 1984. *Everyday Life in the Modern World.* New Brunswick, NJ: Transaction Publishers.

Lefebvre, Henri. 1991, 2002, 2005. *The Critique of Everyday Life,* 3 vols, trans. Gregory Elliot and John Moore. New York: Verso.

Lefebvre, Henri. 2004. *Rhythmanalysis: Space, Time, and Everyday Life,* trans. Stuart Elden and Gerald Moore. New York: Continuum International.

Leland, John. 2004. *Hip: The History.* New York: Ecco.

Leonard, Marion. 1997. "Rebel Girl You Are the Queen of My World: Feminism, Subculture, and Grrrl Power." *Sexing the Groove: Popular Music and Gender,* ed. Sheila Whiteley. New York: Routledge.

Lévi-Strauss, Claude. 1966. *The Savage Mind,* trans. John Weightman and Doreen Weightman. Chicago: University of Chicago Press.

Levine, Noah. 2003. *Dharma Punx: A Memoir.* New York: HarperSanFrancisco.

Lipsitz, George. 1990. *Time Passages: Collective Memory and American Popular Culture.* Minneapolis: University of Minnesota Press.

Lipsitz, George. 1998. *The Possessive Investment in Whiteness: How White People Profit from Identity Politics.* Philadelphia: Temple University Press.

Lloyd, Richard. 2006. *Neo-Bohemia: Art and Commerce in the Postindustrial City.* New York: Routledge.

Lott, Eric. 1993. *Love and Theft: Blackface Minstrelsy and the American Working Class.* New York: Oxford University Press.

Lukács, György. 1971. *History and Class Consciousness: Studies in Marxist Dialectics,* trans. Rodney Livingstone. Cambridge, MA: MIT Press.

Maffesoli, Michel. 1996. *The Time of the Tribes.* London: Sage Publications.

Mailer, Norman. 1959. *Advertisements for Myself.* Cambridge, MA: Harvard University Press, 2005.

Males, Mike. 1996. *The Scapegoat Generation: America's War on Adolescents.* Monroe, ME: Common Courage Press.

Mandel, Ernest. 1975. *Late Capitalism.* London: NLB.

Mannheim, Karl. 1952. "The Problem of Generations." *Essays on the Sociology of Knowledge,* ed. Paul Kecskemeti. London: Routledge and Kegan Paul.

Marcus, Greil. 1989. *Lipstick Traces: A Secret History of the Twentieth Century*. Cambridge, MA: Harvard University Press.

Marcus, Greil. 1993. *Ranters and Crowd Pleasers: Punk in Pop Music, 1977–92*. New York: Anchor Books.

Marcus, Greil. 2001. "Sleater-Kinney." *Time*, July 9.

Marin, Rick. 1992. "Grunge: A Success Story." *New York Times*, November 15.

Marx, Karl. 1978. *Capital*, vol. 1. *The Marx-Engels Reader*, ed. Robert Tucker. New York: Norton. (*Unless otherwise indicated, the texts are translations that have appeared in editions published by the Foreign Languages Publishing House or Progress Publishers in Moscow.*)

Karl Marx. 1978. *The Eighteenth Brumaire of Louis Bonaparte, The Marx-Engels Reader*, ed. Robert Tucker. New York: Norton.

Marx, Karl and Friedrich Engels. 1978. *Manifesto of the Communist Party. The Marx-Engels Reader*, ed. Robert Tucker. New York: Norton.

McAdam, Doug, John D. McCarthy, and Mayer Zald (eds.). 1996. *Comparative Perspectives on Social Movements: Political Opportunities, Mobilizing Structures, and Cultural Framings*. New York: Cambridge University Press.

McCarthy, John D. and Mayer N. Zald. 1977. "Resource Mobilization and Social Movements: A Partial Theory." *American Journal of Sociology* 82 (6) (May): 1212–41.

McChesney, Robert W. 1999. *Rich Media, Poor Democracy: Communication Politics in Dubious Times*. Urbana: University of Illinois Press.

McClary, Susan. 1991. *Feminine Endings: Music, Gender, and Sexuality*. Minneapolis: University of Minnesota Press.

McClary, Susan and Robert Walser. 1990. "Start Making Sense! Musicology Wrestles with Rock." *On Record: Rock, Pop, and the Written Word*, eds. Simon Frith and Andrew Goodwin. New York: Pantheon Books.

McGirr, Lisa. 2001. *Suburban Warriors: The Origins of the New American Right*. Princeton, NJ: Princeton University Press.

McNeil, Legs and Gillian McCain. 1996. *Please Kill Me: The Uncensored Oral History of Punk*. New York: Penguin Books.

McRobbie, Angela. 1991. *Feminism and Youth Culture: From* Jackie *to* Just Seventeen. London: Macmillan.

McRobbie, Angela (ed.). 1991. *Zoot Suits and Second-Hand Dresses: An Anthology of Fashion and Music*. London: Macmillan.

McRobbie, Angela. 1994. *Postmodernism and Popular Culture*. New York: Routledge.

McRobbie, Angela and Jenny Garber. 1997. "Girls and Subcultures." *The Subcultures Reader*, eds. Ken Gelder and Sarah Thornton. New York: Routledge.

Melucci, Alberto. 1996. *Challenging Codes: Collective Action in the Information Age*. New York: Cambridge University Press.

Mertes, Tom (ed.). 2004. *A Movement of Movements: Is Another World Really Possible?* New York: Verso.

Middleton, Richard. 2006. *Voicing the Popular: On the Subjects of Popular Music.* New York: Routledge.

Miller, James. 1999. *Flowers in the Dustbin: The Rise of Rock 'n' Roll, 1947–1977.* New York: Simon and Schuster.

Miller, Timothy. 1991. *The Hippies and American Values.* Knoxville: University of Tennessee Press.

Mishel, Lawrence, Jared Bernstein, and Sylvia Allegretto. 2007. *The State of Working America, 2006/2007.* Ithaca, NY: Cornell University Press.

Mitchell, Tony (ed.). 2001. *Global Noise: Rap and Hip-Hop Outside the USA.* Hanover, NH: Wesleyan University Press.

Modleski, Tania. 1986. "Femininity as Mas(s)querade: A Feminist Approach to Mass Culture." *High Theory/Low Culture: Analyzing Popular Television,* ed. Colin McCabe. Manchester, U.K.: Manchester University Press.

Moore, Ryan. 2005. "Alternative to What? Subcultural Capital and the Commercialization of a Music Scene." *Deviant Behavior* 26 (3): 229–52.

Moore, Ryan. 2007. "Friends Don't Let Friends Listen to Corporate Rock: Punk as Field of Cultural Production." *Journal of Contemporary Ethnography* 36 (4): 438–74.

Mort, Frank. 1996. *Cultures of Consumption: Masculinities and Social Space in Late Twentieth-Century Britain.* New York: Routledge.

Muggleton, David. 2002. *Inside Subculture: The Postmodern Meaning of Style.* New York: Berg.

Muggleton, David. and Rupert Weinzierl (eds.). 2004. *The Post-subcultures Reader.* New York: Berg, 2004.

Newman, Katherine. 1993. *Declining Fortunes: The Withering of the American Dream.* New York: Basic Books.

News from Nowhere (ed.). 2004. *We Are Everywhere: The Irresistible Rise of Global Anticapitalism.* New York: Verso.

Nixon, Sean James. 1996. *Hard Looks: Masculinities, Spectatorship, and Contemporary Consumption.* New York: St. Martin's Press.

Oberholzer-Gee, Felix and Koleman Strumpf. 2007. "The Effect of File Sharing on Record Sales: An Empirical Analysis." *Journal of Political Economy* 115 (1) (February): 1–42.

Olick, Jeffrey K. and Joyce Robbins. 1998. "Social Memory Studies: From 'Collective Memory' to the Historical Sociology of Mnemonic Practices." *Annual Review of Sociology* 24 (August): 105–40.

Orenstein, Peggy. 1994. *Schoolgirls: Young Women, Self-Esteem, and the Confidence Gap.* New York: Anchor Books.

Park, David J. 2007. *Conglomerate Rock: The Music Industry's Quest to Divide Music and Conquer Wallets.* New York: Lexington Books.

Perry, Imani. 2004. *Prophets of the Hood: Politics and Poetics in Hip Hop*. Durham, NC: Duke University Press.

Peterson, Charles. 1995. *Screaming Life: A Chronicle of the Seattle Music Scene*. New York: HarperCollins.

Peterson, Charles. 2003. *Touch Me, I'm Sick*. Brooklyn: powerHouse.

Peterson, Karla. 1994. "Independents' Days: Concerts, Workshops Offer a Sounding Board for Struggling Musicians." *San Diego Union-Tribune*, October 4.

Peterson, Richard. 1999. *Creating Country Music: Fabricating Authenticity*. Chicago: University of Chicago Press.

Pfeil, Fred. 1995. *White Guys: Studies in Postmodern Domination and Difference*. New York: Verso.

Pilsbury, Glenn. 2006. *Damage Incorporated: Metallica and the Production of Musical Identity*. New York: Routledge.

Pink, Daniel H. 2001. *Free Agent Nation: How America's Independent Workers Are Transforming the Way We Live*. New York: Warner Books.

Pipher, Mary. 1994. *Reviving Ophelia: Saving the Selves of Adolescent Girls*. New York: Ballantine.

Polhemus, Ted. 1997. "Post-subcultures." *The Clubcultures Reader: Readings in Popular Cultural Studies*, eds. Steve Redhead, Derek Wynne, and Justin O'Connor. Malden, MA: Blackwell.

Pough, Gwendolyn. 2004. Check *It While I Wreck It: Black Womanhood, Hip-Hop Culture, and the Public Sphere*. Boston: Northeastern University Press.

Priore, Dominic. 2007. *Riot on the Sunset Strip: Rock 'n' Roll's Last Stand in Hollywood*. Berkeley, CA: Jawbone Press.

Quinn, Eithne. 2005. *Nuthin' But a "G" Thang: The Culture and Commerce of Gangsta Rap*. New York: Columbia University Press.

Reynolds, Simon. 1999. *Generation Ecstasy: Into the World of Techno and Rave Culture*. New York: Routledge.

Reynolds, Simon. 2006. *Rip It Up and Start Again: Postpunk, 1978–84*. New York: Penguin Books.

Reynolds, Simon and Joy Press. 1995. *The Sex Revolts: Gender, Rebellion, and Rock 'n' Roll*. Cambridge, MA: Harvard University Press.

Richardson, James T. 1991. "Satanism in the Courts: From Heavy Metal to Murder." *The Satanism Scare*, eds. James T. Richardson, Joel Best, and David G. Bromley. New York: A. de Gruyter.

Riesman, David. 1990. "Listening to Popular Music." *On Record: Rock, Pop, and the Written Word*, eds. Simon Frith and Andrew Goodwin. New York: Pantheon.

Ritchie, Karen. 1992. "Get Ready for Generation X." *Advertising Age*, November 9.

Ritchie, Karen. 1995. *Marketing to Generation X*. New York: Lexington Books.

Roediger, David. 1999. *The Wages of Whiteness: Race and the Making of the American Working Class*. New York: Verso.

Rogin, Michael. 1988. *Ronald Reagan, the Movie, and Other Episodes in Political Demonology*. Berkeley and Los Angeles: University of California Press.

Rose, Tricia. 1994. *Black Noise: Rap Music and Black Culture in Contemporary America*. Hanover, NH: Wesleyan University Press.

Rosenberg, Bernard and David Manning White (eds.). 1957. *Mass Culture: The Popular Arts in America*. Glencoe, IL: Free Press.

Ross, Andrew. 1989. *No Respect: Intellectuals and Popular Culture*. New York: Routledge.

Ross, Andrew. 2002. *No-Collar: The Humane Workplace and Its Hidden Costs*. New York: Basic Books.

Roszak, Theodor. 1969. *The Making of a Counterculture*. New York: Anchor Books.

Rubin, Lillian B. 1995. *Families on the Fault Line: America's Working Class Speaks About the Family, the Economy, Race, and Ethnicity*. New York: HarperCollins.

Ryan, Michael and Douglas Kellner. 1988. *Camera Politica: The Politics and Ideology of Contemporary Hollywood Film*. Bloomington: Indiana University Press.

Sandler, Lauren. 2006. *Righteous: Dispatches from the Evangelical Youth Movement*. New York: Penguin Books.

Sanneh, Kelefa. 2007. "The Rap Against Rockism." *The Rock History Reader*, ed. Theo Cateforis. New York: Routledge.

Savage, Jon. 1993. *England's Dreaming: Anarchy, Sex Pistols, Punk Rock, and Beyond*. New York: St. Martin's Griffin.

Schippers, Mimi. 2002. *Rockin' Out of the Box: Gender Maneuvering in Alternative Hard Rock*. New Brunswick, NJ: Rutgers University Press.

Schlit, Kristen. 2003. "'A Little Too Ironic': The Appropriation and Packaging of Riot Grrrl Politics by Mainstream Female Musicians." *Popular Music and Society* 26 (1): 5–16.

Schlit, Kristen. 2003. "'I'll Resist with Every Inch and Every Breath': Girls and Zine Making as a Form of Resistance." *Youth and Society* 35 (1): 71–97.

Schloss, Joseph. 2002. *Making Beats: The Art of Sample-Based Hip Hop*. Middletown, CT: Wesleyan University Press.

Schor, Juliet. 1998. *The Overspent American: Upscaling, Downshifting, and the New Consumer*. New York: Basic Books.

Schor, Juliet. 2004. *Born to Buy: The Commercialized Child and the New Consumer Culture*. New York: Scribner.

Schumacher, Thomas G. 2004. "'This Is a Sampling Sport': Digital Sampling, Rap Music, and the Law in Cultural Production." *That's the Joint! The Hip-Hop Studies Reader*, eds. Murray Forman and Mark Anthony Neal. New York: Routledge.

Schwartz, Gary. 1987. *Beyond Conformity or Rebellion: Youth and Authority in America*. Chicago: University of Chicago Press.

Sennett, Richard. 1998. *The Corrosion of Character: The Personal Consequences of Work in the New Capitalism*. New York: Norton, 1998.

Sennett, Richard. 2006. *The Culture of the New Capitalism*. New Haven, CT: Yale University Press.

Shank, Barry. 1994. *Dissonant Identities: The Rock 'n' Roll Scene in Austin, Texas*. Hanover, NH: Wesleyan University Press.

Sharpley-Whiting, T. Denean. 2007. *Pimps Up, Ho's Down: Hip Hop's Hold on Young Black Women*. New York: New York University Press.

Shaughnessy, Rick. 1993. "County Jobless Rate: 9.2%." *San Diego Union-Tribune*, August 28.

Sheff, David and Rob Tannenbaum. 2007 "Rip. Burn. Die." *The Rock History Reader*, ed. Theo Cateforis. New York: Routledge.

Shumway, David. 2007. "Where Have All the Rock Stars Gone?" *Chronicle of Higher Education*, June 22.

Simmel, Georg. 1907. *The Philosophy of Money*, trans. Tom Bottomore and David Frisby. New York: Routledge, 2004.

Simon, William. 1978. *A Time for Truth*. New York: Reader's Digest Press.

Slash, with Anthony Bozza. 2007. *Slash*. New York: HarperEntertainment.

Sloat, Lisa. 1998. "Incubus: Male Songwriters' Portrayal of Women's Sexuality in Pop Metal Music." *Youth Culture: Identity in a Postmodern World*, ed. Jonathan Epstein. Malden, MA: Blackwell.

Smith, Ethan. 2007. "Sales of Music, Long in Decline, Plunge Sharply." *Wall Street Journal*, March 21.

Soja, Edward W. 1989. *Postmodern Geographies: The Reassertion of Space in Critical Social Theory*. New York: Verso.

Sontag, Susan. 1966. *Against Interpretation, and Other Essays*. New York: Farrar, Straus and Giroux.

Spillman, Lyn. 1997. *Nation and Commemoration: Creating National Identities in the United States and Australia*. New York: Cambridge University Press.

Spitz, Marc and Brendan Mullen. 2001. *We Got the Neutron Bomb: The Untold Story of L.A. Punk*. New York: Three Rivers Press.

Stallybrass, Peter and Allon White. 1986. *The Politics and Poetics of Transgression*. Ithaca, NY: Cornell University Press.

Stark, James. 2006. *Punk '77: An Inside Look at the San Francisco Rock 'n' Roll Scene*. San Francisco: RE/Search.

Strausbaugh, John. 2001. *Rock 'Til You Drop: The Decline from Rebellion to Nostalgia*. New York: Verso.

Straw, Will. 1990. "Characterizing Rock Music Culture: The Case of Heavy Metal." *On Record: Rock, Pop, and the Written Word*, eds. Simon Frith and Andrew Goodwin. New York: Pantheon Books.

Straw, Will. 1991. "Systems of Articulation, Logics of Change: Communities and Scenes in Popular Music." *Cultural Studies* 5 (3): 368–88.

Students for a Democratic Society. 1995. "The Port Huron Statement." *'Takin' It to the Streets': A Sixties Reader*, eds. Alexander Bloom and Wini Breines. New York: Oxford University Press.

Tabb, William. 1982. *The Long Default: New York City and the Urban Fiscal Crisis*. New York: Monthly Review Press.

Taussig, Michael T. 1980. *The Devil and Commodity Fetishism in South America*. Chapel Hill: University of North Carolina Press.

Temple, Johnny. 1999. "Noise from Underground: Punk Rock's Anarchic Rhythms Spur a New Generation to Political Activism." *The Nation*, October 17.

Theweleit, Klaus. 1987. *Male Fantasies*, vol. 1, *Women, Floods, Bodies, History*, trans. Steven Conway. Minneapolis: University of Minnesota Press.

Thompson, E.P. 1963. *The Making of the English Working Class*. New York: Pantheon.

Thornton, Sarah. 1994. "Moral Panic, the Media and British Rave Culture." *Microphone Fiends: Youth Culture and Youth Music*, eds. Andrew Ross and Tricia Rose. New York: Routledge.

Thornton, Sarah. 1996. *Club Cultures: Music, Media, and Subcultural Capital*. Hanover, NH: Wesleyan University Press.

Thornton, Sarah. 2006. "Understanding Hipness: 'Subcultural Capital' as Feminist Tool." *The Popular Music Studies Reader*, eds. Andy Bennett, Barry Shank, and Jayson Toynbee. New York: Routledge.

Thrasher, Fredric M. 1927. *The Gang*. Chicago: University of Chicago Press.

Turner, Chris. 2004. *Planet Simpson: How a Cartoon Masterpiece Defined a Generation*. Cambridge, MA: Da Capo Press.

Twenge, Jean. 2006. *Generation Me: Why Today's Young Americans Are More Confident, Assertive, Entitled—and More Miserable Than Ever Before*. New York: Free Press.

Union-Tribune Publishing Company. 1990. *The Union-Tribune's Annual Review of San Diego Business*. San Diego: Union-Tribune.

Vale, V. 1998. *Swing: The New Retro Renaissance*. San Francisco: V/Search Publications.

Vaneigem, Raoul. 2004. *The Revolution of Everyday Life*, trans. Donald Nicholson-Smith. Seattle: Left Bank Books.

Wagner-Pacifici, Robin and Barry Schwartz. 1991. "The Vietnam Veterans Memorial: Commemorating a Difficult Past." *American Journal of Sociology* 97 (2): 376–420.

Waksman, Steve. 1999. *Instruments of Desire: The Electric Guitar and the Shaping of Musical Experience*. Cambridge, MA: Harvard University Press.

Walker, Michael. 1993. "San Diego, Alternatively." *Los Angeles Times Magazine*, October 18.

Walser, Robert. 1993. *Running with the Devil: Power, Gender, and Madness in Heavy Metal Music*. Hanover, NH: Wesleyan University Press.

Watkins, S. Craig. 2006. *Hip Hop Matters: Politics, Pop Culture, and the Struggle for the Soul of a Movement*. Boston: Beacon Press.

Weber, Max. 1905. *The Protestant Ethic and the Spirit of Capitalism*, 3d ed. trans. Stephen Kalberg. Los Angeles: Roxbury, 2002.

Weider, Judy. 1998. "Judas Priest's Rob Halford Is First Heavy Metal Band Member to Say He's Gay." *The Advocate*, May 12.

Weinstein, Deena. 1991. *Heavy Metal: A Cultural Sociology*. New York: Lexington Books.

Weis, Lois. 1990. *Working Class Without Work: High School Students in a De-industrializing Economy*. New York: Routledge.

Widgery, David. 1986. *Beating Time: Riot 'n' Race 'n' Rock 'n' Roll*. London: Chatto and Windus.

Williams, Raymond. 1977. *Marxism and Literature*. Oxford: Oxford University Press.

Williams, Raymond. 2001. "Base and Superstructure in Marxist Cultural Theory." *The Raymond Williams Reader*, ed. John Higgins. Malden, MA: Blackwell.

Willis, Ellen. 1981. *Beginning to See the Light: Pieces of a Decade*. New York: Knopf.

Willis, Paul. 1977. *Learning to Labor: How Working-Class Kids Get Working-Class Jobs*. New York: Columbia University Press.

Willis, Paul. 1978. *Profane Culture*. London: Routledge and Kegan Paul.

Wise, Sue. "Sexing Elvis." *On Record: Rock, Pop, and the Written Word*, eds. Simon Frith and Andrew Goodwin. New York: Pantheon Books.

Witkin, Robert W. 1998. *Adorno on Music*. New York: Routledge.

Witikin, Robert W. 2003. *Adorno on Popular Culture*. New York: Routledge.

Wood, Robert. 2006. *Straightedge Youth: Complexity and Contradictions of a Subculture*. Syracuse, NY: Syracuse University Press.

Wooden, Wayne S. and Randy Blazak. 2001. *Renegade Kids, Suburban Outlaws*. Belmont, CA: Wadsworth.

Zobl, Elke. 2004. "Revolution Grrrl and Lady Style, Now!" *Peace Review* 16 (4): 445–52.

Zukin, Sharon. 1992. *Loft Living: Culture and Capital in Urban Change*. Baltimore: Johns Hopkins University Press.

Index